W9-COH-336

... is a ... at the ... Professor in the Department of Industrial Economics ... Research at the University ... Glasgow. He has published several books on industrial relations and trade unions including the highly successful *Change in Industrial Relations*.

Public sector industrial relations

In recent decades industrial relations in the public sector has come increasingly to the forefront of public policy debate and government policies have sought to bring about significant changes in the attitudes and behaviour of public sector unions. In the 1970s it was the government's attempts to limit the public sector wage increases; in the 1980s the Thatcher government reduced public employment levels and sought to curb the power of public sector unions through such measures as privatization, compulsory tendering and the introduction of private sector arrangements and practices. Such actions have changed the workings of industrial relations.

This book is the first to concentrate on individual relations in the public sector, identifying the distinctive features of management organization, collective bargaining, strikes, and dispute resolution. It offers not only an outline of the major developments in the public sector in Britain but a careful analysis of their effects and implications, comparing them in detail to systems in other countries. This breadth makes the book invaluable for all students of industrial relations and human resource management as well as policy makers, economists and political scientists.

P.B. Beaumont is currently Titular Professor in the department of Social and Economic Research at the University of Glasgow. He has published several books on industrial relations and trade unions including the highly successful *Change in Industrial Relations*.

Public sector industrial relations

P.B. Beaumont

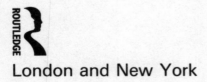

London and New York

First published 1992
by Routledge
11 New Fetter Lane, London EC4P 4EE

Simultaneously published in the USA and Canada
by Routledge
a division of Routledge, Chapman and Hall, Inc.
29 West 35th Street, New York, NY 10001

© 1992 P.B. Beaumont

Typeset in English Times by
Pat and Anne Murphy, Highcliffe-on-Sea, Dorset
Printed in Great Britain by
Mackays of Chatham PLC, Chatham, Kent

All rights reserved. No part of this book may be reprinted
or reproduced or utilized in any form or by any electronic,
mechanical, or other means, now known or hereafter
invented, including photocopying and recording, or in any
information storage or retrieval system, without permission
in writing from the publishers.

British Library Cataloguing in Publication Data
Beaumont, P.B.
   Public sector industrial relations.
   1. Great Britain. Public sector. Industrial relations
   I. Title
   331.04135441

ISBN 0–415–05965–8
ISBN 0–415–05889–4 pbk

Library of Congress Cataloging-in-Publication Data
Has been applied for.

To Pat and Piers
for making it all worthwhile

Contents

Tables

Acknowledgements

I am grateful, as always, to Andrew Thomson for initially encouraging me to undertake some research on public sector industrial relations in Britain. This interest has been sustained over more years than I care to remember by involvement in a variety of research projects in the subject area; I am therefore grateful to the various funding bodies involved, particularly the Royal Institute of Public Administration, and the individuals with whom I have collaborated in this research. In more recent years Geoff White and his colleagues in the IDS Public Sector Unit have been particularly helpful in providing up-to-date information, while the Carnegie Trust for the Universities of Scotland kindly provided a small research grant to assist in some of this work. Finally my thanks go to my long-suffering secretary, Eithne Johnstone, for all her patience, understanding and good humour.

Preface

In late 1989 the media in Britain contained numerous items concerning public sector industrial relations. For example, a single issue of *The Times* (27 September) mentioned the overtime ban in the ambulance service, the demand of the nurses' unions for a minimum 12 per cent pay rise and the prediction of leaders of the two largest teachers' unions that strike action would be the likely result of the government's announcement of a 7.5 per cent limit on pay rises for 400,000 teachers in England and Wales. During 1989 industrial action in British Rail, the London Underground, London buses, the BBC and the local government sector was largely responsible for the fact that in July of that year there were some 2,371,000 working days lost through strike action; this was the highest level for some five years, being only some 500,000 less working days lost than in January 1979, the so-called 'winter of discontent' (*Sunday Correspondent* 24 September 1989). The occurrence and outcome of such public sector strikes undoubtedly contributed to the general mood at the annual meeting of the TUC in September, which was held to be considerably more optimistic than had been the case for a number of years. At the same time, however, the government produced in the subsequent months a Green Paper seeking to curb unofficial disputes and introducing a cooling-off period in disputes involving essential services; the nature of the London Underground dispute was held to be a major influence on these provisions. The 'newsworthy' nature of public sector industrial relations has not been confined exclusively to Britain in recent years, as strikes and other public sector industrial relations developments in other countries, both developed and developing ones, have also frequently been reported in the British press.

In 1978 I co-authored a book with Andrew Thomson on public sector collective bargaining in Britain.[1] The major changes that have occurred in public sector industrial relations since that book was written, together with the absence of a competing volume on the subject in Britain, led me to think about producing a new version. My initial intention was to produce a book not too dissimilar to the original one; I would simply update the major facts and figures, and incorporate the new developments and trends of the 1980s, all within the basic organizational framework of the original work. However, as the work evolved, it soon became apparent that the new version was going to differ from the 1978 book in a number of regards. First, I found that a rather different organizational framework for the book was useful in order fully to incorporate and capture the essence of many of the new developments of the 1980s, which were so vastly different from those of the preceding decade. Second, the study of public sector industrial relations (or at least certain aspects of it) is no longer essentially dominated by researchers who would define their main field of interest or study as that of industrial relations. For example, political scientists became considerably more interested in this subject area in the 1980s than was the case in the 1970s. As a result there is considerably more reference to the arguments and findings of such individuals here than was the case in the 1978 book. And third, in order to put public sector industrial relations in Britain in a wider context I began to look more and more at relevant developments in other countries and to read books and articles on public sector industrial relations in national systems other than Britain's. In the course of this reading I was continually struck by the fact that so many of the contemporary issues and developments in public sector industrial relations, which are of interest to both researchers and practitioners alike, appear to transcend individual national systems of industrial relations.[2]

In view of this fact I have sought, wherever possible, (i) to provide some facts and figures on selected features of the public sector in countries other than Britain, (ii) to identify some notable similarities and/or differences between public sector industrial relations in Britain and elsewhere, and (iii) I have attempted in some cases to offer explanations of a particular feature of public sector industrial relations which appear to transcend the institutional features of particular national systems. That being said, I would in no sense claim that this volume is a comparative study of public sector industrial relations. Admittedly I did at one stage toy with the idea of trying to produce a genuinely comparative study of public sector industrial relations. This did not, however, prove to be a practical proposition because of the imbalance in the literature across countries. That is, I found that the considerable volume of research on public sector industrial relations in Britain, the USA and Canada was not matched by anything like a similar-sized volume of analytical material for other countries; for many other countries I could find (at least in the English language journals) only relatively descriptive statements of laws, structures and individual events. Nevertheless the book does, compared to the 1978 one, contain a significant amount of information for other countries which will, hopefully, be useful in illustrating both similarities to and differences from the public sector industrial relations position in Britain. The book, however, is very much one about British public sector industrial relations, with all of the core material being used to show structures, patterns of behaviour, aspects of change, etc. being drawn from the experience in Britain.

Chapter 1

Introduction

SETTING THE SCENE

The analysis and recommendations of the Donovan Commission (1965–8) viewed the problems of British industrial relations as being very much private sector ones. The Commission's view that public sector industrial relations were in a relatively satisfactory state (and hence in need of little detailed discussion) can be attributed to the fact that in the mid- to late 1960s the public sector was an area of employment where authoritative, national-level collective bargaining was subject to little challenge or threat from fractional bargaining or unofficial industrial action at the level of the individual workplace. And at the same time, formal comprehensive incomes policies were in their relative infancy in Britain so that the wage outcomes of the public sector had not, as yet, been subject to any sustained and substantial 'attack from above'. The result was that the public sector hardly figured at all in discussions of the desired direction(s) of reform in British industrial relations in the 1960s.

More than twenty years after the Report of the Donovan Commission, the position has changed to such an extent that many commentators now view any industrial relations problems in Britain as being overwhelmingly centred in the public sector. For example, Dennis Boyd, as Chief Conciliation Officer of the Advisory, Conciliation and Arbitration Service (ACAS) observed in 1987, 'one particular area of employment however – the public sector – continues to be beset with conflict. There has been a succession of major public disputes since 1979 and no agreement exists between the various interested parties as to how such conflict may be avoided in the future.'[1] Moreover, the 1984 workplace industrial relations survey reported that 'the picture of industrial action in 1983−84 was characterized by short strikes by non-manual workers in the public services sector'[2] while a study based on Department of Employment figures revealed that the proportion of working days lost through strikes in the public sector had ranged from a low of 43.7 per cent in 1981 to a high of 88 per cent in 1984.[3]

The majority of mainstream industrial relations researchers would undoubtedly subscribe to the view that some level of strike activity is both inevitable and desirable, with the result that the level of strike activity (measured according to number of strikes, working days lost, workers involved in strikes or whatever) can only be an imperfect, single measure of the complex, multi-faceted notion of the overall climate or quality of industrial relations. Nevertheless it has been the level of strike activity in the public sector in Britain in both the 1970s and 1980s that has been so prominent in academics', practitioners' and policymakers' discussions of the problems of public sector industrial relations. Indeed, 'worries' about public sector strikes have been expressed from a wide variety of positions along the political spectrum. From the political right have come calls for the removal of the right to strike in 'essential services'. A report to this effect by the Centre for Policy Studies in the mid-1980s, for example, called for this right to be removed in the case of the health service, the fire service, gas, electricity and water, and local authority workers responsible for burials and cremations.[4] While at the other end of the political spectrum Hobsbawm has argued that

we now see a growing division of workers into sections and groups, each pursuing its own economic interest irrespective of the rest. . . . In fact it now often happens not only that groups of workers strike, not minding the effect on the rest, but that the strength of a group lies not in the amount of loss they can cause to the employer, but in the inconvenience they can cause to the public, that is, to other workers, by power blackouts or whatever. This is a natural consequence of a state monopoly capitalist system in which the basic target of pressure is not the bank account of private employers but, directly or indirectly, the political will of the government. In the nature of things such sectional forms of struggle not only create potential friction between groups of workers, but risk weakening the hold of the labour movement as a whole.[5]

Such concerns about public sector strikes in the 1970s and 1980s have not been confined to Britain. Indeed although public sector strike restrictions of some form or another exist in many countries, it has been observed that

> the predominance of restrictive and prohibitory provisions points to the existence of a growing gap between law and practice. Most of the laws specifically aimed at prohibiting or limiting the right of public servants to strike were passed in the 1940s and 1950s, i.e. before the sustained increase in the frequency of strikes that has occurred over the past two decades. Whether because existing provisions are outdated or reflect a purely administrative approach to a socio-political phenomenon, the fact remains that in most countries legal prohibitions and restrictions have been powerless to prevent strikes. Public service work stoppages have been a contemporary fact of life that places them beyond simple legislative assertions of their legality or illegality.[6]

There are a number of comments that can usefully be made at this stage about the above observation. First, it is difficult systematically and comprehensively to document 'the sustained increase in the frequency of strikes that has occurred over the past two decades' in the public sector across countries. This is because the available strike statistics for individual countries are frequently not provided on a public–private sector basis. Moreover in countries where such information is available, the pattern or trend observed does not always conform to the alleged one of a steadily rising level of strike activity through time. In the USA, for example, the volume of public employee strikes grew rapidly in the late 1960s, fell in the mid-1970s, fell and rose again in the late 1970s, and then fell once more during the early 1980s.[7] In short, it is difficult to examine and document any suggestion of a major, sustained 'strike explosion' in the public sector across a wide range of countries.

Nevertheless, there is no denying that the issue of public sector strikes has become of increased concern in a number of countries in recent decades. Many general discussions of public sector strikes across countries have typically drawn a distinction between the major causes of such actions in the 1970s and those of the 1980s.[8] For example, three of the leading industrial relations features of advanced industrialized economies in the 1970s were public sector employment growth, the increased passage of industrial relations legislation and relatively high inflation rates, all of which have been alleged to have been important factors in public sector strikes in that decade. First, the growth in public sector employment (and the associated increase in public sector unionization) was held to have exposed certain major weaknesses and deficiencies in the existing consultation, negotiation and dispute settlement arrangements of some countries, as such arrangements were not designed for or appropriate to a relatively highly unionized sector of employment. Second, the industrial relations legislation of the 1970s is held to have diluted some of the leading, traditional public sector employment advantages (particularly in relation to job security) by spreading and transferring similar substantive and procedural rights to the private sector. And third, the high inflation rates of the 1970s introduced a second element or component into the definition of the 'public or social interest' in industrial relations: to the traditional (procedural) element of keeping down the level of strike activity was added a second (substantive) element, namely that of keeping down the level of wage settlements. The institutional manifestation of this new, second element was incomes or wage control policy and in a number of countries, including Britain, it was argued that the government of the day consistently sought to enforce the restrictions of such policies most vigorously on public sector employees.

The 'awkward' relationship between the public sector and wage control or incomes policies appears to be common to the 1970s and 1980s. For example, Cordova has commented that

> Since the beginning of 1982 public service pay has been frozen or salary increases limited in, for instance, Canada, Denmark, France, Ireland, Japan, the Netherlands and Portugal. In some Latin American countries such as Brazil and Peru, where inflation has reached three digits, public employees have been excluded from the indexation system applied to other groups of workers. Clearly, the public service has been used both to initiate stringent economic policies and to set the pattern for moderate wage policies in the private sector.[9]

The 1980s also saw public sector employment growth checked and reversed in a number of countries as a result of budget cuts, taxpayers' revolts, privatization and competitive tendering or contracting-out moves. Furthermore, there have been attempts to remove or downgrade the importance of certain traditional public sector industrial relations arrangements and practices and to replace them with more private sector-like arrangements (e.g. performance-related pay). And finally, in some countries there have been substantial government criticisms and attacks on public section union organization, facilities and collective bargaining arrangements. In 1984, for example complaints relating to restrictions on collective bargaining or trade union activities were lodged with the International Labour Office (ILO) by public sector employee organizations in Barbados, Burkina Faso, Canada, Chile, Costa Rica, Honduras, Japan, Papua New Guinea, Portugal and Britain.[10]

The 1980s were not, however, solely years of problems or gloom for public sector unions in many countries, particularly when some comparison is made with the position of their private sector counterparts. For instance, the fastest growing individual unions in many countries in recent years are in the public sector. In the USA, for example, the two fastest growing unions since 1970 (leaving aside union growth through mergers) have been in the public sector: between 1970 and 1983 the State, County and Municipal Employees union increased its membership by nearly 409,000, while the American Federation of Teachers nearly tripled in size.[11] The largest individual unions in Canada in the mid-1980s were the Canadian Union of Public Employees, the National Union of Provincial Government Employees and the Public Service Alliance of Canada, all of which have experienced substantial membership growth from the mid-1970s.[12] Furthermore, the proportion of total trade union membership which is accounted for by the public sector is rising in many advanced industrialized economies. According to some calculations by Freeman the public sector share of total union membership increased in the USA by 22 per cent between 1970 and the mid-1980s, by 5 per cent in Britain, 6 per cent in Italy, 8 per cent in Sweden and 9 per cent in the Netherlands.[13] These figures led Freeman to argue that

The shift to white collar and public sector membership has begun to change the face of union movements traditionally dominated by industrial workers. In the US the locus of power in the AFL-CIO is shifting to public sector organizations while the non-affiliated National Education Association has achieved considerable national influence. It Italy the new autonomous public sector organizations and quadri pose a challenge to the three traditional confederations. In Sweden and Denmark the white collar unions have shown an increased willingness to develop their own economic agenda rather than to follow the lead of blue collar manufacturing unions.[14]

Such developments suggest that the earlier cited union complaints of attacks on public sector collective bargaining arrangements in a number of countries need to be viewed in the light of some private sector experience. In the USA, for example, the extent and nature of management opposition to union organization in the private sector in recent decades stands in marked contrast to the position in the public sector where it has been commented thaᵢ

> although public sector employers may have grown more resistant to union demands after the mid-1970s, they did not aggressively try to remove their unions. As a result, the institutions of collective bargaining in the public sector have exhibited much more stability in recent years than their counterparts in the private sector.[15]

This sort of public sector—private sector comparison can be taken a stage further by considering the question of whether there is any sign of convergence between public and private sector industrial relations arrangements. This question has been of particular interest in countries where public sector union organization has been a relatively recent phenomenon, with a good deal of academic and practitioner attention being given to the issue of whether earlier developed private sector arrangements and practices are relevant and appropriate for adoption in the public sector. A recent review of this question for a number of countries has suggested that there has been an increased convergence between the public and private sector models of industrial relations, at least in the sense that 'forms of bipartite determination of wages and working conditions, particularly through collective bargaining, gained ground over unilateral determination by the employing authority'[17] in the public sector. However, a number of important exceptions and qualifications to this broad trend were noted:

1 the unilateral determination of terms and conditions of employment still remained important for Japanese civil servants, the *Beamte* [civil servants] in West Germany and to some extent in the French public service;

2 even where collective bargaining has become the major method of determining terms and conditions of employment, additional (supplementary) methods still remain more significant in the public than in the private sector;

3 there is more legal regulation of the various methods of determining terms and conditions of employment in the public sector than is the case in the private sector;

4 the scope or subject matter of the methods for determining terms and conditions of employment tends to be generally narrower in the public than in the private sector;

5 the nature of dispute settlement procedures in the public sector tend to differ from those in the private sector in the following ways:

   i the process is highly sensitive to political circumstances;

   ii the procedures are more highly regulated;

   iii there is a greater variety of dispute settlement means;

   iv there is more regulation, and even outright prohibition, of industrial conflict.[17]

There are, however, some interesting divergent tendencies between individual countries in recent years as regards the direction of transference of public and private sector working practices and arrangements. For example, a recent volume on public sector industrial relations in the USA has suggested that the innovations and success of collective bargaining in the public sector in the 1970s and 1980s have been such that 'the time would seem to have come for researchers and practitioners to begin to ask what the private sector might learn from public sector experience rather than the converse'.[18] This sort of view needs, however, to be seen in the light of the more general tendency throughout the 1980s of governments seeking increasingly to open up and expose the public sector to the influence of 'market forces' via, among other means, the adoption of private sector-like employment practices and arrangements.

The various issues and themes touched on to date constitute some of the matters more fully explored in this book. In the remainder of this chapter, however, I discuss some practical, conceptual and empirical questions concerning the nature and definition of the public sector, briefly consider the state of public sector industrial relations research and then set out the basic framework of analysis which guides the subsequent order and subject matter of individual chapters.

WHAT IS THE PUBLIC SECTOR?

In any study concerning the role of the public sector it is essential to consider the questions of how the public sector is to be defined, and what kinds of statistics are appropriate for measuring it; such questions are particularly important when some comparison is being attempted across countries. There have been a number of review articles which have addressed these two questions in recent years,[19] with the following sorts of points typically being made.

1 The major problem involved in producing a reasonably comparable definition of the public sector across countries tends to involve the treatment of public enterprises. This is because relatively few countries tend to identify public enterprises separately in their national accounts and those that do so often tend to provide only limited information concerning the criteria used for including (or not) an enterprise in the public sector.
2 In principle it has been suggested that the size of the public sector can be variously measured by value added, compensation of employees, employment, capital formation, saving and net lending figures. In practice, however, there are relatively few studies which have used all of these measures in examinations of the size and growth of the public sector across countries.
3 Those relatively few studies which have used a variety of measures have indicated that judgements about the size of the public sector in an individual country that are highly sensitive to the definition and measures used.[20] For example, it has been suggested that the USA has a medium-sized public sector when measured by government consumption expenditure or government employment, but a much smaller one if the measure used is total public sector final demand or total public sector employment.

The use of even a single measure of the size of the public sector still frequently poses problems for ensuring that 'like is being compared with like' across countries. For example, a study by the International Monetary Fund (IMF) of public sector employment across countries in the early 1980s noted that problems arose concerning the definition of a unit of government, the definition of what constitutes a government employee, and the classification of employees by function.[21] Specifically, they highlighted the following problems involved in trying to produce a reasonably comparable set of public sector employment figures across countries:

1 The frequent lack of employment data at a sufficiently disaggregated level.
2 Different governments implemented comparable policies in different ways. For example, in some countries the government directly operates the health system, whereas in others the government is heavily involved in financing the health system but it allows its ownership and operation to be in the private sector.
3 Differences in the structure of government also create problems in cross-country comparisons, particularly where one is seeking to look at individual parts of the public sector. For example, in some countries the central government may perform functions that in other countries are carried out by the state and local government levels. A particularly important distinction here is between countries that are unitary states and those that are federal states; the latter have three major levels of government (federal, state and local), whereas the former have only a central and local level.[22]
4 In defining a government employee, questions arise as to whether the number of employees should be measured in terms of man-years worked, in terms of the total number of employees, whether full time or part time, or in terms of full-time equivalent employees. (And in the latter case, how is a full-time equivalent employee defined?)
5 The treatment of defence employees also poses a problem in defining the size of the public sector workforce.
6 There is difficulty in classifying government employees by function given that the division of functional responsibilities varies widely across countries. The result is that any figures on public sector employees by function across countries are likely to be less suitable and reliable for comparison than figures for the total size of public sector employment.

In addition to the above issues and difficulties, the experience of the 1980s also raised the question of expanding the definition of public sector employment to include temporary employment opportunities provided through direct job creation schemes.[23] This became an increasingly important issue as governments introduced such schemes in the relatively high unemployment environment of the 1980s. For example, in Britain in the years 1982–8 local authority employment rose by 7.5 per cent on a headcount basis (4.6 per cent in full-time equivalents), but if community programme employees are excluded, the increase is only of the order of 4.4 per cent (1.7 per cent).[24] It is also worth noting at this stage that in most countries the longest and most satisfactory time series figures for public sector employment tend to be for the central civil service, although even here redefinitions and information system changes can be a source of problems in attempting to produce an accurate and comprehensive set of figures over an extended time period.[25] In Britain, for example, employment figures for the non-industrial civil service extend back to 1902 when there were some 50,000 civil servants, compared to the figure of 507,000 in 1987.[26]

The various points made in this section to date are ones that will be recalled in later chapters when any figures on public sector expenditure and employment are presented for various countries. In addition to these definition and measurement issues concerning the public sector, particularly when cross-country comparisons are made, it is also necessary to consider the place of the public sector in organization theory.

A public–private sector distinction is frequently utilized in organization studies, although, as a recent review article has noted, multiple definitions and multiple uses of the construct are apparent.[27] For instance, the use of a public sector variable has been based on a variety of definitions, and has been variously used to develop theories of public organization and bureaucracy, to act as a moderator variable in organization studies and as a predictor variable in evaluation studies. Nevertheless there appears to be some consensus in the relevant organization literature on some key distinctions between public and private sector organizations, such as: (i) market information, signals and incentives are relatively absent for public sector organizations, although they are subject to much greater influence by external political and governmental institutions; (ii) public sector organizations are exposed to more external scrutiny and accountability than their private sector counterparts; (iii) public sector organizations' goals are more numerous, intangible and conflicting than is the case in the private sector; (iv) public sector managers have less autonomy due to constraints such as civil service rules; and (v) public sector organizations have relatively more elaborate, formal rules, reporting requirements and more rigid hierarchical arrangements. In Britain, for example, the Aston Group has categorized public sector organizations as personnel bureaucracies, with highly concentrated decision-making procedures concerning the hiring and promotion of personnel.[28] This

particular review article by members of the group went on to urge
the adoption of a research strategy in which there was a more
detailed, disaggregated treatment of the public–private sector
organization distinction (i.e. less use of a simple dichotomy) and
more integration of theoretical and empirical research in order to
identify just why differences exist between public and private sector
organizations.

A BRIEF NOTE ON PUBLIC SECTOR INDUSTRIAL RELATIONS RESEARCH

In considering the current state of public sector industrial relations
research, much of which will be examined in subsequent chapters,
it is important to note certain criticisms and reservations that have
been expressed about it. For example, in the USA, Freeman has
claimed that

> perhaps the biggest gap in the economic analysis of public sector
> unionism has been the tendency of most researchers to apply the
> same models and tools as have been used to analyse the economic
> impact of private sector unionism, giving short shrift to the dis-
> tinctive aspects of the government as an employer.[29]

Specifically, Freeman contends that the political nature of public
sector collective bargaining means that unions will be interested in
trying to influence budget and employment levels, as well as in
raising wages. As a consequence of these different union goals
between the public and private sectors, there is a need for much
more research on union effects in shifting the demand curves for
labour in the public sector, and hence their effects on budgets and
employment levels – rather than simply pursuing the traditional
private sector research theme of the union impact on wages in the
public sector. If public sector industrial relations research should
more accurately reflect the distinctive industrial relations features
of the public sector, then it is obviously essential to identify just
what are these distinctive features. To this end researchers have frequently produced 'check-lists' of public–private sector industrial
relations differences for individual countries.[30] These differences
typically concern environmental characteristics (e.g. absence of
market forces in the public sector), union organizational characteristics (e.g. higher unionization levels in the public sector),
management organizational characteristics (e.g. divisions within

the management side for negotiating purposes), and dispute resolution facilities (e.g. greater use of third-party intervention in the public sector). In Britain the use of such static, descriptive variables for distinguishing public and private sector industrial relations has been criticized by Ferner for its failure to illuminate differences in the dynamic, behavioural processes of industrial relations in the two sectors over the course of time.[31] And, according to Ferner, the identification of such processes in the public sector requires that researchers pay particular attention to the fact that the public sector employer is basically a political institution. Similarly, a recent review in Canada has argued that 'most of the distinctive features of public sector labour relations stem from differences between public employers and private employers'.[32] The *political* nature of the government as the key factor leading to differences in public and private sector industrial relations is well recognized by researchers, although the precise mechanisms and means by which political forces influence public sector industrial relations structures, processes and outcomes have certainly not been identified and researched in sufficient depth and detail. This is a point to which I will return early in the next chapter.

THE PLAN OF THE BOOK

In chapter 2 I examine the influence of the external environment on public sector industrial relations. This chapter will especially focus on the all-important role of the political environment, although the role of the economic and legal environments will also be considered. Chapter 3 is concerned with union organizational characteristics where the issues discussed include the extent of union organization in the public sector, changes in the 'character' of public sector unions and the determinants of union bargaining power in the public sector. Management organizational characteristics are the subject matter of chapter 4 where I consider matters such as the nature of the public sector employer, the role of the personnel management function and relationships between the different levels of the government. Chapter 5 examines the extent of collective bargaining in the public sector, the structure of bargaining, the scope or subject matter of bargaining and the issue of the public or social interest in relation to public sector collective bargaining. In chapter 6 strikes and third-party dispute resolution procedures are discussed, while chapter 7 looks at the outcomes of collective bargaining, particularly on the wages front. And, finally, in chapter 8 I seek to draw together the major themes and conclusions of my work.

The contents of the individual chapters and their sequence have been considerably influenced by the analytical framework of Kochan's work in the USA.[33] The essence of Kochan's approach is that certain independent variables, notably the external environment, the organizational characteristics of unions and of management, together with bargaining structure (an intervening variable), have an impact on certain dependent variables associated with collective bargaining, namely the negotiations process, bargaining outcomes, the administration of the agreement and the union—management change process which, in turn, feed through to shape the goal attainment of the parties concerned and the public at large. Although not without its critics, this framework of analysis has been utilized in work on public, as well as private, sector industrial relations in the USA.[34] I, too, have relied on it to a significant degree, although inevitably some departures are made from it as a result of either deficiencies or gaps in the existing literature being reviewed or in order to take account of certain issues and considerations that are more a feature of the British, rather than the American, public sector scene. The latter point is an all-important one because, as mentioned earlier, this book is very much about public sector industrial relations in Britain, although wherever possible relevant material from other countries will be introduced.

Chapter 2

The environment of public sector industrial relations

INTRODUCTION

The leading single grand theory of industrial relations relations still remains the systems approach of Dunlop.[1] The essence of Dunlop's approach is that unions, employers and the government interact in an environmental context consisting of three interrelated components, namely technology, product market constraints (or budgetary ones in the public sector) and power relations (and status), the result of which is the 'web of rules' concerning the determination and regulation of the terms and conditions of employment. The model is very much an environmental dominated one in which the industrial relations parties are held to respond in a relatively uniform and mechanical manner to a given environmental change. This relatively long-standing criticism of the Dunlop model has recently been taken a stage further by a number of American researchers who have argued that such a framework of analysis needs to be broadened in order to allow for the role of 'strategic choice' on the part of all of the interested parties in the industrial relations system.[2] That is, one needs to recognize that unions, employers and the government all have some degree of discretion or choice as to how they respond in industrial relations terms to the fact of a changing environment, and that the nature of their responses will be at least in part influenced by 'values' (e.g. historical attitudes towards unions) and by broader considerations (e.g. nature of competitive strategy) than simply industrial relations specific ones. Such discretionary action is held to be particularly important in accounting for major (i.e. non-marginal, non-incremental) changes in the structures and processes of any industrial relations system.

In this particular chapter I will especially emphasize the role of strategic choice by the government (motivated by values and larger macro-economic management considerations) in shaping the nature of the political environment which, in turn, is such an all-important influence on the nature of public sector industrial relations. The majority if this chapter will be concerned with the role of the political environment, although some attention will also be given to the role of product and labour market forces and the legal environment. As mentioned in the previous chapter, industrial relations researchers have invariably acknowledged the importance of political influences in public sector industrial relations, but all too often they have limited their discussion to the presentation of some facts and figures on the size of public expenditure, cited examples of wage control or incomes policies that were specifically directed at public sector employees, discussed public sector strikes as instruments of political, rather than economic (as in the private sector) pressure, or have referred to the use of lobbying tactics (outside of formal collective bargaining) by unions designed to exploit differences within public sector management.

The approach adopted here seeks to depart from this rather fragmented and partial treatment of the role of political influences in public sector industrial relations by discussing, in turn, some theories of the state (including 'fiscal crisis theory') and some views (with their all-important macro-economic management implications) that 'the public sector has become too large' in recent decades. The basic purpose of this discussion, which is one that only rarely features in books on public sector industrial relations, [3] is to make the following points:

1 The state is not just the neutral representative of the public or social interest in industrial relations. Indeed the growth of public sector employment has been one of the most important factors that have made it clear that the state is a separate, self-interested party in the industrial relations arena.
2 The state is not simply a mechanism which reacts to pressures generated within civil society. It has a degree of relative autonomy, which increases considerably in periods of economic crisis.
3 The state's assumption of a greater range of responsibilities in the economic and industrial relations systems increases the likelihood that it will be subject to some degree of inter-role conflict. For

example, the introduction of incomes or wage control policy (as an instrument of macro-economic regulation) has frequently caused problems for the state both as a public sector employer and as a party concerned with providing third-party dispute resolution facilities.

4 Some of the major implications for public sector industrial relations have resulted from the particular macro-economic management strategies adopted by governments; in other words, a number of key government decisions (which, via the political environment, have had a major impact on public sector industrial relations), have been decisions which were not taken solely, or even largely, for industrial relations reasons.

In the course of the discussion concerned to illustrate these and other points concerning the influence of the political environment, some empirical evidence will be presented for a number of countries on the size of public expenditure and public sector employment.

THEORIES OF THE STATE

Traditionally, the major political science perspectives on the state (which in principle comprises government, the judiciary, parliament, the police and the military) have been, first, the liberal-democratic one in which the state is conceived of 'as an autonomous complex of institutions, politically neutral and external to structurally determined social forces. It is then "up for grabs" to be "captured" by elected regimes and used as an instrument for their own specific political purposes.'[4] This pluralist perspective essentially focuses on the political system, rather than on the state, as the major agent of policy formation. The alternative view is the marxist approach which sees the state as the tool of the ruling class, designed to assist both the processes of capital *accumulation* and capital *legitimation*, with the structure and functions of the state being overwhelmingly shaped by the global (economic and political) requirements of capital. There are in fact a number of variants of marxist thought here, some of which stress the economic functions which the state performs for capitalism (i.e. reproduction of the capitalist economy), whereas others primarily emphasize the importance of its political functions (i.e. to maintain political stability). One of the most well-known marxist theories which makes reference to both of these state functions is the work of

O'Connor on the fiscal crisis of the state.[5] According to O'Connor, state activities and expenditures seek to achieve two basic, but often contradictory functions: social capital expenditure (e.g. public investment in infrastructure) is designed to provide the conditions for private capital accumulation, whereas social expenses expenditure (e.g. the welfare state) is intended to legitimize the state and maintain political stability in the system at large. The social capital expenditure function of the state increasingly provides the basis for the growth of the private sector, but the costs of this uneven growth (e.g. unemployment) requires still further social expenses expenditure to legitimize and stabilize the system. However, although the state increasingly assumes the responsibility for financing economic growth and political stability, the profits from such activities accrue almost entirely to the private sector. The problems involved in trying to tax these private sector profits (in order to finance state expenditure) result in a growing divergence between state expenditure and state revenues – hence the fiscal crisis of the state. This crisis is held by O'Connor to be largely played out in urban areas where conflicts emerge between (i) business interests seeking to avoid tax increases and reduce social expenses expenditure and (ii) working-class interests seeking to preserve such services, with public sector unions being particularly prominent in this regard. The debate around compulsory competitive tendering, or contracting-out (see chapter 3) can arguably be viewed as a useful 'microcosm' of this sort of conflict.

Industrial relations researchers have in recent years begun to make more of a contribution or input to conceptual discussions of the role and nature of the state.[6] The general view which has emerged from such work is that the state is not simply a captive of class forces, economic forces or the capitalist mode of production, in that it has some degree of relative autonomy. But it must also be recognized that the state is not a completely independent, homogeneous or all-powerful force, as it experiences internal divisions, the constraints of history, and contradictory demands from (internally) heterogeneous capital and labour groups. Admittedly such work to date has only yielded a small handful of reasonably specific, potentially testable hypotheses, although there is a strong consensus to the effect that crisis situations (e.g. economic depressions) substantially increase the capacity for relatively autonomous action by the state. The approach of the Thatcher government in Britain in the 1980s in attempting to break sharply with certain government traditions in the economic and industrial relations spheres of activity is certainly not inconsistent with this prediction. In the following section I consider some of the factors and considerations which appear to have importantly influenced the Thatcher government's macro-economic strategy, with all the important implications for the public sector industrial relations that that implies, when the Conservatives came to power at a time of 'economic crisis' which significantly enhanced the government's area of discretionary choice.

THE NOTION OF BIG GOVERNMENT AND MACRO-ECONOMIC STRATEGY

Two of the major influences on the approach of the Thatcher government towards the public sector were 'values' and certain key assumptions about how the economy can and should operate, which have been usefully brought together under the notion or heading of 'Big Government'. This notion was central to the work of Bacon and Eltis,[7] a study that 'was exactly right for the prevailing political mood of the country, and it had a powerful influence, perhaps not by creating opinion, but by reinforcing it and giving it academic respectability'.[8] The essence of the Bacon and Eltis argument was that the British economy suffered from the fact that too few people were involved in producing marketed goods and services. Basically they viewed the British economy in terms of two sectors, a marketed and a non-marketed goods and services sector, with the basic problem being, as they saw it, that employment in the non-marketed sector had increased by over 40 per cent in the years 1961–75. This growth of the non-marketed sector had to be financed by the market sector of the economy, which, in turn, so the argument went, had reduced the capacity of the market sector to produce wealth. In practice they tended to equate the public sector with the non-market sector and argued that: (i) public sector employment growth had been directly at the expense of the private, market sector (i.e. there was a physical 'crowding out' effect); (ii) the growth of public sector employment in Britain was greater than in comparable countries; (iii) wage settlements in the public sector were particularly high; and (iv) high levels of public sector employment were associated with slow economic growth.

This general line of argument and its associated individual

elements have been subject to considerable criticism along the following lines:

1 the figures cited by Bacon and Eltis concerning the growth of local government employment do not take account of the fact that much of this increase involved part-time employees;
2 the evidence for the years 1950−80 does not fully support their claim that the public sector enjoyed a relatively high rate of wage increase;
3 one cannot automatically equate the public sector with the non-market sector, as approximately a third of local government current income is derived from marketing activities;
4 the rate of public sector employment growth in Britain was essentially similar to that of other OECD countries;
5 the slowing down of private sector growth seems to have led to the growth of the public sector, rather than the opposite relationship alleged by Bacon and Eltis.[9]

Nevertheless, the general view of Bacon and Eltis concerning the adverse role of the public sector in the macro-economic performance of the British economy in the 1960s and 1970s has been an influential input in the Conservative government's economic strategy since 1979. It is to some of the major elements of this strategy that I now turn, on the grounds that the government's choice of such a strategy has had a major impact on the political environment of public sector industrial relations in recent years. The essence of the Thatcher government's *initial* macro-economic strategy was that the elimination of inflation was its priority concern and that the traditional roles of fiscal and monetary policy needed to be reversed (in favour of the latter) in order to achieve this aim. As the Conservative party's pre-1979 election manifesto put it:

To master inflation, proper monetary discipline is essential, with publicly stated targets for the rate of growth of the money supply. At the same time a gradual reduction in the size of the Government's borrowing requirements is also vital. It will do yet further harm to go on printing money to pay ourselves without first earning more. The state takes too much of the nation's income: its share must be steadily reduced. The reduction of waste, bureaucracy and over-government will yield substantial savings. We shall cut income tax at all levels to reward hard work, responsibility and success.[10]

In addition to the setting of monetary targets (originally introduced by the previous Labour administration) the Government's approach has involved various measures of structural readjustment, trade union reform and a fiscal strategy compatible with financial stability, all of which constituted 'a pot-pourri of different strains of right wing economic thinking'.[11] Political scientists have been particularly interested in the sources of ideas and proposals that have influenced the Thatcher government, and in how the electorate have responded to various government initiatives,[12] while economists have tended largely to focus on the question of whether the government's macro-economic strategy is based on well-established empirical relationships that can be readily controlled by the government.[13] These are important and interesting issues and questions, although they are not pursued in detail here, where my concern is essentially with the place of the public sector in this overall strategy of macro-economic management.

The public sector figures prominently in this strategy in that, first, the government is committed to restricting the size of the Public Sector Borrowing Requirement (PSBR). This is deemed to be essential because of the government's belief that an increase in the PSBR will lead to a rise in interest rates which would limit the government's ability to control the money supply through interest rate changes, and which would constrain private sector investment. An increase in the PSBR is also held to lead to an increase in the money supply, hence the PSBR/GNP ratio needs to be lowered. Second, if a smaller proportion of public expenditure is to be financed from borrowing, and taxation is not to be increased (indeed the government is committed to trying to lower it), then public expenditure as a proportion of GNP needs to be reduced. The latter is also held to be desirable as an end in itself, with the Bacon and Eltis contention that countries with a faster growing public sector tend to have slower economic growth, being particularly influential here.

It needs to be recognized that the Thatcher government's macro-economic strategy did undergo some notable changes in the years since 1979. For example, as one commentary has observed:

> The original 'monetarist' strategy was based on the supposed stability of the income velocity of £M3 and the supposed ability of the authorities to control that aggregate by appropriate adjustments in the PSBR and the level of interest rates. This was

set out clearly in the Financial Statement and Budget Reports (FSBR) 1980/81 and 1981/82. The framework of policy in 1987 is very different. In the FSBR this year, pride of place is given to the medium-term path for money GDP. Both fiscal and monetary policy are set out so as to reduce the growth of that magnitude, if only very gradually. In discussing monetary policy, exchange-rate stability is both assumed and advocated. The monetary aggregates are also mentioned but only the monetary base now merits a target range. The PSBR is now projected as a constant percentage of GDP. The reference to declining interest rates as an objective of policy has been dropped.[14]

The various changes in the particular indicators (e.g. M3, M1, PSL) used to try and control the growth in the money supply and in basic public expenditure objectives (i.e. reduce it in real terms, contain it in real terms, allow it to grow in real terms, although as a declining proportion of GDP) have led some individuals to argue that the government has effectively abandoned a monetarist strategy, at least as that strategy is conventionally understood.[15] Nevertheless, the generally hostile position of the government (for economic, ideological and industrial relations reasons) towards the public sector has essentially remained constant, albeit with some significant changes in the way this has been tangibly manifested. For example, the privatization of public enterprises was hardly pro-minent in the Conservative agenda at the time of their initial election in 1979. However, a Channel 4 programme ('The Thatcher Audit') in August 1990 noted that some thirty sizeable organizations have been privatized since 1979. This privatization programme has been hailed, by economists sympathetic to the Thatcher strategy, as one of the government's major success stories,[16] although political scientists have reported that the early relatively favourable response from the electorate[17] has tended to diminish over time.[18] The government's major arguments in favour of privatization have essentially been as follows:[19]

1 It contributes to the general aim of restraining the size of the PSBR, by generating an immediate cash flow to the Exchequer, and in the case of hybrid enterprises (where the government retains a partial shareholding) allows their borrowing to be excluded from the figures. The PSBR in the financial year 1987−8 was provisionally estimated to have been minus £3.5 billion (i.e. a

net debt repayment), with privatization proceeds having totalled some £5 billion.[20]

2 Privatization will contribute to increased efficiency. This argument follows from the belief that public enterprises are inherently less efficient because of the essential absence of market forces.

3 The programme will contribute to economic freedom by increasing consumers' freedom of choice and spreading share ownership more widely throughout the population.

4 Privatization by introducing market disciplines will provide an important constraint on the level of wage settlements in the organizations concerned.

The validity and strength of some of these arguments have been challenged,[21] although it is apparent that privatization has become a more common practice in a number of OECD countries in recent years. Some actual and proposed moves along these lines in the late 1980s included the following:

1 In Germany, the energy company VEBA and Volkswagen have been recently privatized, and the government will be selling its remaining shares in VIAG (an industrial conglomerate) in 1988.

2 In Canada, Northern Canada Power Commission, Teleglobe Canada and Fishery Products International were removed from the public sector in 1987.

3 In Spain, the state holding company sold SEAT and fifteen other smaller firms in 1987–8.

4 In France, since November 1986, four major industrial enterprises (GGE, St Gobain, CGCT and Matra) have been privatized.

5 In Portugal, there is to be a partial privatization of profitable public enterprises (tobacco, beverages and cement).

6 In Turkey, a telecommunications equipment manufacturer, Teletas, has been privatized, and Petkion (petrochemicals) and Sumarbank (textiles) are scheduled to be sold to the public sector in 1988.[22]

It is important to recognize that the adoption of a particular macroeconomic management strategy which has important political implications for public sector industrial relations may not constitute a completely unconstrained choice on the part of the government in any country. In the case of Britain in the mid-1970s, for example, it has been commented that, the Callaghan–Healey administration had run up a series of large public sector deficits in an attempt to deal with stagflation. This resulted in a run on the pound sterling as international speculators anticipated runaway inflation and a devaluation of sterling. In order to balance the books the IMF was approached for a loan. This loan was granted on the condition that the UK Government would undertake to cut back its public spending, control the money supply, and reduce the public sector deficit. The first UK monetarist government was, in fact, a Labour government.[23]

The role of the International Monetary Fund (IMF) in shaping the nature of individual governments' policies towards the public sector has been particularly important in developing countries. For example, a survey of seventy-eight adjustment programmes in developing countries supported by IMF resources in 1980–3 reported that almost 90 per cent involved proposed public expenditure reductions, with fully two-thirds of these involving some form of public sector wage restraint.[24] Indeed the highly controversial role of the IMF in such programmes is well evidenced by the following summary statement:

Critical versions suggest an institution lying in wait to get control of the nation's economic policies to reshape them in a monetarist, market-orientated, conservative model. More positive versions emphasise the original function of the Fund: to provide emergency credit to help countries avoid drastic contraction threatened by temporary problems, and technical advice on how to get the deficit under better control if the problem seems likely to be more than temporary. In between, perhaps the most common criticism of the Fund is that it applies a standard package of remedies to all countries, whether it is appropriate or not, leaning to the side of deflation for financial safety whether it is really needed or not.[25]

This observation about the role of the IMF was made in relation to Latin American countries, although essentially similar criticisms have been made about its policy role in relationship to Asian and African countries.

To date, I have outlined some conceptions of the role of the state in the economic (and industrial relations) system, and discussed the position of the public sector in the Thatcher government's view of macro-economic strategy, a view which had had such a significant impact on the political environment of public sector industrial relations in Britain. The next section attempts to put this discussion into context by outlining the results of some research on trends in public expenditure. The importance of public expenditure follows from the fact that budgetary constraints are held to substitute for those of the product market in public sector industrial relations, with the level of public expenditure being such a major component of any government's macro-economic management strategy.

RESEARCH AND TRENDS IN PUBLIC EXPENDITURE

One of the most comprehensive studies of the growth of public expenditure examined the position in a substantial number of western industrialized countries for the years 1960–79.[26] This exercise involved a comparison of the average annual growth rates of general government expenditures with the corresponding growth rates of GDP for the overall period 1960/2 to 1977/9, and for the two sub-periods 1960/2 to 1967/9 and 1967/9 to 1977/9. Among the main individual results or findings to emerge from the exercise were the following:

1 For all countries the growth of public expenditure was greater than that for GDP, thus increasing the size of the public sector.
2 The expenditure ratios for the whole period (1960 to 1979) ranged between 1.12 for Iceland, the slowest growing, to 1.44 for Sweden, the fastest growing. (The UK figure was 1.18, which was below the unweighted average for the countries as a group.) Sweden and Belgium were among the four fastest growing countries for both sub-periods of time, while France and the USA were among the four slowest growing ones for both sub-periods. (The UK was among the four fastest growing countries in the sub-period 1960/2 to 1967/9, but was among the four slowest growing ones in the sub-period 1967/9 to 1977/9.)
3 For the three years 1960–2, general government expenditure as a percentage of GDP averaged 33.4 in the UK. This figure was above the unweighted average for all countries studied (29.5), being exceeded only by West Germany (34.5) and France (36.7). In the three years 1977–9 the average figure for the UK was 45.1 which was again above the unweighted average for the group (43.3), but was here exceeded by Austria (47.4), Belgium (48.2),

France (45.6), West Germany (46.4), Italy (45.2), Sweden (61.1), the Netherlands (57.6) and Norway (51.5).

4 The growth of transfers was the fastest growing component overall of general government expenditure, with the expenditure of state/local government being the second fastest growing component.

As to the determinants of public expenditure growth, this particular study was essentially characterized by the relative absence of significant relationships. First, the variation in the level of and growth in general government expenditure at the aggregate level between countries in the period 1960–79 was not related to the level of economic development, nor to differences in the relative size of the public sector at the outset of the study period. Second, neither the level nor rate of growth in public expenditure was significantly related to the rate of inflation in these years. Third, the years in office of left/centre-left governments did not appear to be significantly associated with larger than average increases in general government expenditure: the political complexion of government was, however, rather more strongly associated with an above-average growth of transfer payments. Admittedly, this study did suggest that the rate of growth of public expenditure, although not its level, was negatively related to differences in economic growth among countries.

There are a number of well-known conceptual treatments of the growth in public expenditure over the course of time. This work has typically involved economists who have variously argued that changes in the relative share of public expenditure can be related to the longer run development cycle of economies, that there is a positive relationship with the growth in per capita income (the so-called 'Wagner law'), or that relative upward shifts in the growth of public expenditure are disproportionately associated with periods of 'social turmoil', such as wartime years; in Britain, general government expenditure as a percentage of GDP reached around 60 per cent in the Second World War years. However, all of these explanations have been held to be inadequate to the task of satisfactorily explaining the growth of public expenditure in most countries during the post-1950 years.[27] Indeed a number of commentators have increasingly argued that attempts to try and explain the overall growth of public expenditure through time are essentially misplaced exercises;[28] instead, it has been contended, one needs to adopt a much more disaggregated approach of trying to explain public expenditure growth on an individual programme-by-programme basis. Political scientists have also contributed to the discussion of the relevant determinants of public expenditure growth by focusing on the question of whether the particular political party in power makes a difference to such growth. In general the results of such studies, both across countries and for individual countries over a period of years, find that the individual party in office contributes relatively little to explaining the growth of public expenditure over the course of time.[29] Finally one particular study of the relationship between the growth of public expenditure and the growth of public sector employment is worthy of note. This was an OECD study of fourteen member countries in the period 1960−78 which reported that:

> There is typically a less than proportionate response of public sector employment to a given increase in *total* public expenditure at constant prices. The mean elasticity value for this sample of countries implies that a 1 per cent increase in public expenditure is associated with a 0.6 per cent increase in public sector employment. The results suggest, moreover, a great deal of variation in the magnitude of the elasticity across countries, ranging from a low of 0.3 in Japan and the Netherlands to a high of 1.1 in Denmark. Sweden is the only other case where the elasticity is very close to unity, indicating that the rapid growth in public expenditure since 1960 has been associated with an equally rapid build-up of public sector employment.[30]

The same study also concluded that (i) the magnitude of the public sector employment response tends to increase the narrower is the measure of public expenditure used and (ii) there was no evidence of the public sector employment elasticity having increased in years of rising unemployment. A fuller discussion of public sector employment is presented on p. 32 in this chapter. I conclude this section by making some brief reference to the movement in public expenditure in Britain in more recent years. These figures should be seen in the wider context of the attempt of governments in a number of European countries to reduce the size of public sector deficits, and public expenditure more generally, from the early 1980s − a tendency which has been noted in a number of surveys.[31]

In Britain public expenditure as a proportion of GDP was 40.7 per cent in 1971, 48.5 per cent in 1975, 42.4 per cent in 1977, 46.5 per cent in 1982 and 43.3 per cent in 1986;[32] in 1987 the figure was 40.5 per cent, the lowest level since 1970,[33] and 38.2 per cent in 1988, the lowest level since 1966.[34] In the public expenditure plans announced early in 1990, general government expenditure was expected to be about 39 per cent in 1991, slightly higher than the 38.75 per cent forecast for 1990.[35] As with so much of the Thatcher economic (and industrial relations) strategy, there have been widely varying assessments as to the performance of the government in the area of public expenditure control. Broadly speaking, one can distinguish between the government's own view and those of a heterogeneous group of critics who have variously argued that (i) the government has not done enough to cut public expenditure, (ii) has failed to achieve its own targets or (iii) has produced unfortunate, discriminatory effects within the public expenditure total; individuals in all groups can and have pointed to various individual statistics to support their particular case. For example, the then Chancellor Nigel Lawson stated in late 1988 that public expenditure (excluding privatization sales) would be less than 40 per cent of national income for the first time in twenty years, and that since 1982−3 public expenditure had fallen as a share of national income by some 7 per cent, the most sustained fall in the post-war years.[36] The government could also cite as evidence of its 'achievement' the fact that the central government borrowing requirement has fallen from over 11 per cent of national income in 1983 to under 6 per cent in 1986.[37] However, at least one Conservative MP has been highly critical of the fact that public expenditure was planned to increase by 6.5 per cent between 1988/9 and 1989/90, and that spending per public sector employee had increased in real terms by 12 per cent between 1978/9 and 1987/8;[38] the call here was for genuine, as opposed to 'mythical', public expenditure cuts. Other commentators have noted that the government's plans to achieve real reductions or broadly constant levels of public expenditure have not in fact been realized, as (once the effects of asset sales are excluded) real departmental spending grew by just under 1.75 per cent per year on average in the period 1979/80 to 1986/7.[39] And finally, others have stressed the adverse, 'discriminatory' effects of certain intra-public expenditure changes introduced by the government. For example, Newton and Karran have observed in relation to the local authority sector that

There is a strong school of thought which argues that the Government has stumbled, by miscalculation and mismanagement, from one set of events to the next, seemingly unaware of the fact that it was trying to achieve the impossible, but at the same time compromising its own efforts by arbitrary decisions and political discrimination. The full measure of the failure can be judged from the fact that the Government has not managed to achieve its main policy objective of cutting local spending. Some services (housing) have been reduced in real terms, but others (police) have expanded, and although the rate of increase of total current spending has been slowed, it is still higher in constant money terms in 1983 than 1979. Whatever success the Government has had with cuts has fallen largely upon capital spending, which was less than half (in constant money terms) in 1983 what it had been in 1973.[40]

One of the major mechanisms for trying to control local government expenditure in Britain is the system of central government grants, and in 1979 such grants accounted for 61 per cent of general local government spending, whereas in 1985 the figure had fallen to 48 per cent.[41] The result of such changes in the local government sector produced, not surprisingly, a decade of very 'awkward' and 'uneasy' central–local government relationships in Britain, which will be further discussed in chapter 4.

So far in this chapter I have adopted very much a 'macro' perspective on the role of political influences in public sector industrial relations, emphasizing the importance of the nature of a particular government's macro-economic management strategy and the place of the public sector in such a strategy. This theme will be pursued further in other chapters where I discuss the nature of the government as public sector employer (chapter 4) and the impact of incomes policies on the relative wages of public sector employees (chapter 7). A more 'micro' perspective on political influences in public sector industrial relations is also present in the relevant literature which tends to focus on (i) the nature of public sector strikes as an instrument of political, as opposed to economic, pressure and (ii) union lobbying activities which arise as a consequence of divisions within public sector management. These particular issues will also be pursued in later chapters, while here I continue to concentrate on the more macro-level environmental influences by considering the role of the product market, labour market and the legal environment. As the remainder of this chapter will, hopefully, indicate, the importance of political considerations figures prominently in these 'other' environmental influences. For convenience one may discuss various aspects of the environmental context of public sector industrial relations separately, but in practice it is political influences that permeate all of these other environmental sub-headings.

THE PRODUCT MARKET ENVIRONMENT

In general discussions of differences in public and private sector industrial relations, the relative absence of product market forces in the former sector is invariably mentioned. Indeed it is the very remoteness of product market influences which features centrally in arguments concerning the comparatively powerful bargaining position of public sector unions (this is considered more fully in the next chapter). The view typically taken in the literature is that product market influences, treating the public sector as a whole, can only have an *indirect* effect on the outcomes of public sector industrial relations, as a result of the operation of, for example, the comparability principle in public sector wage determination arrangements. In other words, if product market conditions influence private sector wages then such influences can, in theory, have some indirect (and lagged) effect on public sector wages in situations where the criterion of comparability or the prevailing wage principle is important in public sector wage determination. However, the problems of precisely defining, measuring and implementing comparable wages between the public and private sectors (see chapter 7) have often led to the claim that even this indirect effect rarely comes about in practice.

The one part of the public sector where product market forces would, in principle, seem directly relevant is in the public enterprises sub-sector; it is these particular enterprises which, as noted in the previous chapter, have frequently been the major problem area for studies seeking to produce a comparable definition (and measurement) of the public sector across countries. The size of the public enterprise sub-sector does in fact tend to vary considerably between countries, generally being smaller in developed than in developing ones; an IMF study in the early 1980s, for example, estimated the mean share of non-financial public enterprises employment as some 4 per cent in OECD industrialized countries, compared to a figure of nearly 14 per cent in the case of developing ones.[42] Moreover, as mentioned earlier in this chapter, there is currently considerable government interest in privatizing certain public enterprises in a number of OECD countries. These privatization moves can be seen against the background of considerable academic and policy-maker discussion of the organizational effectiveness and industrial relations record of public enterprises in several nations.

In Britain, for instance, public enterprises are essentially the trading, as opposed to the non-trading, portion of the public sector, and some reports have stressed that such enterprises differ significantly from private sector enterprises.[43] The differences frequently mentioned include the strategic position of such enterprises in the economy at large, their multiple (and potentially conflicting) goals and objectives (which, above all else, are a reflection of political influences), and the relative absence of external financial market pressures. Nevertheless, over the course of time there has been increased government pressure on nationalized industries and public enterprises in Britain to set and report on the achievement of performance targets. This particular development has attracted the research attention of some organization theorists. For example, one recent examination of the published performance indices of the gas, rail and coal industries in 1981−2 argued that these measures yielded only limited information on management performance and organizational effectiveness, largely as a result of a misapplication of a private sector analogy.[44]

It has been suggested that the nationalized industries have frequently constituted the wage leaders in the annual round of wage bargaining in Britain. This particular contention has attracted the interest of some economists, with one recent study providing some empirical support for such a relationship.[45] However, another researcher utilizing a different model specification and data source, found no evidence of public corporations acting as wage leaders.[46] The particular issue which has caught the attention of industrial relations researchers is the relative roles of market and political influences in shaping the overall state of industrial relations in the nationalized industries. Pendleton, in his study of British Rail in 1988, argued that political uncertainty, as opposed to market forces, was the primary determinant of the overall state of industrial relations there;[47] he specifically highlighted the fact that the 1970s 'tacit alliance' between unions and management to limit the effects of government intervention had broken down in the 1980s, largely as a result of government intervention which was more explicitly concerned with industrial relations matters. The railways in Britain, as well as in Spain, have also been examined in a comparative industrial relations study by Ferner which was explicitly concerned with the nature of union–management responses to the increased commercial pressures which have come to bear on the two systems.[48] The different modes of response to this common set of pressures were viewed as largely resulting from the different political environment facing the railways in the two countries. Finally, a review of industrial relations in public enterprises throughout the 1980s in Britain re-emphasizes many of these points by indicating that the Conservative government's rhetoric of non-intervention is very different from the reality:[49] the extent of government intervention to bring performance pressure on management has been very considerable which, in turn, has made for highly 'confrontational' patterns of industrial relations behaviour.

There is also some relevant research on industrial relations in public enterprises in other countries. For example, a review of such enterprises in Canada[50] concluded that: (i) the industrial relations legislation covering public enterprises was drawn from both the public and private sector models; (ii) actual industrial relations practices were largely determined by industry and regional-specific, as opposed to ownership, influences; and (ii) the degree of government influence in industrial relations decisions in these organizations was highly variable, depending on the extent to which an enterprise was financially self-supporting, its visibility in the community and its economic importance. The importance of the visibility issue was particularly stressed in that

> stoppages or even threatened strikes in a public enterprise that injure or inconvenience the public almost guarantee a response from government. These pressures are especially strong within provincial Crown corporations because disruptions may affect a large proportion of the electorate. It is not uncommon for cabinet ministers, including premiers, to take a direct part in negotiations which may be politically sensitive. The dominant concern of politicians in these situations seems to be to minimise political costs, even if they have to 'buy' a settlement.[51]

In contrast to the position in Britain, industrial relations considerations had little initial influence in the establishment of Crown corporations in Canada, but as the above quotation indicates, essentially similar political considerations and influences have frequently been at work in the industrial relations of public enterprise in both systems. In short, public enterprises may be the part of the public sector most exposed to the influence of product market forces, but in practice their basic industrial relations patterns have, in a number of countries, been greatly affected by political considerations and forces, although there will inevitably be some variation in this respect both between and within individual countries over the course of time.

The following section considers the role of the labour market in public sector industrial relations. The intention here is to consider the size of the public sector workforce, and some of the workforce characteristics particularly associated with employment in the public sector. As always, the focus is mainly on Britain, although some facts and figures for other countries are also presented.

THE LABOUR MARKET

Various individuals and organizations in the 1980s sought to build up reasonably comparable public sector employment data sets for a number of countries. For example, an IMF study for the early 1980s produced the following major findings:

1 General government (central, state and local) employees averaged 7 per 100 inhabitants for OECD countries and only 3 for developing countries. The mean employment share of the central government in total general government employment in developing countries was approximately 85 per cent, with the relevant figure for OECD countries being 42 per cent.
2 Employees of non-financial public enterprises in developing countries averaged 14 per cent of non-agricultural sector employment, in contrast to only 4 per cent in the OECD countries.
3 Public sector employees averaged 44 per cent of non-agricultural sector employment in developing countries compared with a 24 per cent average figure for the OECD countries.[52]

This particular study was especially useful in providing information for developing countries, but all of its data was essentially for the early 1980s. That is, it provided no indication of changes in the size of the public sector workforce over the course of time. Some limited time perspective on the size of public sector employment is provided by a number of OECD publications, although this is only for member countries and only for the category of general government employment (i.e. it excludes employees in public enterprises). One such publication indicated that the mean share of the public sector in total employment in member countries was 11.6 per cent in 1960, 14.2 per cent in 1970 and 17.7 per cent in 1979.[53] A subsequent OECD study reported that the general government share in employment in 1982 was an average of 18.4 per cent, but with a range of below 7 per cent in Japan to over 31 per cent in Sweden and Denmark.[54] Relative to the position in 1960, general government employment had risen most rapidly in Austria, Sweden and (after 1970) Denmark, while the slowest growth was in Canada, France, Japan and the USA. The work of Rose, which covers Britain, France, Germany, Italy, Sweden and the USA, has also made a significant contribution to our understanding of the growth of public sector employment over time.[55] Among his major findings were the following:

1 public sector employment as a proportion of the non-agricultural workforce in the early 1980s was 32.2 per cent in Britain, 35.6 per cent in France, 27.4 per cent in West Germany, 28.1 per cent in Italy, 38.8 per cent in Sweden and 18.9 per cent in the USA.
2 Public sector employment grew only relatively slowly from the mid-nineteenth century to the Second World War. In Britain the mid-nineteenth century figure of 2.4 per cent rose to 10.8 per cent prior to the Second World War. The highest mid-nineteenth century figure was 7.2 per cent for Germany, with Germany also having the highest figure (12.9 per cent) prior to the Second World War.
3 The years 1951−81 saw public sector employment double as a proportion of the workforce in most major western countries. This was most obviously the case in Sweden where the public sector employment share increased from 15.2 per cent in 1951 to 38.2 per cent in 1980. The USA was a notable exception in this regard.
4 Public sector employment growth since 1951 has been disproportionately concentrated in 'social programmes', particularly in the education and health areas. Their share of total public sector employment increased by more than 23 per cent in Britain, France, Sweden and the USA in these years.
5 The growth of nationwide social welfare programmes has had the effect of reducing the relative importance of central ministries as public sector employers, and conversely increasing the importance of the local and regional levels.

Similarly, some figures for Canada in the mid-1980s indicate that public sector employment is very much dominated by health care (26 per cent) and education (30.7 per cent) workers who account for more than 1 in 2 public sector employees.[56] The fact that reasonably comparable public sector employment data across countries have only begun to be built up in the 1980s has inevitably limited the extent of research concerned to identify the determinants of changes and variations in public sector employment levels between countries. Nevertheless one or two findings and observations can be made. First, the IMF study tested a variant of 'Wagner's law', and found that total government employment per capita tended to increase as per capita income rose.[57] Second, a study of public sector employment for twenty OECD countries covering the years 1965—83 found that an 'index of union power' (which included components such as the level of bargaining and the unity of labour) was positively correlated with both the proportion of public employment and the rate of change in these proportions across countries.[58] It is, however, important to note that some commentators, such as Rose,[59] have strongly argued that the determinants of public sector employment change need to be studied on a programme-by-programme (or functional area) basis, rather than seeking to explain variation in the level of or changes in public sector employment as a whole.

A number of studies have made reference to the particular characteristics of the public sector workforce which appear to transcend individual countries. For example, the relatively high proportion of women workers in the public sector is often mentioned. This was an issue examined in an OECD report which, using data on the proportion of women in public sector employment (excluding public enterprises) in eight member countries over the period 1965—77, concluded that

There is a wide differential between the female-intensity of public sector employment across the countries in this sample. Typically, the public sector is very female-intensive in the Scandinavian countries where seven out of every ten workers are female while Japan and Australia are at the other extreme with a ratio of two males to every one female employed in the public sector. Indeed, for this sample of countries there is a positive correlation between the female-intensity of public sector employment and the size of the public sector; the larger the share of public employment in total employment, the greater is the female-intensity of the public sector. Second, there is also a clear tendency for the public sector to become more female-intensive over time. In each of the eight countries the percentage of public sector employment accounted for by females has increased.[60]

This study indicated that the proportion of women workers in public sector employment in the United Kingdom rose from 48.8 per cent in 1971 to 54.3 per cent in 1977. This increase in Britain is also associated with the growth of part-time work in the public sector. For example, one article which was highly critical of the Bacon and Eltis argument for exaggerating the extent (and financial implications) of public sector employment growth in Britain, noted that a major labour shift in the local government sector involved the relative growth of women and part-time workers.[61] Specifically it was noted that (i) in 1961 some 20 per cent of women workers in the manufacturing sector were part-time employees, compared to 17 per cent in central and local government, whereas by 1981 some 31 per cent of women in central and local government (49.7 per cent in local government) were part-time, compared to 23 per cent in manufacturing; and (ii) in 1952 there were more full-time than part-time women employees in local government, but by 1969 there were as many part-time as full-time women workers and by 1972 part-timers outnumbered full-timers by a ratio of 1 to 1.05. A number of publications also refer to the general tendency across countries for the public sector to have a more highly educated workforce than the private sector,[62] while for individual countries there are frequently indications of other differences between the workforces of the public and private sectors. In Britain, for example, the average age of public sector employees tends to be higher than that in the private sector, particularly in the case of manual employees. For instance in 1983 the average age of male manual workers in central government was 42.3, 42.4 in local government, 42.3 in public corporations, whereas it was 37.7 in the private sector.[63] These sorts of differences in the characteristics of the workforce in the public and private sectors need continually to be borne in mind when comparisons (e.g. of wages) are made between the two sectors of employment.

To complete this section, I consider some of the changes that have occurred in the size of the public sector workforce in Britain since the 1960s. To this end Table 2.1 sets out some figures for the

Table 2.1 UK public sector employment 1961−89, by major categories
(thousands)

Head-count	Central government	Local authorities	Public corporations	Total public sector
1961	1,790	1,870	2,200	5,860
1962	1,785	1,940	2,196	5,921
1963	1,788	2,008	2,136	5,932
1964	1,794	2,088	2,079	5,961
1965	1,816	2,154	2,025	5,995
1966	1,842	2,259	1,962	6,063
1967	1,896	2,364	2,164	6,424
1968	1,909	2,444	2,069	6,422
1969	1,890	2,505	2,041	6,436
1970	1,931	2,559	2,025	6,515
1971	1,966	2,652	2,009	6,627
1972	2,005	2,771	1,929	6,705
1973	2,024	2,890	1,890	6,804
1974	2,140	2,782	1,985	6,907
1975	2,301	2,917	2,035	7,253
1976	2,364	2,956	1,980	7,300
1977	2,358	2,921	2,089	7,368
1978	2,364	2,932	2,061	7,357
1979	2,387	2,997	2,065	7,449
1980	2,393	2,956	2,038	7,387
1981	2,419	2,899	1,867	7,185
1982	2,400	2,865	1,756	7,021
1983	2,384	2,906	1,662	6,952
1984	2,359	2,942	1,610	6,911
1985	2,360	2,958	1,261	6,579
1986	2,337	3,010	1,199	6,546
1987	2,312	3,062	996	6,370
1988	2,322	3,081	924	6,327
1989	2,303	2,934	844	6,081
Full-time equivalent				
1977	2,140	2,324	2,058	6,522
1978	2,140	2,325	2,060	6,525
1979	2,188	2,368	2,034	6,590
1980	2,196	2,343	2,007	6,546
1981	2,225	2,306	1,862	6,393
1982	2,198	2,274	1,736	6,208
1983	2,181	2,301	1,641	6,123
1984	2,149	2,320	1,589	6,058
1985	2,144	2,325	1,247	5,716
1986	2,116	2,352	1,182	5,650
1987	2,091	2,377	980	5,448
1988	2,084	2,379	905	5,386
1989	2,072	2,269	824	5,165

Source: A. Fleming, 'Employment in the public and private sectors', *Economic Trends*, No. 434, December 1989, p. 94

major categories of public sector employment in Britain for the years 1961–89.

Taking the head-count figures for the public sector as a whole, Table 2.1 indicates that the peak level of public sector employment was reached in 1979. Indeed total public sector employment grew by some 27 per cent in the years 1961–79, whereas in 1979–89 it declined by some 18 per cent. The extent of the reduction in public sector employment since 1979 has, however, varied a great deal between the different parts of the public sector. The local authority sector declined by some 2.1 per cent in 1979–89, central government declined by 3.5 per cent, whereas the level of employment in public corporations fell by fully 59 per cent. Furthermore, substantial variations in the extent of employment decline since 1979 were also apparent within these broad categories. For example, within central government, the level of employment increased in the National Health Service by some 6.0 per cent in the years 1970–89, whereas the number of civil servants declined by 20.7 per cent. And within local authorities the numbers in education fell by 6.4 per cent, whereas the level of employment in social services and the police rose by 19.5 and 11.4 per cent respectively.

In 1979 approximately 7.4 million employees or 29.8 per cent of the British workforce were in the public sector, a figure which was made up of 2.1 million (8.2 per cent) in public corporations, 2.3 million (9.3 per cent) in central government and 3.1 million (12.3 per cent) in local authorities. However, by 1989 public sector employment as a proportion of the workforce was down to some 6 million (24.9 per cent), comprising 2.9 million (11.1 per cent) in local authorities, 2.3 million (8.8 per cent) in central government and 0.8 million (3.2 per cent) in public corporations. It is clearly the public corporations which have borne the brunt of public sector employment cuts in the years since 1979. The concentration of employment reductions in this particular area is very much associated with the government's privatization programme. The following examples illustrate the size of some of the employment reductions in the public corporations sub-sector associated with privatization moves: (i) the privatization of British Aerospace in 1981 reduced employment in public corporations by some 23,000; (ii) the privatization of both Cable and Wireless (1981) and the National Freight Corporation (1987) reduced employment in public corporations by approximately 28,000; (iii) the transfer of Britoil (1982) and the Associated British Ports (1983) to the private sector reduced employment in public corporations by some 14,000; (iv) British Telecom (1984) and Trust Posts (1985) reduced public corporations employment by about 25,000; (v) British Gas (1986) involved an employment reduction of 89,000; (vi) British Airways (1987) reduced employment by 36,000; (vii) BAA (1988) involved a reduction of some 7,200; and (viii) the privatization of National Bus Company subsidiaries (1987–8) reduced public corporation employment by some 30,000. Furthermore, the level of employment in public corporations fell by some 80,000 between 1988 and 1989, with nearly three-quarters of this being due to the privatization of British Steel, and that of certain former Passenger Transport Executives. The significance of such moves can be gauged from the fact that total public sector employment fell by 12.5 per cent (head-count), and by 15.6 per cent (in full-time equivalent terms), in 1983–9, but if the employment effects of privatization are excluded, then the scale of the reductions was 5 per cent on a head-count and 8 per cent in full-time equivalents in these years. Table 2.2 contains some more detailed figures for employment change in the years 1983–9.

Table 2.2 Employment changes by sector, 1983–9

	000s	*% change*
Total workforce in employment	+2,703	+11.4
Private sector	+3,111	+18.7
Public sector	−871	−12.5
Public corporations	−818	−49.2
General government	−53	−1.0
Central government	−81	−3.4
HM forces	−14	−4.3
National Health Service	−6	−0.5
Other	−61	−7.3
Local authorities	−28	−1.0
education	+6	+0.4
social services	+51	+14.2
police	+9	+4.8
other	−38	−4.1

Source: A. Fleming, 'Employment in the public and private sectors', *Economic Trends*, No. 434, December 1989, p. 91

THE LEGAL ENVIRONMENT

The final aspect of the environment of public sector industrial relations to be discussed is the legal one. And here one finds that

Britain has a somewhat unusual system in the sense that legal regulation has played relatively little role in shaping the nature of public sector industrial relations.[64] This is essentially a reflection of the following facts; (i) statute, as opposed to common, law has historically been of comparatively minor significance in the traditional (pre-1970s) British system of industrial relations as a whole; (ii) the public sector was the most highly unionized part of the British system well before statute law began to play a more important part in the system of industrial relations as a whole in the 1970s and 1980s; and (iii) the provisions of the statute law that were increasingly passed in the 1970s and 1980s have rarely contained any significant distinctions between the public and public sector systems of industrial relations. Indeed, as Fredman and Morris have commented

> Labour lawyers have not traditionally drawn a distinction between public and private employment law. Indeed, despite the fact that the State is the largest single employer in the country, many labour law works, both practical and theoretical, have all but ignored the public services. The myriad of laws and regulations applicable specifically to public services are seen as a mere exception, or as a footnote, to labour law's central concerns. This approach has also been reflected in industrial relations writings. . . . Turning from theory to the law itself, we find that no consistent distinction has been drawn between the State and private employers. Unlike some systems there is no separate body of administrative law which exclusively governs public service employment. In some contexts, public and private employees are treated alike. For example, most of the statutory employment protection rights specifically apply to civil servants. In the sphere of industrial action, English law stands out from other systems in giving public service workers largely the same freedoms as those in the private sector. In other respects, however, public service workers, particularly civil servants and police, are set apart from private sector employees. For example, obligations of loyalty and confidentiality in relation to their employment are enforced by the criminal as well as the civil law.[65]

Fredman and Morris go on to provide a detailed, wide ranging discussion of a number of aspects of individual and collective employment law in the public services, although the more usual approach in Britain has typically involved little more than passing reference being made to the following matters: (i) in individual employment law there is the long-standing issue of 'Crown immunity', which involves the question of whether a civil servant has a contract of service;[66] (ii) the post-war Nationalisation Acts placed management under a legal obligation to recognize and negotiate with unions; (iii) the Trade Disputes and Trade Unions Act 1927 prohibited civil service unions from affiliating to either the TUC or the Labour Party, and prohibited closed shops in the public sector (repealed in 1946); (iv) the Police Act 1964 provides for criminal sanctions against police going on strike, and the Post Office Act 1953 provides for criminal sanctions against employees who wilfully detain or delay the passage of the mail; (v) the Conspiracy and Protection of Property Act 1873 and the Electricity (Supply) Act 1919 provided for criminal sanctions against strikes in the gas, electricity and water industries (repealed by the Industrial Relations Act 1971); and (vi) the Emergency Powers Act 1920 (amended in 1964) allows the government to take special measures to safeguard essential supplies and services, with these powers having largely been invoked in cases of public sector strikes.

However, even in these few cases where there are legal measures specifically concerned with aspects of public sector industrial relations, it has generally been argued that in practice their impact and significance has been relatively limited. For example, the industries which were nationalized in the post-war years were already highly unionized ones so that the obligation on management to recognize unions was of little practical consequence. Similarly, although the ultimate right of the Crown to dismiss at will has been retained, the early, well-developed dismissal procedures in civil service departments have been hailed as an excellent illustration of the 'salutary effects of formal procedures in preventing arbitrary dismissal.'[67] And finally, when criminal sanctions for strike activity did exist in the public utilities they were rarely invoked. Moreover even the substantial programme of industrial relations legislation passed by the Conservative government since 1979 has not particularly involved provisions which are either exclusively concerned with the public sector or likely to have major differential effects between the public and private sector systems of industrial relations.

As a consequence, even in the much more legally regulated, contemporary system of industrial relations in Britain, legal scholars interested in public sector industrial relations can do little more than first, point to one or two public sector specific provisions in the Thatcher programme of industrial relations legislation (e.g. the outlawing of union labour only contracts and the rescinding of the Fair Wages Resolution of the House of Commons); second, note the questions raised by the Mercury telecommunications case about the distinction between 'political' and 'industrial' action in the public sector,[68] and third, suggest that the EEC directive on equal pay for 'work of equal value' may be of particular interest in a sector with a relatively high proportion of women employees. It is, however, important to recognize that certain pieces of non-industrial relations specific legislation passed by the Thatcher government may have some important public sector industrial relations implications. The nature of the contracting-out provisions of the Local Government Act 1988 are a case in point, which I discuss in chapter 3.

In contrast to Britain, legal regulation of various aspects of public sector industrial relations, such as the extent of unionization, the means of determination of terms and conditions of employment, the right to strike and procedures for dispute resolution, has been much more important in many other countries. In some cases major pieces of legislation (e.g. the Co-determination of Working Life Act 1977 in Sweden) are equally applicable to the public and private sectors, but many countries have pieces of legislation which are solely concerned with aspects of public sector industrial relations. West Germany's Federal Civil Servants Act of 1953 regulated the terms and conditions of employment of the *Beamte*; in Japan, Decree 201 of 1948 removed the right of public sector employees to strike; in Italy, Act 93 of 1983 provides a common bargaining framework for all parts of the public service; in Sweden the Act on Public Employment 1977 contains provisions concerning the contents of agreements in the public sector; while in the USA Title VII of the Public Law Act 95–454 of 1978 provides for the right of federal sector employees to organize and bargain over conditions of employment, although pay and fringe benefits are explicitly excluded from the scope of bargaining. In short, what one observes elsewhere in the developed world is a mixture of law, both within and between individual countries, variously designed to facilitate and/or constrain the structures, processes and outcomes of public sector collective bargaining.

The role of legal regulation in public sector industrial relations seems particularly important in systems of industrial relations which are characterized by (i) relatively decentralized bargaining arrangements (in the system of industrial relations as a whole) and (ii) the relatively late emergence (i.e. from the 1960s) of public sector unionization. The obvious examples here are Canada and the USA. In Canada there has been the establishment of a distinct public sector legislative model of industrial relations which differs from private sector practice as regards the degree of regulation of bargaining structure, limitations on the scope of bargaining, and restrictions on the right to strike.[69] For instance, Canadian federal civil servants are statutorily divided into more than a hundred bargaining units, with legislation in that sector specifying that certain items (e.g. criteria for promotion, pensions, technological change) are non-negotiable, while compulsory interest arbitration arrangements have been the quid pro quo for the removal of the right to strike by police, firefighters, civil servants, teachers and hospital employees.[70] In the United States there has been considerable debate and disagreement about the importance of changes in the legal environment as a major cause of the increased public sector unionization of the 1960s and 1970s. According to Freeman such changes were all important; he cited the fact that in 1959 fully thirty-nine states had no explicit policy on public sector collective bargaining and only one state required such bargaining, whereas in 1984 only four states had no explicit policy and fully thirty-four required such bargaining.[71] This view has been strongly challenged by Burton and Thomason who are more inclined to believe that the growth of public sector unionization led to the passage of such legislation, rather than the relationship being the other way round.[72]

SUMMARY

I have been particularly concerned in this chapter to emphasize the importance of the political environment in shaping the nature of public sector industrial relations. This is a theme that pervades the book, with later chapters providing various illustrations of the impact of political influences on the structures, processes and outcomes of collective bargaining. Indeed such influences are among those developed in the next chapter's discussion of union organizational characteristics in the public sector.

Chapter 3

Unions in the public sector

INTRODUCTION

In this chapter I consider the organizational characteristics of unions as an independent influence on the processes and outcomes of collective bargaining in the public sector. The leading individual themes examined are, first, the relatively high level of union membership and density in the public sector and second, the changing 'character' of public sector unions in the 1970s and 1980s. In addition I will also outline two a priori views of the determinants of union bargaining power in the public sector, and illustrate the nature of the union response to the competitive tendering or contracting-out initiatives of the government in recent years. The latter material usefully illustrates a government strategy which is seeking to reduce the bargaining power of unions in the public sector, while the nature of the union response to this particular strategy indicates the use and limits of existing union power in the public sector.

UNION MEMBERSHIP IN THE PUBLIC SECTOR

Unions emerged at a relatively early stage in the public sector in Britain; the Webbs, for instance, suggested that there were more than a hundred trade unions of state employees by the second decade of this century.[1] Some of the earliest examples of public sector unions in Britain included: (i) teachers' unions, which emerged in the 1860s as a protest against school managers being given the unilateral right to appoint and dismiss teachers; and (ii) civil service departmental associations, which were established in the Post Office in 1854 and in Taxes and Excise in 1858 as a response to departmental reorganization and employee discontent over pay and conditions.[2] The Civil and Public Services Association had some 383 members in 1903, a figure that rose to 1,704 in 1910, to 5,368 in 1920, to 29,278 in 1930 and to an estimated figure of some 85,000 in 1940.[3] The National Association of Local Government Officers was reported to have a membership of more than 100,000 by 1938, following the enactment and establishment of certain legislation and inquires concerning the local government sector in the 1920s and 1930s and the absorption of the Poor Law Officers Association in 1930.[4]

Clegg has produced some union density figures for the ten most highly unionized industries in Britain in 1910, 1920 and 1933[5] which reveal the following picture: (i) in 1910 the Post Office (53.4 per cent union density), local government and education (32.7 per cent) and national government (18.8 per cent) were represented among the top ten industries in terms of the level of union density, despite the absence of national-level recognition of unions for collective bargaining purposes in these areas of employment; (ii) in 1920 the Post Office (76.6 per cent) was the only public sector industry among the ten most highly unionized industries; and (iii) in 1933 national government (84 per cent) was the most highly unionized industry in Britain, with the Post Office (63.5 per cent) and local government and education (51.9 per cent) also being in the top ten industries. Furthermore, in 1948 the level of union density in national government was 66.4 per cent, and 61.9 per cent in local government and education, compared to a private sector average of 37.6 per cent, while in 1974 union density in the public sector averaged 83.1 per cent (compared to an overall workforce figure of 50 per cent), with the figures for national government, education and local government, and the health service being 90.5 per cent, 61.9 per cent and 60.9 per cent respectively.[6]

In seeking to account for the fact that the public sector has for long been the most highly unionized part of the British system of industrial relations it is useful to make some comparison with the position in other countries. Table 3.1 presents some relevant figures, all of which have been drawn from a number of explicitly comparative studies.

Looking at those countries with multiple entries in Table 3.1 reveals the following general picture or pattern: (i) countries where historically public sector unionization has been greater than in the private sector – a situation which still persists in more recent years

Table 3.1 Public sector unionization in a comparative context

Study (and year)	Countries (and year)	Findings
Clegg (1976)	Australia (1972)	77% in the public sector (53% overall)
	France (1973)	75 (25)
	Sweden (1972)	95 (87)
	UK (1973)	85 (50)
	USA (1973)	28 (28)
	West Germany (1972)	93 (37)
Rose (1980)	Sweden (1951)	83% in the public sector (42% in the private sector)
	Ireland (1951)	49 (20)
	Britain (1951)	54 (35)
	Italy (1951)	38 (22)
	USA (1951)	13 (23)
	Sweden (1976)	81 (71)
	Ireland (1976)	81 (51)
	Britain (1976)	72 (34)
	Italy (1976)	39 (39)
	USA (1976)	25 (27)
Treu (1987)	West Germany (1982)	75% public service (38% overall)
	Italy (1983)	52% (45% in private industry)
	Japan (1982)	66.9% in public service (25.3% in private sector)
	Sweden (early 1980s)	80–90% overall (no significant public–private sector difference)
	UK (1979)	80% public sector (55% overall)
	USA (1978)	23.1% in public sector (23.4% in private sector)

Sources: H. Clegg, *Trade Unionism under Collective Bargaining*, Oxford, Blackwell, 1976, p. 12; R. Rose, 'Changes in public employment: a multi-dimensional, comparative analysis', *Studies in Public Policy No. 61*, Centre for the Study of Public Policy, University of Strathclyde, 1980, p. 41; T. Treu *et al.*, *Public Service Relations: Recent Trends and Future Prospects*, Geneva, ILO, 1987.

(e.g. Britain, Ireland, West Germany); (ii) countries where historically the level of public sector unionization has been greater, but where in more recent years there appears to be little difference between the public and private sectors (e.g. Italy, Sweden); and

(iii) countries where historically the level of public sector unionization has been below that of the private sector, but where in more
recent years this traditional difference has been removed and the
public sector is now moving ahead of the level of unionization in
the private sector (e.g. USA). Canada would also come into the last
category. As the majority of countries cited in the table are in categories (i) and (ii) it would appear that there are certain influences
making for relatively high levels of public sector unionization
which appear to transcend the institutional details of individual
national systems of industrial relations; for countries (such as the
USA and Canada) where public sector unionization has been a
comparatively late developer, it would appear that some of these
natural forces for high unionization were originally held back by
legal restrictions, which were then replaced by legislation which
allowed such factors to become operative. The influences which
have been cited as accounting for the relatively high level of union
density in the public sector across individual countries include first,
the concentration of public sector employment in a relatively small
number of individual large-sized undertakings; second, the bureaucratic operation and decision-making processes of public sector
organizations; third, the unionization of public sector managers
which limits their opposition to the unionization of subordinates;
and fourth, the need for practice in the public sector to be consistent with any overall public policy measures in favour or union
recognition and organization.[7] The relevant influence of all four
factors can be usefully illustrated with reference to British
experience.

The first two sets of influences can be discussed together, as
bureaucratic operations are typically held to be a feature of large-
sized employment undertakings or establishments. This explanation of the relatively high level of public sector unionization is
essentially analogous to the 'large plant size' effect reported in
many studies of private sector unionization. That is, a relatively
high level of union density is positively associated with industries in
which employment is concentrated in large-sized establishments
because the bureaucratic operations of such establishments limit
the feasibility of individual bargaining and can generate an above
average level of employee demand for union representation (due to
non-monetary sources of job dissatisfaction); it is also more cost-
effective for unions to concentrate their organizing activities on
such establishments. According to Lockwood the reorganization of

the civil service in the 1920s, which reduced individuals' promotion opportunities and produced a standardization of terms and conditions of employment, provided the basis for the growth of the Civil Service Clerical Association,[8] while a more recent study of union organization in the British Broadcasting Commission argued that the nature of union behaviour was essentially 'a reaction to the growth of more bureaucratic forms of administration'.[9] There is no question that the level of management unionization in the public sector is considerably above that in the private sector in Britain. For example, in 1978 some 90 per cent of male managers in the public sector had their pay determined (directly or indirectly) by collective bargaining arrangements, compared to only 27 per cent in the private sector,[10] while a study of the determinants of the union status of managers in the 1980s found that such status was strongly associated with employment in the public sector.[11]

The particular influence on public sector unionization in Britain that is arguably of major importance is the fact that the government has historically adopted the quite unusual stance, as an employer of labour, of actively encouraging its employees to be union members. According to Bain, for example, the sizeable differential between public sector (i.e. 80 per cent) and private sector (i.e. 10 per cent) white collar union organization in the early 1960s provided 'the best illustration of the importance of employer policies and practices as a factor in union growth'.[12] There are a number of comments to make about this employee encouragement of union organization in the public sector. The first point is that it needs to be seen in the context of a system of industrial relations in which there was historically relatively little in the way of tangible public policy support for union organization; statutory union recognition provisions, for instance, were only introduced in Britain in the 1970s. Second, this encouragement of unionization only followed the government's adoption of Whitley Council arrangements as the basis of national-level recognition of unions for collective bargaining purposes in the non-industrial civil service in 1918–19. Interestingly, the government was initially reluctant to apply the recommendations of the Whitley Committee to the civil service, but was persuaded to do so on the grounds that it needed to set an example of 'best practice' for private sector employers.[13] In fact, over the course of time, this encouragement of unionization came to be viewed as an integral part of the government's commitment to act as a 'good employer' of labour. This commitment to encourage unionization in the public sector has taken a number of tangible forms: (i) as mentioned in the previous chapter, the management of nationalized industries in the post-war years were legally obliged to recognize and negotiate with unions; (ii) the civil service staff handbook has explicitly urged all employees to join unions on the grounds that such organization was essential to facilitate collective bargaining;[14] (iii) essentially similar statements of encouragement have been issued in other parts of the public sector;[15] and (iv) union recognition rights and facilities were frequently granted at lower levels of union membership than has been the case in the private sector.[16] Although few commentators have doubted such encouragement to be an important influence on the level of union membership in the public sector, there have been suggestions that it has had some 'adverse' consequences for the 'character' of the unions concerned. For example, Prandy noted that government encouragement resulted in many public sector unions being 'less protest bodies than administrative unions [whose] function is not so much to challenge the system as to make it work more effectively by providing for the representation of staff opinions and reactions'.[17] The question of the character of public sector unions will be considered in more detail on pp. 50–9.

In view of the fact that the size of the trade union movement as a whole in Britain has declined by more than 3 million members in the years since 1979, it is important to consider the current level and state of public sector unionization. This was a matter investigated in a study by the IDS which produced the following findings:

1 The level of public sector unionization was estimated to be 81 per cent, compared to 38 per cent in the private sector.
2 Thirty of the 88 unions affiliated to the TUC are purely, or overwhelmingly, public sector based ones, with a further nine TUC affiliates having a significant public sector membership. In addition there were some 641,600 members of 16 non-TUC unions in the public sector.
3 Women members constituted some 25 per cent of the total TUC affiliated union membership, with some 73 per cent of all TUC women affiliated members being in the public sector.
4 Only 4 out of 16 listed unions in the public sector recorded membership increases in the years 1979–85.
5 As a result of the privatization of some of the highly unionized, nationalized industries, some public sector unions now have

members in the private sector. For example, some 93 per cent of the membership of the National Communications Union is in the private sector, while the National and Local Government Officers Association's private sector membership (i.e. British Gas) constitutes approximately 5 per cent of its total membership.[18]

In addition to these findings the General Household Survey for 1983[19] reported that the percentage of persons with trade unions at their place of work which they were eligible to join was 95 per cent of men and 97 per cent of women in the public sector; the relevant figures for the private sector were 58 per cent and 49 per cent respectively. Table 3.2 sets out some recent membership figures for a number of the leading individual unions represented in the public sector in Britain.

Table 3.2 Unions in the public sector, membership figures 1979 and 1988

Union	1979	1988	% change 1979–88
Transport & General Workers' Union	2,086,281	1,312,853	– 37.07
General & Municipal Boilermakers' & Allied Trades Union	967,153	789,556	– 18.36
National & Local Government Officers' Association	753,226	754,701	+ 0.20
National Union of Public Employees	691,770	635,070	– 8.20
Royal College of Nursing	161,962	281,918	+ 74.06
National Union of Teachers	290,740	216,614	– 25.50
Confederation of Health Service Employees	212,930	218,321	+ 2.53
National Union of Mineworkers	372,122	169,661	– 54.41
National Association of Schoolmasters & Union of Women Teachers	152,222	159,256	+ 4.62
Civil and Public Services Association	223,884	143,062	– 36.10
National Union of Railwaymen	170,294	120,291	– 35.23

Source: extracted from *Annual Reports of the Certification Officer*, London, HMSO, relevant years

The vast majority of the individual unions in Table 3.2 have suffered membership declines in the years since 1979, with some of these having experienced very substantial membership reductions. (Such adverse movements in membership figures are clearly a major factor in proposed union mergers, such as that between NALGO, NUPE and COHSE; this would be the largest union merger ever in Britain.) However, the position of these (and other) unions in the public sector needs to be seen in the context of an overall union membership decline in Britain of more than 25 per cent in these years. In fact overall union membership decline in Britain in the 1980s has been heavily concentrated in the manufacturing sector with the result that (i) a substantial number of public sector unions have experienced below average membership declines and (ii) as noted in chapter 1, the proportion of total union membership which is accounted for by public sector unions has actually increased in recent years. In Table 3.2 the one union which stands out, as having grown dramatically in the 1980s is the Royal College of Nursing. This is a union which is not affiliated to the TUC or to the Labour Party, and which has an explicit non-industrial action clause as part of its constitution. The growth of this non-militant union, as well as that of the Assistant Masters' and Mistresses' Association in education (whose membership in 1986 totalled 123,601), when placed in the context of overall union decline in Britain, is an issue which I take up in the next section in the discussion of union character in the public sector.

THE CHANGING CHARACTER OF PUBLIC SECTOR UNIONS

The importance of looking at the character of public sector unions can be justified on a number of grounds. First, industrial relations researchers have frequently been highly critical of studies by economists of the average impact of unions on, for example, wages, which tend to view the union movement as an essentially homogeneous one in terms of attitudes, administration and patterns of behaviour. Second, and more specifically, is the view of Prandy, who suggested that government encouragement of union membership in the public sector in Britain tended to produce unions, at least among white collar grades of employees, that were more akin to staff association bodies. Third, a number of commentators, referring to Britain and other countries, have suggested that the

1970s saw many public sector unions begin to undertake certain actions that were very different in nature from their traditional patterns of behaviour. And finally, in the 1980s there appears to be, at least in the case of Britain, a change of a rather different type to that of the previous decade, namely the substantial membership growth of a number of non-militant unions, such as the Royal College of Nursing.

The term 'union character' is one that has been frequently used by industrial relations researchers, although often with little attempt being made to define it precisely and to indicate the criteria to be used in its measurement.[20] However, as a starting point for considering the meaning and value of the concept of union character in the public sector in Britain, there are two studies which can be usefully noted. The first is by Blackburn in which it was argued that the performance of an individual union as a bargaining agent is a function of its level of workforce organization and its position along the spectrum of 'unionateness', the latter being an ordinal measure of the level of an organization's commitment to the general ideology and principles of trade unionism.[21] This notion of 'unionateness' consisted of the following elements: (i) the organization concerned regards collective bargaining and the protection of the interests of members, as employees, as its main function, rather than professional activities or welfare schemes; (ii) the organization is independent of employers for purposes of negotiation; (iii) the organization is prepared to be militant, using all forms of industrial action which may be effective; (iv) the organization declares itself to be a trade union; (v) the organization is registered as a trade union; (vi) the organization is affiliated to the TUC; and (vii) the organization is affiliated to the Labour Party. The first four elements are concerned with the function and behaviour of the organization, while the remaining three (which are essentially British specific in nature) are measures of the level of identification with the labour movement as a whole.

The second study, by Undy *et al.* used the term union 'character' to refer to the strategies and tactics used in the process of job regulation, and they argued that

all the unions in the sample, blue and white collar, experienced some change in the character of job regulation over the period studied in at least two respects: a growth of political action and a growth in militancy, largely in response to increased government intervention in collective bargaining arrangements. Whereas for the majority of unions this was simply a further development along well established lines, for white collar unions in general, and particularly for those in the public services, it involved a major qualitative change. For NALGO and the NUT it involved a change from a position of eschewing militant action and participation in the wider trade union movement prior to 1960, to one that involved affiliation to the TUC and the willingness to take militant action in pursuit of bargaining aims.[22]

Table 3.3 provides a summary statement of the leading manifestations and causes of the changing character of the National and Local Government Officers' Associations, as identified in this particular study.

Table 3.3 Manifestations and causes of the changing character of NALGO

Manifestations

1 Affiliation to the TUC in 1964 (previous attempts to affiliate in 1920, 1921, 1942, 1945, 1948, 1955, 1962 had been defeated).
2 The adoption of a strike clause in its constitution in 1961.
3 1967, 1970 and 1974 saw major examinations of strike policy. In 1970 the size of the strike fund was increased, and in 1974 shortened procedures for calling strikes were introduced.
4 The authorization of first official strike in 1970.
5 The first use of industrial action in support of a major wage claim in 1974.

Causes

1 (External) The operation of incomes policy which appeared to favour low paid workers and sought to downgrade the importance of comparability (vis-à-vis productivity) as a wage-setting criterion in the public sector. The result being a perceived decline or squeeze in wage differentials.
2 (Internal) Extensive use of provisions in the constitution to change existing policy where it interfered with the attainment of more militant objectives. The increased occurrence of branch level initiated special conferences being a particular case in point.
3 (Internal) The reduced extent of chief officer presence and influence within the National Executive Committee, and a change of general secretary.
4 (Internal) The activities of the NALGO Action Group, a 'ginger group' of younger aged activists well represented in certain key local branches.

Source: derived from R. Undy, V. Ellis, W.E.J. McCarthy and A.M. Halmos, *Change in Trade Unions*, London, Hutchinson, 1981, pp. 223–38

The importance of these changes in NALGO is highlighted in a recent study of unionization among social workers where it was commented that

The 1974 dispute was part of a definite trend in NALGO. The workload of the union's Emergency Committee, a committee of the National Executive Council (NEC) with the formal authority of the union to make industrial action official, increased substantially in the 1970s. Between 1968 and 1972, it considered an average of eight cases per year; whereas between 1973 and 1976 this figure increased to thirty. This trend towards militancy was urged on by NAG supporters who were very influential at the union's conferences in 1972 and 1973. The growing militancy seemed to be rewarded by even higher rates of membership growth. In 1975, the membership of NALGO increased by an astonishing 15 per cent, which was the biggest annual increase in the whole period from 1970 to 1985 and more than double the average annual increase for the 1970s.[23]

In both of these treatments of union 'character' (or 'unionateness' in Blackburn's terminology) what is essentially argued is that the change observed (in a union as an organizational entity) involved (i) increasingly militant attitudes and patterns of behaviour and (ii) an increased integration, and sense of identity, with the larger, mainstream trade union movement. And, specifically, in the case of public sector unions among white collar groups of employees, it is contended that such unions became increasingly similar (along these two basic dimensions), from the late 1960s, to blue collar unions in both the public and private sectors. Chapter 6 will discuss the issue of industrial action and strike activity in the public sector in some detail so here, in order further to illustrate this contention concerning a change in character, I first concentrate on the relationship between public sector unions and the TUC.

There are three major elements involved in this particular relationship: public sector union affiliations to the TUC, the representation of public sector unions on the General Council of the TUC, and the existence of any special arrangements within the structure of the TUC which particularly cater for the needs and interests of public sector unions. Taking the first of these elements, the unions organizing blue collar workers and even some white collar unions (e.g. CPSA in 1920) in the public sector have been longstanding affiliates of the TUC. However, it was the 'incomes policies years' of the 1960s and 1970s which were particularly associated with white collar, public sector unions affiliating to the TUC, largely on the pragmatic grounds of their need to obtain access (via the TUC) to the centres of government decision-making which were so important in the administration of such policies. The affiliation of NALGO in 1964 has already been mentioned and this was followed by the affiliation of the National Association of Schoolmasters in 1968, the National Union of Teachers in 1970, the Society of Civil and Public Servants in 1973, the Institution of Professional Civil Servants and the Association of University Teachers in 1976, and the Association of First Division Civil Servants in 1977; in fact all members of the (then) Council of Civil Service Unions were TUC affiliates by the end of the 1970s.

Second, the relative growth of white collar and public sector union membership in the 1970s was increasingly, albeit slowly, reflected in the composition of the General Council of the TUC and the overall organizational structure of the body. For example, the number of white collar representatives on the Council in the early 1970s was double that of a decade previously, the non-manual workers advisory conference was abolished (as inadequate to their growing presence) in 1975, and from the early 1980s unions with more than 100,000 members were to be automatically represented on the General Council (very approximately in 1986–7, some 15 per cent of members were from private sector unions, 36 per cent from public sector unions, and the remainder from unions with members in both sectors). Furthermore, there has been a growth in the number of industry committees from nine in 1972 to fifteen in 1985. These industry committees provide the unions concerned with an important element of 'freedom to manoeuvre' in the overall TUC structure, and a number of them are based in the public sector: fuel and power, health service, local government, steel and transport. These committees are primarily for union lobbying purposes, although the steel one also engages in collective bargaining. In addition the eleven joint committees of the TUC include one for the nationalized industries and one for public services. The latter (established in 1979) has been prominent in recent years in attempting to stimulate and facilitate moves towards more of a co-ordinated, bargaining strategy in the public sector; it has, for instance, sought to encourage a concentration of public sector wage settlements in April of each year, and has issued annual guidelines for a common core approach to collective bargaining.

Third, in addition to these changes in the character of public sector unions being reflected in an increased integration and sense of identity with the larger union movement (at the level of the TUC), public sector unions in the 1970s increasingly emulated private sector union organizational developments of the 1960s, in the sense of seeking to develop shop steward arrangements. In many cases these were 'planned', national-level, union initiatives, albeit in response to growing grass-roots developments. Although differences in bargaining structure between the two sectors of employment (see chapter 5) have inevitably made for differences in this regard, there is no doubt that the presence of shop stewards in the public sector increased noticeably in the 1970s. For example, one study commented that

> On the employee side representation through shop stewards was rare in the 1960s in local government, existing only in isolated pockets among self-contained groups of workers such as refuse-collectors. In the 1970s more devolved patterns of worker representation have developed, with the gradual establishment both among blue and white collar workers of shop steward systems. In the case of the General and Municipal Workers Union (GMWU) it has been estimated that the number of shop stewards trebled in the ten years from 1968 to 1978. The National Union of Public Employees (NUPE) and the Transport and General Workers' Union (TGWU), both with strong membership among local government manual workers, gave greater power to their shop stewards. NUPE in particular made strong attempts to expand the strength and depth of its shop steward organisation.[24]

Similarly on the non-manual workers' front the study of unionization among social workers, which was referred to earlier (p. 53), observed that the 1978−9 social workers' dispute, concerning the right to negotiate social workers' grades locally, was the culmination of a process of growing union activism which,

> although initially narrowly-based in certain types of local authority . . . began to express itself in workplace union organisations that seemed to be moving closer and closer to the shop steward form found in the private manufacturing sector. Official trade union approval was given for these changes in 1977: when the main union, NALGO, issued a circular to its branches giving advice on the introduction of shop steward systems, thereby formally marking the arrival of the shop steward movement.[25]

Indeed the extent of movement along these lines has been such that the 1984 workplace industrial relations survey observed that in the years 1980–4:

> Taking all representatives, both manual and non-manual, in the economy as a whole, our estimates indicate a slight increase in the total number from about 317,000 to around 335,000, a rise of some six per cent. This is composed of a very substantial decline in manufacturing of some 27 per cent, a substantial increase in private services of 18 per cent and very substantial rise in the public sector of 31 per cent. . . . The result of these various changes is that non-manual union representatives were nearly as common as manual shop stewards in 1984 and a clear majority of trade union representatives in the economy as a whole were employed in public sector establishments. The stereotype of the trade union representative as a manual shop steward in manufacturing industry evidently needs revision.[26]

The major cause of the changed character of public sector, white collar unions in Britain from the late 1960s has been the operation of incomes policies. The general contentions under this heading are that public sector wage settlements have come in for particularly close scrutiny by the relevant administrative bodies; that such bodies have frequently been highly critical of the role of comparability in wage determination procedures; that flat rate increases have squeezed salary differentials; that the productivity or efficiency exceptions to the general limits of such policies tended to favour private sector employees; and that the public sector as a whole, or at least certain groups within it, suffered wage losses relative to private sector employees in such policy years. Chapter 7 discusses the wage impact of incomes policies in more detail, although here it is relevant to note that male employees in central and local government certainly reported much less satisfaction with all matters relating to pay than did other employees in a national survey in 1978, whereas in the early 1970s there was little apparent difference between the two groups of workers.[27] This employee dissatisfaction with pay is likely to have been particularly important in triggering off certain internal changes in the leadership and administration of a number of white collar, public sector unions (see Table 3.3). For example, the decision of the Civil Service Clerical Association to remove the no-strike clause from its constitution in 1969 has been linked to a change of General Secretary in 1967. Indeed a 'leftward' or 'radical' shift in the leadership of a number of civil service unions from the late 1960s has been identified as one of the causes of their changing character,[28] although other commentators may see this particular tendency as more of a manifestation, rather than a cause, of the change in union character.

This basic direction of change in the character of white collar, public sector unions has been noted in some other countries. For example, in the United States a distinction in the literature is often drawn between unions and bargaining associations in the public sector. Although both rely on collective bargaining, the latter are more likely to emphasize the importance of political action, to include supervisors as members, to be less willing to endorse strike action and are not affiliated to the AFL–CIO.[29] However, throughout the 1970s there was a general tendency for bargaining associations to become more union-like; this point has frequently been made in relation to the National Education Association which has become increasingly similar to the American Federation of Teachers, although the former still remains outside the AFL–CIO.[30] A 1989 review of public sector industrial relations in Canada has also documented the movement from an association-consultation model to one of unionization-collective bargaining from the mid-1960s.[31] In other national systems of industrial relations this change of character may be manifested in rather different ways. For instance, rather than joining the 'mainstream' union movement (as represented by the leading union confederation) the white collar, public sector unions may take an increasingly independent line of their own. In Sweden, for example, the Central Organization of Salaried Employees–Federation of Civil Servants has been more and more reluctant during the 1980s to follow the national wage bargaining pattern set by the Swedish Employers' Confederation and the Swedish Confederation of Trade Unions, while in Italy some independent unions for white collar employees in the public sector have enjoyed recent membership gains and been increasingly active outside of the three major union confederations.[32]

Finally, one needs to ask whether this character change by white collar, public sector unions in Britain has continued into the 1990s. The answer to this question is not entirely straightforward, as developments seem to have been mixed. On the one hand, it is apparent that it is the non-militant unions, such as the Royal College of Nursing and the Assistant Masters' and Mistresses' Association (which is currently close to being the second largest teachers' union in Britain), which have experienced the exceptional, substantial increases of membership in these years. This is a very different situation to that in the 1970s, when individual union membership increases were held to be positively correlated with militancy, and many commentators felt that unions like the Royal College of Nursing had little future.[33] At present, however, it is clear that new entrants to nursing and teaching appear disproportionately to favour membership of these less militant organizations, and that substantial numbers of existing employees have switched their membership to them following the occurrence of strike action in both the health service and education in the 1980s; the nature of this change between the 1970s and 1980s is clearly a subject area worthy of further research.[34] This being said, one needs to recognize, first, that such organizations as the Royal College of Nursing have become increasingly union-like and, second, that other public sector, white collar unions have, in a number of ways, continued to move along, in Blackburn's terminology, the 'unionateness' spectrum. For example, the Royal College of Nursing remains unaffiliated to the TUC and the Labour Party and retains its non-industrial action clause, but in 1977 it was certificated as an independent union, has balloted its members on the questions of both TUC affiliation (1979–80 and 1982) and the repeal of its non-industrial action clause (1982 and 1988), has declared its unwillingness to be involved in any attempt to establish a rival union confederation to the TUC, and has indicated its intention to consider admitting untrained nursing staff to membership. Second, the increased 'politicization' of the TUC-affiliated white collar unions in the public sector in the 1980s can be observed in relation to the requirement of the Trade Union Act 1984 that membership ballots be held on the question of the retention of political funds. All thirty-eight unions with political funds at the time voted to retain them, while a further seventeen unions have established (since the Act) such funds for the first time.[35] No fewer than fourteen of the seventeen unions concerned were public sector ones, with all of the major civil service unions being to the forefront in their establishment; the National Association of Schoolmasters/Union of Women Teachers also voted at their annual conference in 1989 to establish such a fund.

The discussion in this section of the increased 'militancy' of public sector unions from the late 1960s leads logically to the next section, which essentially outlines two views of the determinants of union bargaining power. The emphasis of the discussion will be on identifying what these two views suggest about the bargaining power of public sector unions relative to that of their private sector counterparts.

UNION BARGAINING POWER AND THE PUBLIC SECTOR

One view of the determinants of union bargaining power, which has been particularly favoured by economists in relative wage studies, makes extensive reference to the concept of the elasticity of demand for labour.[36] This particular concept was in fact central to the position adopted by Dunlop in the early 'Dunlop–Ross' debate concerning the determinants of union aims in wage bargaining.[37] According to Dunlop, a union is essentially a supplier or seller of labour services and hence, as the supply side counterpart to the firm, can be treated as an economic decision-making unit whose primary objective is the maximization of some wage/employment dimension of its membership. The essential aspect of virtually all of the possible union aims outlined by Dunlop was that the union would take explicit account of the level of employment (of its current membership) that was associated with various possible wage demands. In other words, the union would make some estimate of the elasticity of demand for the services of its members when framing its basic wage demands, and the more inelastic the demand for labour function (i.e. the less employment changes in response to a given change in its price) the more the union could make higher wage demands without risking a displacement of members from employment. And, according to the Marshallian-derived demand conditions, a labour demand function will be more inelastic: (i) the more essential is (union) labour to the production of the final product; (ii) the more inelastic is the demand for the final product; (iii) the smaller is the ratio of (union) labour cost to total production cost; and (iv) the more inelastic is the supply of other factors of production.

This basic framework of analysis has led a number of economists to predict that the size of the union relative wage effect associated with public sector unions will be greater than that for private sector unions,[38] largely as a result of condition (ii) above. However, as Kochan and Katz have argued, it is essential to consider all four of the above conditions in any assessment of differential union bargaining power between the public and private sectors.[39] And in their view conditions (i) and (ii) point to a difference which favours public sector unions, while for condition (iv) there is no obvious public–private sector difference, and in the case of condition (iii) the relatively high labour cost ratio of public sector employment suggests that public sector unions will be relatively disadvantaged. In short, not all four determinants of the elasticity of demand for labour consistently point in the direction of relatively greater union bargaining power in the public sector.

Moreover, most mainstream industrial relations researchers would be highly sceptical of the view that union bargaining power is solely, or even largely, determined by this elasticity of demand for labour framework of analysis. In conceptual terms industrial relations researchers have tended to favour the view of Chamberlain who has defined bargaining power in terms of the costs to each party of agreement relative to the costs to them of disagreement,[40] which has inevitably led such individuals to emphasize the importance of 'strike leverage' as a major determinant of union bargaining power. There has in fact been considerable discussion and disagreement over the question of whether the strike leverage of public sector unions is greater (lesser) than that of private sector unions due to the greater (or lesser) costs imposed on public sector employers. The absence of a close relationship between strikes and employer revenue, unlike the position in the private sector, would seem to accord public sector employers a relative advantage in taking strikes. However, this influence may be more than offset by a number of other considerations. The nature of these other considerations can be usefully illustrated by considering Chamberlain and Schilling's argument that the output costs of any strike will depend upon three basic factors: (i) the ability of consumers of the products of, and suppliers of the raw materials to, strike-affected establishments to switch their orders and supplies to alternative firms or industries; (ii) the level of stocks which the strike-affected establishments consume, and suppliers are able to run down and build up respectively during the stoppage; and (iii) the 'necessity' of the product concerned.[41]

The fact that much of the output of the public sector consists of services (rather than goods) which are by definition non-storable, and for which there are no alternative, short-run sources of supply (i.e. the public sector is a monopoly producer), provides, according to the Chamberlain and Schilling factors, something of an a priori case for believing that the costs of public sector strikes will be relatively high cost ones. Furthermore, the national or industry-wide bargaining structure of the public sector – at least in Britain – means that a strike's impact will be nation-wide, which is one of the pre-conditions which has been proposed for defining a 'national emergency' dispute.[42] It is, however, the third factor (i.e. the necessity or essential nature of the product) in Chamberlain and Schilling's framework of analysis which has figured so prominently in discussions of the 'high cost' nature of public sector strikes. Specifically, it has been argued that the essential nature of publicly provided goods and services means that the effects of strikes in the public sector cannot be confined to the immediate parties in dispute, and hence the strike in the public sector does not perform the traditional private sector function of exerting a reciprocal economic (wage and profit loss) pressure on unions and management which causes them to modify their negotiating positons to the extent necessary to bring about agreement. Instead public sector strikes are held to be essentially a political weapon designed ultimately to bring pressure on the government as the ultimate pay-master, through adversely affecting third parties and the public at large. Indeed it has been contended that the greater the adverse effect on the public the more likely it is that the government, through fear of electoral disfavour, will settle public sector strikes relatively quickly and on terms relatively favourable to the union position.[43]

There are, however, a number of important qualifications which need to be attached to this particular line of argument. The first is that the essentiality of goods and services, for maintaining the short-run economic and social welfare of the public at large, will obviously vary considerably between the different parts of the public sector. It has, for instance, been suggested that one can distinguish in the public sector between (i) essential goods and services (e.g. police and fire services), (ii) intermediate services (e.g. sanitation), and (iii) non-essential services.[44] Second, the pattern of public sector strikes will tend to vary between different national systems of industrial relations, as a result of differences in, for example, the nature of bargaining structure. In the USA for instance, where bargaining structures are relatively decentralized in the public sector, public sector strikes are typically of shorter duration than in the private sector, whereas in Britain exactly the opposite relationship tends to exist. Third, some public sector strikes have only disrupted, as opposed to eliminated, the supply of public sector services, as a result of the use of, for example, army personnel in maintaining a certain level of service provision.[45] And finally, it needs to be emphasized that there has been remarkably little systematic, empirical research concerning the actual costs of public sector strikes in Britain and elsewhere. As a consequence, arguments concerning the allegedly high costs of public sector strikes are overwhelmingly a priori as opposed to empirically based ones.

An examination of the government's competitive tendering or contracting-out approach in the public sector would seem (as well as being important in its own right) to constitute a useful empirical input to discussions of the nature and determinants of public sector union bargaining power. This is because such an approach can be viewed as an attempt to reduce such power, with the nature of the union response (and its degree of success) to such initiatives providing some indication of the existing extent of such power. In other words, if compulsory competitive tendering poses a threat to the organizational (e.g. high level of union density) basis of union power in the public sector, will there be certain behavioural manifestations of this power (e.g. strikes) which can offset or disrupt the introduction and effects of such tendering? Accordingly it is to this subject area which I now turn.

THE UNION RESPONSE TO COMPETITIVE TENDERING IN THE PUBLIC SECTOR

The Conservative government's programme of 'privatization' has frequently been categorized as follows: (i) denationalization of public corporations and the sale of public assets (e.g. British Telecom); (ii) liberalization, or the removal of restrictions on private competition for public services (e.g. the Transport Act 1985 and the deregulation of public passenger road transport); and (iii) contracting-out.[46] The latter, which is the concern of this section, has involved, first, *mandatory* competitive tendering for certain specific services in the civil service and the NHS. For example, it was reported that by early 1987 some 84 per cent of cleaning contracts in the civil service (73 per cent of laundry and 81 per cent of maintenance ones) had been contracted-out to the private sector.[47] In the NHS competitive tendering has been required for cleaning, laundry and catering services, although in practice some 85 per cent of the contracts put out to tender have been awarded in-house.[48] An important difference between the civil service and the NHS initiatives is that in the former case the in-house work-force have been given little opportunity to tender for the contract. In the case of the local government sector, contracting-out was initially a voluntary process associated with a small number of Conservative-controlled local councils, with mandatory competitive tendering only applying in relation to construction, direct labour organizations (1980) and municipal buses (1985). However, the Local Government Act 1988 contains compulsory competitive tendering provisions for a range of services, including refuse-collection, cleaning of buildings and other cleaning, school meals and welfare catering, other catering, repair and maintenance of vehicles and ground maintenance. (A NALGO pamphlet estimates that 'contracting out six major council services would lead to the loss of over 73,000 jobs nation-wide'.) The increasingly mandatory nature of competitive tendering moves in the public sector in Britain should be viewed in the light of one review of local government and NHS experience which suggested that such initiatives are likely to be most effective in 'non-political' environments, where they arise naturally in response to local needs.[49]

For the individual employees concerned, competitive tendering is seen as likely to involve job losses, pay reductions and a general decline in the conditions of service. Indeed as one review of the experience to date put it:

> There can certainly be no doubt that contracting-out does lead to a decline in terms and conditions of employment. Pay rates do not necessarily suffer, the NHS has been particularly successful to date in obtaining basic Ancillary Staffs General Whitley Council hourly rates in the contract with the tendering organiza-tions, but even here cost savings are made by a worsening of conditions of employment such as pensions, standard hours, sickness pay, holidays, and through the eradication of bonus schemes.[50]

Furthermore, competitive tendering poses a threat to unions as organizational entities because of its capacity to reduce member-ship levels. This is because competitive tendering

> generally results in a smaller number of staff being proposed to undertake the contract by both in-house and external bidders. Regardless of whether the contract is awarded in-house or to a

contractor, less jobs result from the exercise and the unions must increase their penetration among re-employed workers to sustain membership totals. If the contract is awarded externally, the effect upon membership is likely to be more dramatic as a high percentage of union members will not apply for jobs with contractors. Those who do and are hired privately are not always interested in renewing their subscriptions, especially if the fight to save the in-house service has been a particularly bitter one. New workers hired externally by the contractor, particularly part-timers, are usually reluctant to enter into any formal association with a trade union. Retention of both old and new members is difficult as staff turnover with contractors' organisations is high.[51]

These concerns and dilemmas for trade unions in the public sector have produced a pattern of response, of which the major components are set out in Table 3.4.

There has been scant conceptual discussion of the particular criteria which should be used for evaluating the 'success' of the union responses to competitive tendering, and little systematic research concerning the degree of success actually obtained. The relevant literature typically contains hardly more than some figures for (i) the extent of job losses and (ii) the number of contracts awarded in-house. However, Ascher does summarize a range of essentially impressionistic evidence, which leads her to conclude that the unions have had essentially mixed fortunes in their campaigns against competitive tendering. In essence she points to the following effects and outcomes:

1 The efforts to discredit the contractors have been highly visible and have focused considerable political and media pressure on them (e.g. in October 1989 a COHSE official was reported as claiming that 'masses of bacteria' had been found in one Glasgow hospital cleaned by private contractors). For example, the managing director of one contracting firm claimed in 1985 that nearly a quarter of his time was spent in responding to union complaints and criticisms in the media.
2 Although industrial action has been less successful than the unions had hoped, it has helped to publicize any resulting declines in employment standards, has caused some disruptions in ancillary services following tendering exercises and may have caused some authorities to avoid using private contractors.

Table 3.4 The nature of the union response to competitive tendering

1 Internal union campaign to mobilize both membership and lower level officer support against such initiatives.
  (i) Individual national unions have issued policy guidelines of opposition, designed to delay the tendering process, although any decision taken about the specific forms of opposition rests essentially with the local branches of the union(s).
  (ii) Workshops, seminars and short training courses have been provided for local level officials and shop stewards. The material in these initiatives has sought to indicate the sort of provisions which should ideally be included in the contracts, and to assist individuals who may be involved in reviewing the contract bids submitted (e.g. assist in identifying any 'unrealistic' bids).
  (iii) A network of internal communication arrangements has been established often via the research department of the individual union, to circulate material on the 'lessons learned' in particular parts of the country. The NUPE network in this regard is held to be especially impressive in terms of the range and quality of information provided.
2 External strategies designed to influence public opinion concerning the worth and value of public services.
  (i) Extensive publicity of the poor performance of private sector contractors.
  (ii) Various local level strikes against competitive tendering (e.g. those in the London hospitals, Hammersmith and Barking, in 1984) which have attracted considerable media attention.
  (iii) The attempt to establish formal and informal links with political and pressure groups at the local level who are likely to favour the maintenance of in-house public services (e.g. the 'resistance 83' grouping in Basingstoke).
  (iv) A number of legal rulings sought in the courts (e.g. the legal standing of the government's circular on competitive tendering in the NHS in 1983–4).

Source: compiled from K. Ascher, *The Politics of Privatisation*, London, Macmillan, 1987, pp. 113–23

3 The impact of links with other community based groups is difficult to measure, although such arrangements have rarely prevented a 'determined' authority from either seeking tenders or contracting-out.
4 Legal rulings have helped raise the morale of union members and have been well covered in the media, which may have dissuaded certain contractors from putting in particular tenders.[52]

The basic conclusion reached by Ascher is essentially that:

Overall, the unions' campaign has been successful on a number of fronts. It has helped to push the issues surrounding competitive tendering to the forefront of many local political agendas; this has generally meant that the process itself is undertaken more slowly and more carefully than might otherwise be the case. The unions' campaign has also had a recognizable impact upon the thinking of both authority members and officers. The dramatic portrayal of potential changes in the individual worker's environment has inspired many authorities to include fair wages clauses in their tendering documents; likewise the detailed descriptions of contractors' 'failures' have prompted many to include 'protective' clauses which place extra costs on the outside tenderers. Both developments have helped to improve the competitive position of in-house labour forces.[53]

The developments noted in the above quote are clearly an important part of the background to the provisions of the Local Government Act 1988 which rule out the possibility of inserting any clauses in contracts which are designed to achieve certain minimum standards of personnel practice and conditions of service. That is, local authorities are to be prevented from taking into account 'noncommercial considerations' when awarding a contract. Although Ascher holds that the unions have achieved certain 'procedural victories' in the competitive tendering process she believes that more substantive gains have not been realized as a result of co-ordination difficulties and problems both within and between unions.[54] For example, reference is made to the limited co-operation and co-ordination between NUPE and COHSE at the local level in opposing competitive tendering in the NHS. The 1988 Local Government Act does, however, appear to have stimulated some enhanced inter-union co-operation, at least at the national level, as indicated by the GMB, NALGO, NUPE, TWGU publication 'Who Cares Wins'. This document sets out some detailed guidelines for union negotiators at all stages of the tendering process.

In summary, competitive tendering is an important initiative directed against what the government view as 'excessive union power' in the public sector, but it appears that the exertion of this existing level of power has done little more than (i) delay the tendering process and (ii) result in the insertion of some procedural clauses and arrangements which have favoured in-house bids; the latter arrangements will, however, be reduced in the future, at least in local government, as a result of the recent legislation. However, the initial experience under the 1988 Act indicates that a majority of contracts have been awarded in-house. For example, Manchester City Council reported that 81 per cent out of 448 contracts had remained in-house, a figure that varied from 98 per cent in the case of school meals and welfare catering to 70 per cent in the case of building cleaning contracts.[55] The major factors in accounting for the early stage success of the in-house bids have been first, major reorganizations of council services into 'quasi'-companies (Direct Service Organizations) in many councils, and second, a significant renegotiation of terms and conditions of employment at local level (e.g. employment reductions, consolidation of bonus schemes, changes to working hours and practices).[56] However, the unions are clearly concerned as to whether this sort of in-house success level can be maintained over time, and at what cost to the employees and themselves.

SUMMARY

In this chapter I have examined the organizational characteristics of unions as an independent influence on the process and outcomes of collective bargaining in the public sector. The focus here has been very much on the relatively high level of union organization in the public sector, and the changes observed in the character of many public sector unions, particularly white collar ones, in recent decades. The issue of union bargaining power has been raised, although the extent and determinants of such power can only be more fully appreciated once we have considered a number of other factors, most notably the management role in collective bargaining. It is to this subject that I turn in the next chapter.

Chapter 4

Management organization for industrial relations purposes in the public sector

Introduction

The decision of management to recognize unions for collective bargaining purposes will inevitably result in certain structural changes within the management hierarchy of the organizations concerned. The leading structural change in this regard will be the establishment of a specialist management function for dealing with personnel and industrial relations matters. As a result, researchers concerned with collective bargaining in the private sector have devoted considerable attention to questions concerning the role, power and performance of the personnel management function.

In the public sector, however, the fact that the employer is essentially a political institution raises a question that rarely (if ever) has to be posed in private section industrial relations research, namely, who is management for the purposes of collective bargaining? This is the first question considered here, which is then followed by a discussion of some concepts of the government as an employer of labour and an examination of the personnel management function within the management organization of the public sector.

WHO IS MANAGEMENT IN THE PUBLIC SECTOR?

The public sector in most parliamentary democracies is characterized by a diffusion of management responsibility which arises from constitutional divisions, which reflect 'assumptions about the value of checks and balances, political versus nonpolitical decision-making, and local versus central control',[1] and the multiple funding sources of many public sector organizations. The result is frequently shared management authority, with formal responsibility and actual responsibility often differing, which has a number of important consequences for the operation of collective bargaining, some of which are indicated below.

In Britain, civil servants are the direct employees of the government and in this part of the public sector the unions have historically negotiated solely and directly with representatives of the Treasury. In contrast, elsewhere in central government, such as the NHS, the unions have long complained about the lack of direct Treasury representation on negotiating bodies. However, the fact that the civil service unions are in the unusual position of directly negotiating with the Treasury has not always been viewed as an unmixed blessing for them. For example, the academic Harold Laski argued more than forty years ago that

> a separation will have to take place between the financial and establishment functions of the Treasury. A separate Minister of Personnel is required to whom all questions of recruitment, training, promotion, pay and other conditions of service will be entrusted. The present fusion of functions in the Treasury has the undesirable result of making financial considerations unduly influential in personnel problems.[2]

Arguments along these lines resulted in the period 1968–81 being an important exception to the fact of sole negotiations with the Treasury, as the responsibilities for the management of the civil service were placed in the hands of the Civil Service Department in these years; the creation of this department followed upon the Report of the Fulton Committee of Inquiry into the Civil Service in 1968. However, co-ordination difficulties with the Treasury, together with the belief that the Civil Service Department was not sufficiently efficiency-orientated in outlook, increasingly built up under the Thatcher government and finally 'the CSD's apparent inclination to appease the unions during the civil service strike of 1981 ensured its death later that year'.[3] The decision to abolish the Civil Service Department in November 1981 resulted in its responsibilities for manpower matters and negotiations on pay and conditions of service being returned to the Treasury with some minor sharing of responsibilities with the Management and Personnel Office, the latter being part of the Cabinet Office structure.

The unions in the nationalized industries of public corporations also appear to have the advantage of facing a unitary management side on negotiating bodies, which is free to conduct and conclude negotiations without any need to refer matters to the government for approval. In practice, however, this management freedom from government influence in the pay negotiations of the nationalized industries has been more apparent than real. This situation has been most obvious in the case of British Rail where from the early 1960s management has regularly consulted with the Treasury about the size of 'acceptable' wage increases before entering into negotiations with the unions.[4] However, if one looks beyond the details of individual wage negotiations, particularly during episodes of incomes policy, to government attempts to reorientate the larger business and industrial relations strategies of management in public enterprises, one cannot automatically assume that the political authorities' objectives will always be implemented and accomplished in full. For example, Ferner's study of British Rail indicates that the political authorities have inevitably experienced control problems as a result of the following factors and considerations: (i) there is some degree of managerial discretion in such enterprises which gives rise to internal (managerial) interests and agendas that may differ from those of the political authorities; and (ii) public enterprises have some degree of countervailing power because their activities have significant economic and political implications for the perceived performance of the government.[5] As a result, the attempt of the Thatcher government to have the management of British Rail adopt a more commercially orientated business strategy in the 1980s was not a straightforward and simple exercise in external control. Indeed, as Ferner illustrates, a number of problems and contradictions arose 'in the course of translating external pressures into managerial strategies'.[6]

The NHS is, like the civil service, part of central government but, unlike the civil service, the unions in the NHS do not face a unitary management side on negotiating bodies. The important management side division on negotiating bodies in the NHS is, in McCarthy's words, that between 'employers who do not pay and paymasters who do not employ'.[7] For instance, in 1982 the NHS Ancillary Staffs Council contained 24 management side members, of whom 19 represented the health authorities and 5 represented the central government funding departments. Although the former group was vastly superior in numerical terms, the unions have consistently argued first that the central government department representatives have a disproportionate influence in the determination of the management side agenda and second, that the really powerful influence in the determination of this agenda is the Treasury, which is not directly represented at the bargaining table. According to the unions, the major decisions affecting the outcome of negotiations in the NHS are made outside the operation of the joint negotiating bodies, a situation which has resulted in (i) especially harsh wage treatment under incomes policies, (ii) a general worsening of union–management relations, (iii) confrontations arising from frustration, (iv) the increased substitution of lobbying for collective bargaining, (v) delays in decision-making and (vi) ultimate negotiated outcomes which are seen to bear little relationship to the validity and importance of arguments advanced across the bargaining table.[8] For these reasons, the unions in the NHS have periodically urged a number of reforms to their existing bargaining arrangements, such as the need for direct representation of Treasury on the Whitley Councils or the transfer of the health service to national authority status.[9]

There are also important management side divisions on negotiating bodies in the local government sector. For example, in the case of the Burnham Committee for Teachers in England and Wales (a body actually abolished by the government in 1987) there were 27 management side representatives in the mid- to late 1980s, consisting of 13 for the Association of County Councils, 10 for the Association of Metropolitan Authorities, 2 for the Welsh Joint Education Committee and 2 representatives from the Department of Education and Science. This mixed management side involved first, a party-political difference in that the Association of Metropolitan Authorities was usually Labour-controlled, whereas the Association of County Councils had a Conservative majority until the mid-1980s. And second, there was the division between actual employers and the central, funding department. The latter division had resulted in an agreed arrangement whereby the representatives of the Department of Education 'had a veto over global sums the employers could offer during salary negotiations and a weighted vote over the distribution of any award'.[10] However, the intra-management difficulties within this particular negotiation body reached such a stage in the 1980s that the local authority representatives effectively 'tore up' this agreement in 1985; this was clearly an important part of the background to the government's decision to abolish this joint negotiating committee in 1987.

The relationship between central and local government, as paymasters and actual employers respectively, is one that requires some additional discussion and comment, first because, as indicated in chapter 2, the local government was particularly significant in the overall growth of public expenditure and public employment during the 1960s and 1970s in a number of countries, and second, because central government finance is so important in the provision of local government services in many countries. On the latter point, Newton and Karran have observed:

> Local authorities in Britain have to lean heavily upon the financial support of central government, primarily because their range of responsibilities is unusually large, and because their own revenue-raising capacities are unusually limited. Consequently central government has had to underwrite the cost of local services on an ever-increasing scale throughout the twentieth century. During this period grants rose steadily year by year until they reached a peak level in the late 1970s, when they made up more than 45 per cent of total current income. Even as late as 1950 local government raised as much money through the rates as it received in grants but in the following 30 years rates declined to less than a third of income while grants continued to grow.[11]

Indeed some figures for 'grants from higher levels of government as a percentage of total expenditure of local government' for twelve countries in the years 1979–80 indicated that the UK with a figure of 44.6 per cent was exceeded only by the Netherlands (83.8 per cent), Belgium (52.1 per cent), and Denmark (50.7 per cent);[12] the eight countries below the UK included France (39.6 per cent), West Germany (30.7 per cent), and Sweden (27 per cent).

The relatively high level of dependence of local government on central government grants is obviously a potentially important weapon of central government control. This has become particularly apparent in the years of the Conservative government in which various pieces of local government legislation have changed the basis of the local government grant system, introduced penalties for 'overspending' authorities, and set an upper limit to the size of rate increases. In fact, between 1980/1 and 1983/4 the proportion of planned expenditure borne by grants and rates which was provided by grants actually fell from 61 per cent to 52.8 per cent.[13] However, this grant control mechanism has not fully achieved the government's aims in that it is a relatively blunt instrument which has hurt 'political friends' (i.e. the Conservative-controlled county areas) as well as 'political enemies' (i.e. the Labour-controlled metropolitan centres) and has led authorities, following an initial cut in capital expenditure, to increase fees, charges and local taxes as an alternative to cutting services and jobs.[14] However, these changes in the nature of central–local government financial relations, as well as the introduction of other measures to increase directly or indirectly the centralization of power (e.g. the 1980 legislation compelling local authorities to sell rented accommodation to tenants) and bypass local government,[15] have seriously damaged and undermined the quality of the relationship between these levels of government. Indeed as one commentary put it,

> central government control has coarsened and narrowed, focusing on a dwindling range of financial aggregates and politically salient *idées fixes*, while the capacity for effective long-run policy co-ordination has simply ebbed away from the state sector as a whole.[16]

The attempt of central government increasingly to constrain the expenditure of lower tiers of government through means of financial control is not unique to Britain in the 1980s. In the USA, for example, the Reagan administration's 1981 budget cuts eliminated several federal revenue-sharing programmes (federal revenues as a proportion of total state and local government revenues fell from 22 per cent in 1978 to 17.8 per cent in 1985), while in the late 1980s it was suggested that

> two developments at the federal level suggest that states and localities may have to pick up a greater share of the tab for the provision of various public services. First, congressional actions aimed at reducing the federal deficit threaten to reduce and even eliminate various programs that they now provide to state and local governments. Second, changes in the federal tax law may affect the cost of state and local government borrowing and may change the amount of state tax revenue generated. These forces may compel states and localities to cut public services and institute 'revenue-enhancement' programs.[17]

Central government cuts in the financial resources of lower tiers of government in a number of countries in the 1980s have been widely noted, although as one article has observed, 'in spite of the pervasiveness of funding cutbacks in many public sector organizations, there has been surprisingly little published research on how such organizations respond to externally imposed budget reductions'.[18]

The small but growing body of literature on 'cut-back management' in the public sector is very largely based on American material and experience, and this literature is drawn upon in Table 4.1 to provide a summary statement of the range of possible internal and external response strategies of public sector organizations to imposed budget reductions.

Table 4.1 Internal and external response strategies to budget reductions

Internal Responses

1 Rational priority planning. Those functions in an organization which make the least contribution to the priority objectives of the organization are disproportionately cut.
2 Externally orientated political cuts. Those functions of the organization which will put the most political pressure on funding bodies to stop funding cut-backs are cut the most.
3 Internally orientated political cuts. Those functions in the organization with the least power to resist cuts are cut the most.
4 Across the board cuts. All functions in the organization have their budgets cut by an equal sized proportion.
5 Delay. The decision of where to make cuts in the organization is put off as long as possible.
6 Abdication. The organization looks to other bodies to decide where cuts are to be made.
7 Passivity. The nature of the cuts to be made is imposed on the organization.

External Responses

1 Rational argumentation. The organization uses rational argument and evidence to demonstrate to the funding body that cutbacks must cease because of the havoc caused by such actions.
2 Alternative sources of funds. The organization seeks to offset the effects of funding cutbacks by seeking increased resources from alternative sources.
3 External political threats. The organization seeks to exert pressure on the funding body by threatening to cut politically sensitive functions.
4 External political promises. The organization seeks to obtain more resources from the funding agency by 'voluntarily' changing their functions in the direction desired by the funding agency.
5 Coalition forming. The organization initiates the formation of coalitions with other organizations in order to bring increased pressure on the funding agency.
6 Coalition joining. The organization joins coalitions already established to bring pressure to bear on the funding agency.
7 Passivity. The organization simply accepts the fact of budget cuts.

Source: T.D. Jick and V.V. Murray, 'The management of hard times: budget cutbacks in public sector organizations', *Organization Studies*, 3, 2 (1982), pp; 144–5

The article from which the 'check-list' in Table 4.1 is drawn went on to argue that the choice a public sector organization makes from these various forms of response will be strongly influenced by their perception of whether the cutbacks of the funding agency are 'rationally' as opposed to 'politically' motivated. And if they believe the action to be politically motivated their choice from these response strategies will be further influenced by perceptions of their own power relative to those of other organizations with an interest in the budget reduction decision. This sort of conceptual framework has influenced the a priori discussions of a number of social scientists in Britain concerned with central government funding cutbacks in the local government sector.[19] However, it has rarely been explicitly utilized as the basis for any systematic empirical research in Britain. Moreover, industrial relations researchers have been particularly conspicuous by their absence in discussions of this subject area, which is most unfortunate as both industrial relations (broadly defined) and the union role (in particular) would seem highly relevant in a highly unionized sector of employment to the sort of management choices and responses suggested by the contents of Table 4.1. Hopefully this omission in the relevant body of literature will be rectified in the future.

The discussion to date may be briefly summarized as follows: (i) in the civil service the unions negotiate directly with the Treasury, a department whose concerns and responsibilities are considerably wider than simply those of personnel and industrial relations considerations; (ii) in the nationalized industries the unions negotiate with a management which is itself involved in a complex, negotiating relationship with the state; and (iii) in the NHS and local government sector the unions negotiate with a management side whose representatives have the mixed interests and objectives of direct employers of labour and ultimate 'paymasters', with the latter having to make the case for resources, in competition with other parts of the public sector, to the Treasury.[20]

In view of these three factors, and the discussion in chapter 2 of the importance of the government of the day's economic strategy in shaping the political environment of public sector industrial relations, it is important to ask: is the government of the day ultimately the employer in the public sector, in the sense that its views about 'appropriate developments' in public sector industrial relations will always come to pass? To answer 'yes' to this question is to make a number of very powerful assumptions about the nature of decision-making processes in the public sector, which would include: the government of the day has a coherent, internally consistent economic and industrial relations strategy; the instruments of government control are straightforward, direct and all-powerful, with little capacity to be evaded or offset; the government needs only compliance and not co-operation from the lower tiers of administration; and a highly unionized workforce (including management personnel) has no sources of countervailing power.

In fact, the chances of government policy being translated in a relatively straightforward manner into actual practice is likely to vary considerably between the different parts of the public sector. One can envisage, as Ferner has suggested,[21] something of a spectrum of political (government) control throughout the public sector, ranging from the civil service (arguably strong control) at one end to the local authority sector (much weaker control) at the other; such differences in control strength clearly help account for the fact that civil service employment numbers have fallen by nearly 21 per cent in the years 1979–89, compared to only a 2 per cent fall in local authority employment. In general it would appear that the strength of central government control tends to be relatively less, the greater the number of separate managerial interests and the greater the role of party-political considerations in industrial relations arrangements and also the greater the capacity to substitute for central government funding.

THE NATURE OF THE GOVERNMENT AS AN EMPLOYER OF LABOUR

There has not been a great deal of explicit, conceptual discussion of the nature of the government as an employer of labour.[22] However, numerous general discussions of public sector industrial relations in a number of countries have frequently made reference to two particular notions or concepts, namely those of the government acting as a *sovereign* employer and as a *model* employer of labour. Accordingly, it is around these two notions that the discussion of this section is centred.

The sovereign employer concept, strictly interpreted, precludes the granting of collective bargaining rights to public sector employees as being incompatible with the absolute decision-making authority of the legislature. The strength of the concept at the present time is most apparent in relation to, for example, civil servants in countries such as Germany and Japan whose terms and conditions of employment are laid down by law or by ordinances. However the concept, although prohibiting collective bargaining amd the right to strike, does not necessarily preclude public sector employees from joining unions, which in practice has meant that

> In Japan the legislative determination of pay and working conditions for the local and national civil service has generally . . . followed the recommendation of personnel commissions which regularly meet and confer with the unions. In the Federal Republic of Germany, too, the representatives of *Bea umte* have always exerted a strong influence on the civil service legislation which determines their working conditions, either through formal participation in drafting general legislation or regulations or through informal lobbying.[23]

In short, the sovereign employer concept may preclude formal collective bargaining arrangements for civil servants in these two countries, but it has not prevented union representatives from making some input to the administrative-based determination of their terms and conditions of employment. More generally, the strength of this concept in shaping the means by which the terms and conditions of employment of public sector employees are determined has declined substantially, relative to the influence of collective bargaining (or other joint determination mechanisms) over the course of time. However, the concept has still continued to exert some influence, even in contemporary systems of industrial relations which generally accord collective bargaining rights to public sector employees. It may, for instance, operate to constrain or limit the scope of collective bargaining, such as in the federal government sector of the USA where joint negotiations over wages are not permitted. It may also provide for certain reserved rights of the executive in relation to joint negotiating bodies or third-party dispute resolution procedures. In Britain, for example, the government has retained the right to exclude any claims going to the civil service arbitration tribunal which are incompatible with, or contrary to, government policy of the day. And finally, the sovereign employer notion is important in relation to the right of public sector employees to go on strike. In some countries it remains the traditional (although no longer the exclusive) reason for refusing this right to public sector employees, while in other countries where this right is permitted the sovereign employer notion has often been used by governments for symbolic-tactical purposes in order to try and influence public opinion during the course of a major public sector dispute. For example, during the 1974 miners' strike in Britain the then Prime Minister Edward Heath continually accused the NUM of defying the expressed will of the elected representatives of the people in Parliament.

The second concept frequently referred to in the literature is that of the government acting as a model employer of labour. This particular notion essentially involves the view that both the procedural and substantive aspects or elements of public sector industrial relations should generally be better than those in the private sector in order to provide a 'leadership by example' model for the national system of industrial relations as a whole. Historically, this concept appeared to be first raised in both Britain and the USA in relation to attempts to bring about a general reduction in working hours, although most of the early discussion of it centred around its possible role as a principle of pay determination in the public sector.[24] For example the concept was extensively discussed as a factor in wage determination by a number of early Royal Commissions on the Civil Service in Britain, although the Tomlin Commission of 1929−31 concluded that 'a phrase which lends itself to varied and contradictory interpretations affords no practical guidance for fixing wages or for indicating the responsibilities of the state towards its employees'.[25] This practical difficulty of precisely defining and measuring just what the model employer concept meant in terms of operational wage standards, combined with other criticisms of the concept,[26] has meant that the concept is now rarely explicitly mentioned in contemporary public sector wage determination arrangements in Britain or elsewhere. Nevertheless, some individual results and findings for current public−private sector differences in the level and nature of employee compensation in individual countries still tend to be discussed in terms of this particular influence.[27]

Arguably, however, the notion of the government acting as a model or best practice employer of labour has received more tangible expression in the procedural, as opposed to substantive, aspects of industrial relations in both Britain and elsewhere. Indeed this seemed to be very much the approach desired by the Priestley Commission on the Civil Service in the 1950s which reported that

there has been an extension in the practices which today would lead one to describe an employer as 'good' and that this change suggests that practical guidance can now be secured from the term. The 'good employer' is not necessarily the one who offers the highest rates of pay. He seeks rather to provide stability and continuity of employment, and consults with representatives of his employees upon changes that affect both their remuneration and their conditions of work. He provides adequate facilities for training and advancement and carries on a range of practices which today constitute good management, whether they be formalised in joint consultation along civil service lines or not. Such employers are likely to be among the more progressive in all aspects of management policy.[28]

In chapter 3 it was noted that the encouragement of unionism in the public sector was one tangible manifestation of the government's commitment to act as a model or good employer of labour in procedural terms in Britain. In addition one can point to the relatively early establishment of (i) formal disciplinary procedures in the civil service, (ii) formal procedural arrangements for dealing with redundancies in the public sector, (iii) voluntary joint health and safety committees in the public utilities and, more recently, (iv) the experiments with trade union directors in the British Steel Corporation (BSC) and the Post Office, as examples of procedural innovations associated with the notion of the government acting as a model employer of labour.[29]

The idea of the public sector setting an example in relation to 'industry democracy' developments in particular has certainly not been confined to Britain. For example, in Canada a special report commissioned by the Federal Ministry of Labour in 1976 recommended that federal crown corporations be used to pilot test the feasibility and value of introducing co-determination arrangements along the lines of the West German system,[30] while more recently in Australia the Labour Party, which came into office in March 1983, stated in its election manifesto that it would support the introduction of industrial democracy schemes in public service departments and statutory authorities in order, among other things, to establish models and examples potentially suitable for application in the private sector.[31] The result has been the passage of the Public Service Reform Act 1984 which requires government departments and statutory authorities to develop industrial democracy action plans.

In the particular case of Britain it is important to consider whether there has been any change in the government acting as a

model employer of labour during the years of the Thatcher administration. This is certainly the view of at least one commentator who
has stated quite explicitly that it has been 'deliberate policy, since
1979, of taking government off its pedestal as a model for progressive labour relations policies'.[32] There are two senses in which one
could argue that the Conservative government is no longer acting as
a model employer of labour in the public sector. First, it has very
much sought to encourage the adoption of private sector employment practices in the public sector. This, as will be discussed more
fully in later chapters, is most obviously apparent in relation to the
particular wage determination criteria and the level of collective
bargaining which it would like to see adopted in the public sector.
And second, its behaviour as a public sector employer is very different from the historical tradition and pattern of such behaviour,
a point that will be illustrated below by reference to the issue of
union organization. This being said, one could still argue that the
Conservative government is seeking to act as a model employer in
two senses: that its behaviour as an employer in the public sector is
designed to complement and reinforce the initiatives it has taken as
an industrial relations legislator and macro-economic policy
manager, and that it is trying to set an example for private sector
employers to follow, particularly in relation to the issue of union
organization. In short, the view here is that the Conservative
government has not moved away from the position of trying to use
the public sector to provide a role model with regard to certain
industrial relations developments (quite the contrary); the significant change relates to the nature of the particular pattern or
example it is attempting to set for the private sector. This point can
most obviously be illustrated by reference to some of the government's actions towards union organization in the public sector.

In contrast to the traditional government position of encouraging
union membership and organization in the public sector (see
chapter 3), the Conservative government has sought to reduce
unionization levels in the public sector and to eliminate or minimize
any institutional or organizational sources of 'union power' there.
The obvious initiatives for seeking such a reduction are the privatization, competitive tendering and other employment reduction
measures which have been undertaken, and which were discussed in
previous chapters; these have largely stemmed from the government acting in its macro-economic management role, although its
role as an employer has also been a not unimportant consideration

here. In this respect, one also needs to mention the decision to remove the right of union membership for some 8,000 civil servants working at the Government Communications Headquarters (GCHQ), which has gathered signals intelligence for the British government for over forty years; since 1984 the employees there can only belong to an internal staff association. This highly publicized and controversial instance of union decertification has not been followed by similar actions on any significant scale in the public sector, although senior management staff in British Rail no longer have a union recognized for collective bargaining purposes. A newspaper report in early 1990 also suggested that the government is considering withdrawing the right of civilians employed by the police to belong to a trade union.[33]

The government's initiatives regarding the elimination or minimization of union power in the public sector include, first, the fact that public sector management has been very much to the forefront in the removal of closed shop arrangements. In British Gas, British Telecom, the water authorities (all now privatized), the Post Office and British Rail, management has terminated agreements providing for closed shop arrangements. Second, a government report has encouraged public sector management to revise their existing arbitration arrangements, with a view to removing the right to unilateral access to arbitration, a right that was held to be unduly favourable to the unions.[34] Third, public sector management has in recent years accorded increased representation and status to 'non-militant' unions in various public sector joint negotiating bodies. For example, national-level recognition status has been accorded to the Union of Democratic Mineworkers, the Professional Association of Teachers (with its no-strike clause) and the local government Federated Union of Professional and Managerial Officers (which favours the break up of national level bargaining). Moreover, in the case of the independent pay review that was established for nursing staff and other professional medical workers from April 1984, the government has reserved the right to exclude from the scope of its recommendations any groups that resort to industrial action: this decision may well have significantly enhanced the recruitment appeal of the Royal College of Nursing (with its no-industrial action constitutional clause), which, described in the previous chapter, grew substantially in the 1980s. The government's desire to decentralize bargaining structures in the public sector, which I discuss more fully in chapter 5, has been largely argued on the grounds of the need for more variation and flexibility in wage levels, although one suspects that the government is also looking for moves in this direction in order to reduce unionization levels and limit the numbers of workers involved in any strike action. Furthermore, in the civil service there no longer exists a national agreement on time off for trade union duties for lay union representatives; such arrangements now have to be negotiated on an individual departmental basis, against a background of the government's stated intention to bring expenditure on lay union representatives in the civil service under tighter control. And finally a number of parts of the public sector in the 1980s have seen a reduction in the status and authority of personnel management relative to line management – a development to be discussed in the next section of this chapter.

It is difficult to know precisely just how common such government initiatives to reduce unionization levels and some of the sources of 'union power' in the public sector were in other countries during the 1980s. In chapter 1, for example, I noted a rather mixed set of evidence, with the public sector tending to account for an increased proportion of total union membership in various countries (including Britain) in the 1980s, although at the same time public sector unions from a number of countries have complained to the International Labour Office (ILO) of government interference with union and collective bargaining arrangements. These complaints have frequently followed the imposition of public sector-only pay controls (e.g. Canada in the early 1980s), with the governments concerned claiming that they are seeking to set an example of pay restraint for the private sector to follow: the use of the model employer concept to justify such actions is important in indicating the potentially double-edged nature of this concept for unions in the public sector. Certainly, the American and British situations in the 1980s were very different, as the years of the Reagan administration in the USA did not witness public sector management taking the lead in anti-union activities – in fact, quite the contrary – with only the dismissal of the air traffic controllers in 1981 and the decertification of their union (PATCO) constituting a notable exception in this regard (by 1987 the new controllers had voted in a new union). More generally, however, a number of governments have made attempts to introduce more private sector-like employment practices into the public sector. In New Zealand, for example, the Labour Relations Act 1987, passed by a Labour government, has substantially removed some of the traditional differences in the wage-setting arrangements between the public and private sectors.

Finally, it needs to be recognized that, as with so many aspects of the Conservative government policy approach,[35] there are widely differing views as to the effectiveness (both short and longer term) of its attempt to break sharply with traditional management and industrial relations arrangements and practices in the public sector. Two examples may help to illustrate the nature of the different effects and outcomes perceived by different parties. The first concerns the Financial Management Initiative in the civil service which was introduced in 1982 with the aim of promoting in each department an organization and system in which managers at all levels have: (i) a clear view of their objectives and means to assess and, wherever possible, measure outputs or performances in relation to those objectives; (ii) well-defined responsibility for making the best use of their resources including a critical scrutiny of output and value for money; and (iii) the information (particularly about costs), the training and the access to expert advice that they need in order to exercise their responsibilities properly. The effect of the Financial Management Initiative has been the subject of considerable debate as indicated by the following summary statement:

> Who is right about how the Civil Service has developed during the Thatcher era? We seem to have identified three main interpretations. One is the thesis of the senior civil servant, Anne Mueller, who sees something emerging called the 'new civil service' fashioned in the spirit of the Financial Management Initiative. A second is the Civil Service unions' view that the service has been singled out in the name of ideology for 'deprivileging' and for ruthless cuts in numbers. . . . The third interpretation, that of the Radical Right, represented . . . in the strictures of *The Economist*, argues that the Thatcher Government has fallen down on its ideological job. Evidence of this is that the Career Civil Service, far from being seriously scaled down and discriminated against, has been let off lightly and that it certainly retains sufficient strength to actively obstruct the policies associated with the Financial Management Initiative, which are unambitious anyway.[36]

This wide range of views as to the outcomes of this particular initiative obviously reflect differing initial ideologies, belief systems, as well as the extent of vested interest in seeing a particular outcome emerge (or not). There is also the important question of what indicators or evidence one chooses to emphasize in considering the potentially multiple impacts of a particular initiative. The importance of this consideration is evidenced by the following comment on the second of our examples, namely the industrial relations consequences of privatization:

> The TUC, and affiliated trade unions, have claimed that there has been a worsening of industrial relations in these privatised corporations, and this was given some credence by the British Telecom dispute in early 1987. The TUC claims that managements have become much more aggressive and the previous well-established consultative arrangements have been ignored. It also points to reductions in employment, reductions in employee benefits (such as pensions) and withdrawal of trade union rights. However, the evidence on pay bargaining suggests that, now that they are free of Government pay controls and free to share in the profits of these companies, pay settlements may be better than in the public sector. And employees in some newly privatised organisations can also benefit from profit sharing and employee share option schemes.[37]

In fact views of some leading union officers involved in a number of the early privatization moves suggest the difficulty in generalizing about the direction and extent of industrial relations changes both between and within individual corporations.[38] For example, in the case of Amersham International, union officers reported better changes in bargaining arrangements, easier management attitudes in pay bargaining, but a worsening change in consultation and a toughening of management attitudes towards unions. In contrast, in British Aerospace the union officers interviewed suggested that there had been an accelerated loss of jobs, although the changes in consultation arrangements and in management attitudes to unions were both in the direction of improvement. This 'diversity of results and impacts' view seems to be borne out by a comparison of the post-privatization positions of British Telecom and British Gas, as indicated in Table 4.2.

It is also of interest to note here that in the preparation for privatization of the electricity supply industry nearly 800 senior management personnel have accepted individual contracts of

Table 4.2 The post-privatization position in British Telecom and British Gas

British Telecom

1 Currently some 80 per cent overall unionization rate, although (in contrast to the pre-privatization position) the level of union density is highly variable between the different parts of the company; some subsidiaries (e.g. Mitel and TSL) have refused union requests to be recognized for collective bargaining purposes.

2 In the immediate post-privatization period, BT, without consulting the unions, has sought to bring about employment reductions of some 2.5–3 per cent per year; there has been some recent employment increase, however.

3 1986–7 saw industrial action over the attempt to decentralize bargaining arrangements and attach efficiency measures to wage increases.

4 Some 800 top and senior managers are on individual (i.e. non-union negotiated) contracts of employment, with an attempt being currently made to extend such arrangements to a further 4,000 managers.

5 The proportion of pay which is performance related is being proposed for increase in the case of manual employees.

6 The post-privatization years have seen the introduction of new pension arrangements about which there is considerable union–management controversy.

7 Despite union opposition, some 96 per cent of the workforce accepted the initial free share offer, some 79 per cent of the workforce took up a matching share offer and a third of the eligible employers have opted for a company share-saver scheme. However, the impact of this is seen as only marginal on industrial relations.

8 BT is currently seeking increasingly to communicate directly with individual employees, rather than attempting to achieve this via the trade unions.

9 A toughening of 'management style' is alleged by the unions as witnessed by attempts to undermine national collective bargaining arrangements, reduce employment numbers and increase the extent of sub-contracting.

British Gas

1 Workforce unionization levels have remained relatively high: 95 per cent of manuals, 85 per cent of staff-senior officers and 70 per cent of higher management. Some concern has, however, been expressed by NALGO about the role and activities of the non-TUC affiliated Gas Higher Management Association, which currently claims to represent some 50 per cent of senior managers.

2 Employment numbers have fallen, but this was occurring prior to privatization.

3 There has been little substantive change in salary and benefit arrangements in the post-privatization period; there have been no changes to pension arrangements, and performance-related salaries only exist for the top 25 managers.

continued overleaf

Table 4.2 – *continued*

4 Share ownership among the workforce is quite extensive (i.e. 99 per cent of the workforce took up the free share offer and some 47 per cent of the eligible employees have opted for a share-saver scheme), but the impact on industrial relations is perceived as limited.
5 Management is interested in seeking to communicate more directly with individual employees.
6 There have been union suggestions and claims that management has taken an increasingly tougher stance in relation to discipline, absence control and the introduction of new technology.

Source: derived from *Industrial Relations Review and Report*, 439, May 1989, pp. 12–14

employment, as an alternative to collective bargaining arrangements.[39] More generally, this question of the impact and effectiveness of government changes in public sector industrial relations arrangements and practices will be returned to in the final chapter, whereas the next section concentrates on the position of the personnel management function in the management organization of the public sector.

THE PERSONNEL MANAGEMENT FUNCTION IN THE PUBLIC SECTOR

In conceptual terms the personnel management function has been viewed as an organizational 'boundary spanning unit' designed to insulate the technical core of the organization from sources of environmental uncertainty. The sources of environmental uncertainty that are particularly relevant to the personnel function are (i) tight labour market conditions, (ii) substantial government intervention (via legislation and regulations) in both the individual and collective employment relationship and (iii) organizational and behavioural manifestations of 'union power'. It is these three sets of environmental conditions which significantly shape the extent and nature of the resources accorded to, and activities and influence of, the personnel function (within the management hierarchy of organizations) at any point in, and over the course of, time. Indeed the presence of one or more of these influences has historically characterized periods in which the personnel function has enjoyed relative gains within the management hierarchy of organizations (e.g. during the Second World War and the 1970s in Britain).

However, the fact that the determinants of the power of the personnel function (in relation to other management sub-units within organizations) is essentially exogenous to the function's own control has a number of 'awkward' implications for personnel management. First, it is likely to mean that the function's power is highly variable over time and, second, in successfully coping with a particular source of environmental uncertainty the function paradoxically risks reducing the extent of its own power within the management hierarchy. Furthermore, personnel's gains from external sources of environmental uncertainty in particular periods of time do not appear to have provided an adequate basis for longer term development in the face of other management sub-units' doubts about the particular worth and contribution of the function to organizational effectiveness.

In keeping with this general perspective, one finds in the United States that the growth of public sector unionization and collective bargaining arrangements in the 1960s and 1970s resulted in the establishment and development of specialist labour relations sub-units in city governments. These sub-units were typically associated with the personnel management function; one report in 1986, for example, revealed that more than 90 per cent of the cities surveyed gave the responsibility for collective bargaining to the personnel department.[40] Furthermore, at least one American study has comprehensively tested the 'boundary spanning–environmental uncertainty' framework of analysis outlined above, and found that the establishment of such sub-units was significantly related to factors such as the extent of unionization.[41] In Britain, however, the public sector has, as shown in chapter 3, for long been the most highly unionized area of the economy, but this fact did not result in the relatively early establishment of a personnel management function. Indeed as one commentator observed, 'prior to local government reorganisation in the early 1970s, trying to find a post in local government with the word "personnel" in its job title was akin to searching for a needle in a haystack.'[42] The relatively limited early development of the personnel management function in the public sector has largely been attributed to the strength of its national-level bargaining arrangements; this was a major contention of the Report of the Donovan Commission commenting on the British system of industrial relations in general in the mid- to late 1960s. For example, Alan Fowler has argued that for personnel officers in local government, a significant feature of the whole national industrial relations system is that it provides no formal role for them . . . the whole system is heavily biased towards the establishment and maintenance of national agreements and procedures, and the role of the individual authority is consequently minimal.[43]

As a result of the continued strength of national-level pay negotiations in the public sector there have been detailed studies of the role and impact of central bodies such as the Local Authorities Conditions of Service Advisory Board[44] (which co-ordinates the employer side in all local government collective bargaining), whereas the number of studies of the role of the personnel function at more decentralized levels within the public sector have been comparatively few. Nevertheless, several individual issues and findings have frequently been emphasized in the small, existing body of literature and it is these which constitute the basis of my subsequent discussion. First, it has been noted that the historical origins of the personnel management function differed between the public and private sectors. That is, in the public sector personnel management was historically associated with the employment officer or establishment officer function, whereas in the private sector the function grew out of the welfare work tradition.[45] For example, prior to the 1970s it was establishment officers in local government, with a general administrative rather than personnel background, who were concerned with the day-to-day administration of rules about pay and conditions of service, and who were responsible for controlling and monitoring individual departments' demands for staff. Second, the relatively rapid growth in the number of personnel appointments in local government and the health service in the 1970s[46] largely resulted from the overall administrative reorganizations of the services in these years. In 1974, for instance, following the Local Government Act of 1972, over 1,500 county boroughs, county, urban and rural districts were replaced by 422 local authorities. This basic structure of a smaller number of individually larger-sized authorities necessitated the development of a centralized personnel/industrial relations management function. Indeed the Committee of Inquiry on Local Government Reorganisation, having explicitly argued that local government had lagged behind other employers in the development of the personnel management function, proposed that in the industrial relations field we believe that it is the personnel officer who should be the expert in the design of appropriate procedures and systems of communication with the representatives of the staff. He himself should be the recognised channel of communication between the Council and the trade unions on matters of manpower and industrial relations policy, and he should also advise line managers on the conduct of the more domestic issues which are properly their concern. Such an arrangement would ensure consistency and continuity of industrial relations procedure and would also ensure that management at the centre was aware of the industrial relations climate throughout the organisation.[47]

This recommendation in favour of a centralized personnel function, and away from the departmental autonomy position of the 1950s and 1960s, has clearly borne fruit, as a survey of some 235 local authorities in the early 1980s revealed that: (i) approximately 80 per cent of them had a central personnel/industrial relations management department; (ii) some 90 per cent had a personnel–manpower committee; and (iii) such arrangements were significantly associated with individual authorities characterized by quite considerable industrial relations activity at the local level, as proxied by the number of shop stewards and the number of manual worker bonus schemes in operation.[48] In addition, relatively large sized and Labour-controlled authorities were more likely to have such arrangements. These administrative re-organizations of the 1970s also strongly shaped the characteristics of individuals currently holding comparatively senior personnel management positions in local government and the health service. Such individuals were, in the terms of a popular typology of personnel managers in Britain, overwhelmingly 'late professionals',[49] that is individuals who started their career in non-personnel jobs, but who at some stage (i.e. at the time of re-organization) moved into personnel management; this fact was well evidenced by one study of the personnel function in the NHS.[50] Furthermore, throughout the 1970s personnel managers in the public sector, as in the national system as a whole,[51] perceived an increase in the extent of their influence within management decision-making circles – largely as a result of the passage of industrial relations legislation (particularly that concerning unfair dismissal) and the growth of trade union membership, with individuals in the more senior positions especially concentrating on industrial relations developments.

One or two survey studies undertaken in the 1980s permit some limited comparison between personnel management departments in the public and private sectors. In one such study it was generally argued that any observable inter-sectoral differences between personnel management were relatively few in number and mainly derived from differences in the nature of their larger management control systems.[52] And the 1984 workplace industrial relations survey produced the following individual findings:

1　The public service sector was less likely than average to employ someone with the term 'personnel' in their job title (with the continuing use of the term 'establishment officer' in central government), although they were more likely than average to have someone who spent a substantial amount of time on personnel work.
2　Workplace personnel managers in the public sector were least involved in matters of pay determination, due to the relatively centralized bargaining structures operative there.
3　Personnel management was most heavily centralized in the nationalized industries.
4　There appeared to be few differences between manufacturing, private sector services, the nationalized industries and public services in the extent to which personnel managers reported any increase in the influence of their departments.
5　Public sector personnel managers tended more commonly to report that changes outside the immediate employment establishment were a source of the improved influence of personnel.[53]

The public sector is, of course, unlikely to be a completely homogeneous one as regards the extent and nature of developments and changes in the personnel management function. Indeed one early 1980s examination of personnel management in local government, water, gas, electricity and the NHS argued that there were notable differences in the development stages of the function, which themselves derived from differences in larger organizational structures, the range of functions undertaken, the size of workforces, financial arrangements, political influences and the personnal priorities of management.[54] Table 4.3 indicates this particular study's view of the 'likely challenges and developments in the personnel field over the next 10/15 years in each service'.

The table contains a number of references to the likelihood of an increased role for line management in personnel matters, a

Table 4.3 Suggested future issues facing personnel management in five public sector areas

1 *Local government*
(a) A great need to gain acceptance of the concept of 'organic' personnel management and then to work for its implementation at the individual authority level
(b) The gradual development of an innovative and problem-solving approach in the fields of manpower utilization and costs, individual development, industrial relations and organization development

2 *Water*
(a) The development of a sound manpower information base co-ordinated at national level
(b) Greater attention to the need to provide opportunities for career development in a national service
(c) Following (a), there will be a marked move from national productivity bargaining to regional and district agreements
(d) The status of heads of personnel will improve but slowly

3 *NHS*
(a) There will be a wider recognition of the need for and importance of trained and experienced personnel specialists
(b) Greater opportunities will be afforded for direct personnel specialist input into the most important decision-making processes at all levels
(c) A longer-term view will be taken of the priorities and financing of the NHS in order that manpower requirements may be worked through properly

4 *Electricity*
(a) A much greater degree of co-ordination will arise at national level
(b) There will be increasing public demands that manpower is utilized efficiently,
  – initially, individual boards and trade unions will co-operate much more closely on ways of reducing manpower unit costs; and
  – later, the Electricity Council (or its successor) will be equally involved
(c) The role of the personnel specialist will be under close examination and if there is any development in his role and status this will be achieved only with difficulty against pressures to increase the strength of line management's position in personnel matters

continued overleaf

Table 4.3 – *continued*

5   *Gas*

(a) There will be further reductions in manpower unit costs

(b) A number of behavioural scientists will be recruited at both national and regional levels

(c) There will be a devolution of (personnel) matters to line management to allow personnel specialists to develop a new role:

  (i) analysing manpower problems on an industry-wide basis using information gleaned under (a) and (b) and a more sophisticated manpower information system;

  (ii) determining with employees how these problems shall be approached; and

  (iii) ensuring that the organization as a whole is changed to enable agreed solutions to be effected

Source: I.M. Brown, *Personnel Management in Five Public Services: Its Development and Future*, Birmingham, Institute of Local Government Studies, University of Birmingham, 1982, pp. 252–3

likelihood that has become a reality in several parts of the public sector in the 1980s. For example, following the 1983 review of personnel work in the civil service[55] the emphasis there has been very much in the decentralized direction, with personnel policies and procedures to be developed much more on an individual department-by-department basis, and the balance of decision making at the individual department level to shift in favour of line management *vis-à-vis* the personnel function. The 1983 report on personnel in the civil service in fact contained the following specific recommendations: (i) each department should develop a coherent personnel strategy tailored to its own particular needs; (ii) departments should define explicitly the division of responsibility between line and personnel management and the personnel responsibilities and authority of individual posts; (iii) as far as possible, line managers should be fully responsible and accountable for the management of their staff; and (iv) personnel staff should continue to undertake directly some executive functions, but these should place more emphasis on providing information, support and expert advice to line management in the discharge of its personnel responsibilities. The basic thrust of this report is highly consistent with the well-publicized management approaches of Edwardes at BL and McGregor at BSC and the Coal Board (now British Coal), while in the NHS the proposals of the Griffiths Report to appoint general managers and enhance the authority of unit managers in relation to, for example, the dismissal of employees are also likely significantly to change the sort of relationship that developed between line and staff management in the 1970s. In fact, at the time of writing, in the NHS the government is seeking to decentralize the personnel function from the regional and district levels to the unit level, with unit personnel departments to be built up in order to assume control of manpower planning, employment policies, administration of pay and conditions and industrial relations matters: currently more than 50 per cent of the 3,500 personnel staff in the NHS are employed at district level.[56] These tendencies towards decentralization of personnel management in the public sector will clearly be further stimulated by movements away from national-level bargaining arrangements (in local government), the possible emergence of self-governing hospitals and the establishment of civil service agencies. At Companies House (previously the Companies Registration Offices), one of the first civil service agencies, the personnel department has doubled in size due to increased workload responsibilities.[57]

Finally, the issue of the transference of certain private sector employment practices into the public sector has inevitably raised the question of whether 'human resource management' will increasingly become a feature of public sector practice. A recent review article has noted some individual developments along these lines (e.g. the Audit Commission's criticism of the bureaucratic model of organization, the interest of health authorities in quality circles, individual contracts for managers in British Rail, pro-line management initiatives in the NHS), although it identified a number of important, potential constraints on the ability (and desirability) of the public sector to move more fully in this direction.[58] This is a matter to which I return in the final chapter.

SUMMARY

In this examination of management organization for industrial relations purposes in the public sector I have especially emphasized a number of the important industrial relations implications that follow from the political nature of the government as an employer of labour. However, at a number of points I also made reference to some effects and implications that have resulted from the fact of a national-level bargaining structure in the public sector in Britain.

It is therefore on this issue of bargaining structure that I concentrate in the next chapter.

Chapter 5

Collective bargaining coverage and structure in the public sector

INTRODUCTION

The industrial relations system of Britain has long been based on collective bargaining, with such arrangements constituting the major mechanism of union–management interaction for establishing and regulating the terms and conditions of employment. This chapter is essentially concerned with the coverage of collective bargaining and the nature of bargaining structure, or more specifically the level at which collective bargaining is conducted, in the public sector in Britain. The concept of bargaining structure is in fact the major *intervening* variable in any national system of industrial relations based on collective bargaining in that it is hypothesized to influence the outcomes of the collective bargaining process but is, at the same time, itself influenced or determined by features of the environmental context and by the organizational characteristics of both unions and management. The discussion here will consider both the relevant determinants and effects of bargaining structure in the public sector, topics whose importance has been much enhanced by the Conservative government's strong criticism of the operation of national-level bargaining arrangements in the public sector and indeed in the larger system of industrial relations.

However, before turning to these issues of collective bargaining coverage and structure in the public sector I present in the next section some comments and observations on the nature of collective bargaining in general, and raise some of the important issues associated with the introduction and increased role of collective bargaining arrangements in the public sector.

AN OVERVIEW OF COLLECTIVE BARGAINING

The first point to note is that collective bargaining is more than simply the collective equivalent to, and counterpart of, individual wage bargaining:[1] this is because the role of collective bargaining is to regulate (and not simply determine at periodic points in time) the terms and conditions of employment. In fact collective bargaining has been conceived of as involving the following individual functions: (i) a marketing function which fixes the basic substantive terms of the wage-effort relationship; (ii) an industrial government function which is a system of industrial jurisprudence whereby the procedural conditions under which employees operate are established and administered; and (iii) a method of management by which the views of employees and trade unions are represented in managerial decision-making processes whose outcomes will have implications for their particular concerns and interests.[2] Second, organization and conflict theorists have increasingly argued that a substantial number and variety of inter-personal and inter-group relationships (all of which involve some element of interest conflict between the parties concerned) can be usefully conceived of as, and analysed in terms of, bargaining or negotiating relationships. However, collective bargaining needs to be distinguished from this broader group or family of bargaining relationships because it has the following (inherent) features: (i) the parties are not engaged in a one-off transaction and hence must continue to interact over the course of time (i.e. there is a mutual interest in the survival of the basic relationship); (ii) the issues being negotiated are multiple in nature; hence the possibility of trade offs between individual, negotiating items; (iii) the different interests, and hence potential conflict, involved in the bargaining relationship are not simply inter-personal in nature because the bargainers are organizational representatives (i.e. there is the likelihood of inter-role conflict); and (iv) the parties to the relationship are likely to have internal differences (in matters of strategy, tactics and priorities) among their constituent members (i.e. there is a likelihood of intra-organizational conflict). In fact Walton and McKersie have argued that a collective bargaining relationship typically involves four basic sub-processes of bargaining,[3] namely distributive bargaining, integrative bargaining, intra-organizational bargaining and attitudinal structuring. These particular sub-processes of collective bargaining will be discussed more fully in chapter 6.

The role of collective bargaining as the basis of a national system of industrial relations has attracted considerable criticism from a wide variety of 'political' perspectives. First, those individuals who adopt essentially a unitarist frame of reference towards individual organizations (i.e. organizations are basically co-operative systems) have argued that a union presence and collective bargaining arrangements are both unnecessary and undesirable. That is, such arrangements are alleged to have no positive, inherent gains or virtues because they only arise from a management failure to meet the on-the-job needs of employees and, what is more, they introduce new, multiple sources of conflict into the basic individual employee—management relationship. Second, Marxist writers have argued that collective bargaining arrangements inevitably operate to reinforce the status quo by not challenging the larger structures of ownership and control in society as a whole. In their view collective bargaining is frequently portrayed as an instrument for contributing towards an approximate power balance between organized interest groups in society at large, but in reality such arrangements have the 'adverse' effects of: producing only marginal improvements in the terms and conditions of employment (i.e. largely wages—hours matters); lowering rank and file employee expectations with regard to what is 'realistically negotiable', and hence limiting the extent of any challenge to the scope of managerial prerogative; making industrial conflict more manageable through the process of procedural regulation; and limiting the development of a cohesive working class with a genuine trade-union consciousness orientated towards greater political, social and economic changes.[4]

The natural advocates and supporters of the principle of collective bargaining arrangements are researchers with a pluralist perspective, given the basic view which they take of society in general and of business organizations in particular. That is, such individuals favour the establishment of collective bargaining arrangements in organizations on the grounds that such arrangements (i) are an explicit recognition of the fact that there are inevitably conflicts of interest between employees and employers; (ii) can help to make such conflict 'functional' in the sense of making it a source of potentially constructive change by limiting its manner of expression in 'socially costly' forms; (iii) limit or constrain the extent of unilateral decision-making in individual organizations; and (iv) provide the basis of an important, independent body (i.e. the labour or union movement) which represents the interests of the less privileged elements of a larger, democratic society. However, certain changes in the nature of collective bargaining, and in the environment in which it operates, have led a number of pluralists to question certain aspects of the performance (as opposed to the principle) of such arrangements in different national systems of industrial relations at various points in time. Specifically, some of them have frequently argued that the practice of collective bargaining has taken insufficient account of the 'public or social interest' in industrial relations.[5] The questions of whether there is a genuine public or social interest in industrial relations, what are its individual components and elements, whether they conflict with each other and who gives tangible expression to the concept are, of course, longstanding and controversial ones.[6] Nevertheless, the public interest notion has been particularly important in shaping the position and role of collective bargaining in the public sector in many countries.

As noted in earlier chapters, the government was historically viewed as the neutral representative of the social or public interest in the industrial relations system. However, over the course of time there have occurred some important changes in this perspective. These changes concern, first, the content of the notion of the social interest in industrial relations and, second, the view of the government's role in giving expression to this notion in the system of industrial relations. Traditionally, the social interest in industrial relations involved a single, procedural element, namely the public's concern with the level of strike activity. As a reflection of this particular concern the government in various countries typically established third-party dispute resolution facilities (usually conciliation and arbitration arrangements) to try and limit the impact of strike activity on parties not directly involved in the immediate areas of dispute. However, from the 1960s a new, substantive element was introduced into this notion, namely the public's concern with the size of wage settlements and their implications for inflation. The government gave expression to this second element of the social interest in industrial relations by the introduction of incomes or wage control policies. The operation of these policies, by seeking to limit the operation of 'free' collective bargaining, has had some significant impact in the industrial relations systems of a number of countries (e.g. stimulated changes in the character of white collar, public sector unions) and indeed has

raised the possibility of some degree of conflict with the older, procedural component of the notion of the social interest in industrial
relations.

The incomes policies years of the 1970s also saw the growth of
union membership and collective bargaining arrangements in the
public sector in several countries which has had the effect of first,
calling into question the view that the government's role in the
industrial relations system was simply that of the neutral representative of the social interest in industrial relations; second,
raising the possibility of inter-role conflict for the government in
trying to achieve a reasonably acceptable balance between its
responsibilities (to the public at large) for macro-economic
management and its responsibilities (as an employer of labour)
towards public sector employees; and third, causing governments
to make attempts to shape the nature of collective bargaining
arrangements in the public sector by reference to the notion of the
social interest in industrial relations. In the last case, one can point,
for example, to the imposition of restrictions on the coverage of
collective bargaining, the subject matter or scope of collective bargaining, and the right to strike in the public sector. The quid pro
quo for restrictions on the right to strike was frequently the design
and introduction of specialist, third-party dispute resolution
facilities for public sector employee groups, most notably in the
USA and Canada where a conscious policy attempt was made to
produce collective bargaining arrangements in the public sector
which differed from those in the private sector, especially on the
grounds of the relatively greater need for the social interest in
industrial relations to be relected in the particular arrangements of
the former sector of employment. These conscious government
attempts to fashion public sector collective bargaining arrangements by reference to social or public interest (in industrial
relations) considerations seems to be particularly a feature of
systems in which public sector unionization was a comparatively
recent phenomenon, legislative intervention in industrial relations
was a well-accepted feature of the overall system of industrial
relations, and the national system of industrial relations has
traditionally involved relatively decentralized collective bargaining
arrangements. These are obviously features of the Canadian and
American systems, which are very different from the British ones –
or at least they were at the time when public sector collective bargaining arrangements were established in Britain.

THE COVERAGE OF COLLECTIVE BARGAINING

In Britain, according to Clegg, the coverage of collective bargaining expanded essentially in step with the growth in union membership in the years 1910–20, whereas 'between 1910 and 1933 the coverage of collective bargaining may have increased as much as threefold, while trade union membership rose by only two-thirds'.[7] This changed relationship between these two measures of workforce organization, which initially came about as the district or local area basis of collective bargaining was broadened and expanded to the industry or national level, has continued to exist in Britain. For example, in the mid- to late 1960s the difference between the two measures was estimated to be some 35 per cent,[8] while data for the early 1970s suggested a difference of some 25 per cent;[9] such differences indicate the limited extent of union security arrangements in recognized bargaining units and the existence of non-union firms setting their wages by reference to the provisions of the relevant, industry-wide collective agreement. Nevertheless, one would expect that a relatively highly unionized area of employment would also have a relatively high level of collective bargaining coverage. This is certainly the case in the public sector in Britain, as the figures in Table 5.1 indicate.

In the 1980s the size of the union movement in Britain, as discussed in chapter 3, declined quite considerably, a change that one would expect to be reflected, at least to some degree, in the collective bargaining coverage figures for these years. Indeed a comparison of the collective bargaining coverage figures in the annual *New Earnings Survey* for 1978 and 1985 indicates, for example, that the overall extent of collective bargaining coverage fell from 78.3 per cent to 70.6 per cent for male manual employees, and from 70.9 per cent to 61.9 per cent for women manual employees. However, the strength of national-level collective agreements in the public sector in Britain relative to the private sector raises the possibility that the extent of collective bargaining coverage will have remained comparatively more stable in the former area of employment. This intra-system relationship is suggested by the results of a number of inter-system studies of union membership and collective bargaining coverage in the 1980s which reveal that membership levels and coverage have remained most stable in those countries characterized by national-level bargaining arrangements.[10] This hypothesis receives considerable support from a comparison of some of the

Table 5.1 Collective bargaining coverage in the public and private sectors, male employees, 1978

Occupation groupings by sector	% whose wages set directly or indirectly by collective agreements
Managers – public sector	90.7
– private sector	26.7
Professionals – public sector	93.8
– private sector	34.3
Intermediate non-manuals – public sector	96.7
– private sector	37.7
Junior non-manuals – public sector	97.7
– private sector	46.7
Foremen – public sector	94.8
– private sector	60.3
Skilled manuals – public sector	96.1
– private sector	73.3
Semi-skilled manuals – public sector	96.6
– private sector	67.8
Unskilled manuals – public sector	96.9
– private sector	67.3

Source: based on M.B. Gregory and A.W.J. Thomson, 'The coverage mark up. Bargaining structure and earnings in Britain, 1973 and 1978', *British Journal of Industrial Relations*, XIX, 1, March 1981, p. 28.

Table 5.2 Collective agreement coverage and national agreement coverage only, manufacturing and public administration, 1978 and 1985

	Public administration		Manufacturing sector	
	1978	*1985*	*1978*	*1985*
Collective agreement coverage:				
male manuals	98.5	97.2	79.1	66.9
male non-manuals	98.8	99.2	45.3	36.5
National agreement coverage (only):				
male manuals	62.4	77.5	19.4	19.2
male non-manuals	89.1	86.5	10.6	6.9

Source: *New Earnings Survey*, relevant years

coverage figures in the 1978 and 1985 *New Earnings Surveys*, as shown in Table 5.2.

The traditional role and strength of national, industry-wide bargaining structures in the public sector in Britain, which I discuss more fully in the next section, has meant that the public sector has long been characterized by a relatively small number of individually large-sized bargaining units; the 'visibility' of such units has tended to make them particularly vulnerable to attempted control via incomes policies. Table 5.3 provides some current information along these lines.

Table 5.3 Major public sector collective bargaining groups in the late 1980s

Sector	Number of bargaining units	Number of employees (approximately)
Central government		
Civil Service	2	600,000
National Health Service	9	425,000
Universities	5	102,000
London Regional Transport	20	47,000
Local government		
Manual staff	10	1,000,000
Managerial	3	8,500
Administration, technical and professional	8	630,000
Fire services	2	40,000
Police	5	143,000
Public corporations		
British Coal	7	137,000
Atomic Energy Authority	2	14,000
British Rail	7	140,000
Post Office	5	179,000
British Broadcasting Corporation	1	29,000
Civil Aviation Authority	1	7,000
British Waterways Board	2	3,000

Source: *Industrial Relations in Britain*, Industrial Relations Services, 1988, cited in D. Farnham and J. Pimlott, *Understanding Industrial Relations*, London, Cassell, 1990, p. 156

In reflecting on the extent and nature of collective bargaining arrangements in the public sector in Britain, both prior to and during the 1980s, the following additional points should be noted:

1 In the public sector there have been no legal limitations on the scope of negotiable matters, except in the case of the police and fire services.

2 In the cases of the police, NHS and civil service the outcomes of collective bargaining require ministerial consent before the terms and conditions of the agreement can be implemented.

3 As an alternative to collective bargaining, pay review bodies have long existed for doctors and dentists; judges, senior civil servants and senior officers in the armed forces (the Top Salaries Review Body); and the armed forces. To these were added in the mid-1980s a review body for nurses, midwives, health visitors and professions allied to medicine. As a result of the last, more than 50 per cent of staff in the NHS currently have their terms and conditions of employment set by review bodies, as opposed to collective bargaining.

4 The Teachers' Pay and Conditions Act 1987 abolished the Burnham structure of collective bargaining which had operated since 1919 (from 1944 on a statutory basis). As a result, school-teachers in England and Wales are currently in the unique position of having their terms and conditions of employment determined by the Secretary of State, subject to consultation with interested parties and a report from an advisory committee.

THE CONCEPT OF BARGAINING STRUCTURE

The national-level, industry-wide bargaining structure of the public sector in Britain, which was very much based on Whitley Council lines, was essentially put in place either immediately after the First World War (e.g. the civil service, local authority manuals, education and the water industry) or immediately after the Second World War (e.g. local authority non-manuals, NHS, fire service); the police were the late developers here, with such arrangements only coming about in 1953. In order to provide some feel for these developments the case of local authority manual and non-manual workers is briefly considered. According to Clegg, 'in 1910 formal collective bargaining in the public sector was confined to a minority of local authorities . . . [whereas] by 1933 it was the acknowledged practice of the great majority of . . . local authorities.'[11] This was, however, very much a development concerning manual workers, with the National Joint Industrial Council for Local Authority Manual Workers having been set up in 1919, whereas national-level bargaining for white collar employees in local government was essentially a phenomenon of the Second World War and immediate post-war years. Indeed, one study has noted that of the thirty-seven negotiating bodies in local government in the 1950s fully twenty-nine of them were only established after 1945.[12] In fact, prior to the Second World War the limited organization among employers had produced a situation whereby

> even where agreements were made, they were on a provincial, not a national, basis and, while some local authorities refused to pay the negotiated rates, others considered themselves free to pay above them. Wages and salaries paid, therefore, were determined by random and piecemeal bargaining, and varied in different parts of the country.[13]

As an illustration of the development of national-level collective bargaining arrangements in local government, Table 5.4 provides a chronology of the key events in the establishment of the National Joint Council (NJC) for Administrative, Professional, Technical and Clerical Staffs.

From the late 1940s and throughout the 1950s, both the public and private sectors had essentially the same national-level, industry-wide bargaining structures in Britain. However, the Donovan Commission (1965–8) highlighted the 'breakdown' of these arrangements in the private sector, and subsequent years have seen a sustained movement in the direction of single employer (plant- and company-based) bargaining structures in the private sector.[14] This private sector movement in the 1970s had little real counterpart in the public sector, as indicated in Table 5.5.

In the 1980s, survey evidence has confirmed the continued importance of national-level collective bargaining in the public sector relative to the position in the private sector,[15] although there has been some notable decentralized bargaining activity (to supplement national agreements) in at least certain parts of the public sector in more recent years. For example, supplementary bargaining coverage increased in the period 1978–85 from zero to 24.6 per cent of employees in the case of the technical engineering staff NJB in electricity supply and from 21.6 per cent to 49.3 per cent of employees in the water service staffs NJC. In fact the *New Earnings Survey* for 1985 revealed that for some fifty listed national agreements in the public sector covering male employees, nearly a third of them involved more than a third of the relevant workforce being

Table 5.4 A history of the Administrative, Professional, Technical and Clerical Staffs, National Joint Council, in local government

Period	Events/developments
A Whitley Council meeting in 1920. NALGO submitted a claim for national scales based on civil service pay rates.	Only 11 out of a possible 24 employers' representatives attended. A number of local authorities refused to implement the national scales, and the County Councils Association formally repudiated the agreement.
Inter-war years when pay and conditions set by over 2,000 local authorities at local level.	National Whitley Council founded, but not representative. 15 provincial councils for England and Wales by 1940. Some loss of interest by NALGO in trying to establish national scales, and some suggested alternatives to Whitleyism (e.g. use of statute to set such scales). A survey by NALGO in 1936−7 found that 50 per cent of 890 local authorities had no salary structure of any kind, and 66 per cent had no grievance machinery. The latter findings renewed NALGO interest in trying to establish national-level collective bargaining.
Second World War years. The Conditions of Employment and Arbitration Order in 1940 supported the establishment of national agreements, with the National Arbitration Tribunal being the enforcement mechanism.	NALGO, with government support, met employer representatives to discuss the case for establishing a new national Whitley Council. Talks in 1941−3 involved disagreement about the status of existing national and provincial councils. Agreement reached in October 1943 to establish a new joint council for APT&C grades. A final agreement on uniform national salary scales and conditions reached in 1946. All local government groups, including Chief Officers (1948), had established NJCs by the 1950s.

Source: extracted from IDS Public Sector Unit, *Salaries and Benefits in Local Government*, London, Incomes Data Services, 1988, pp. 47−9

Table 5.5 The nature of collective agreement coverage for wage-setting purposes, public and private sectors, male employees, 1978

	National plus supplementary	National only	Company, district and local	No agreement
Managers:				
public sector	11.3	76.7	2.7	9.3
private sector	8.5	7.7	10.5	73.3
Professionals:				
public sector	12.9	80.0	0.9	6.2
private sector	11.1	7.4	15.8	65.7
Intermediate non-manuals:				
public sector	12.8	82.7	1.1	3.3
private sector	8.8	10.6	18.3	62.3
Junior non-manuals:				
public sector	9.7	86.8	1.1	2.3
private sector	18.7	12.9	14.9	53.3
Foremen:				
public sector	19.3	70.0	5.5	5.2
private sector	21.0	20.8	18.5	39.7
Skilled manuals:				
public sector	27.4	65.1	3.5	3.9
private sector	33.1	24.8	15.3	26.7
Semi-skilled manuals:				
public sector	17.1	78.4	1.1	3.4
private sector	30.5	19.1	18.2	32.2
Unskilled manuals:				
public sector	28.2	66.6	2.0	3.1
private sector	23.0	29.6	14.7	32.7

Source: M.B. Gregory and A.W.J. Thomson, 'The coverage mark up. Bargaining and earnings in Britain, 1973 and 1978', *British Journal of Industrial Relations*, XIX, 1, March 1981, p. 28

affected by supplementary bargaining; the comparable figure for women employeees was four agreements out of the twenty-one listed for that year. The most important areas of supplementary bargaining in the public sector in 1985 are indicated in Table 5.6.

Table 5.6 Percentage of male employees in the public sector covered by a national agreement, but also affected by a supplementary agreement, leading areas, 1985

Particular national agreements	% affected by supplementary agreements
British Steel Corporation – iron and steel and pig iron manufacture	75.8 (male manuals) 75.6 (male non-manuals)
Omnibus Industry – National Council undertakings	85.2 (male manuals)
British Shipbuilders – shipbuilding and ship repair	52.6 (male manuals)
Road Passenger Transport – municipal undertakings NJIC	50.2 (male manuals)
Water – water service staffs NJC	49.3 (male non-manuals)
– water service NJIC (non-craftsmen)	48.8 (male manuals)
Gas – gas staffs and senior officers NJC	42.2 (male non-manuals)
– gasworkers NJIC	41.4 (male manuals)
Electricity supply – workers other than building operatives NJIC	35.0 (male manuals)
Fire services – operational ranks below station officer	33.6 (male non-manuals)
Local authorities services England and Wales – engineering craftsmen and electricians JNC	45.7 (male manuals)
– building and civil engineering workers JNC	40.8 (male manuals)

Source: *New Earnings Survey 1985*, London, Department of Employment, January 1986, Table 187

These relatively high figures for the extent of supplementary bargaining coverage may be contrasted with other areas of the public sector where there is virtually no such additional coverage; leading examples in the latter category include coalmining, British Rail, the civil service, the Post Office and London Regional Transport.

As mentioned earlier in the chapter, bargaining structure, or the level at which collective bargaining is conducted, has been treated by industrial relations researchers as an intervening variable which helps determine the outcomes of the collective bargaining process, but is itself determined by a number of independent variables. The variables which have been held to determine the nature of bargaining structure are, first, certain features of the environmental context in which a particular union–management relationship is situated, and, second, certain organizational characteristics of both the unions and management concerned. The framework of analysis provided by these two sets of variables raises the question of what have been the major factors that have led to the relative importance of industry- or national-level collective bargaining in the public sector in Britain. It has been argued that the comparatively centralized bargaining arrangements of the public sector in Britain are essentially attributable to the fact that most public services are provided by large centralized undertakings operating under parliamentary scrutiny, with generally standardized administrative arrangements and accounting procedures.[16] The problem with this explanation is that it would seem to imply that relatively centralized bargaining structures should be the norm in the public sector across countries, which is not in fact the case. Admittedly in the USA it has been noted that

> in recent years, considerable speculation has emerged concerning the prospects for multi-employer bargaining in government. Such speculation is most commonly focused on teacher–school board labor relations, with some observers and participants foreseeing the development of multi-employer arrangements.[17]

In practice, however, there has been very little actual experience of centralized bargaining structures in state or local government in the USA.[18] At the present time, Britain appears to be in the rather unusual position (compared to most developed countries) of having a substantial difference in the nature of bargaining structure between the public and private sectors. Furthermore, some of the traditional characteristics of national-level, industry-wide bargaining structures (e.g. competitive product markets, a spatial concentration of employment and small-sized employment units) are not features of the public sector in Britain, although relatively high labour cost ratios also favour such arrangements and this is clearly highly relevant in the public sector.

The relatively centralized bargaining structures of the public sector in Britain have been alleged to have had a number of important industrial relations effects on the structures, processes and outcomes of bargaining there. Those effects which are most frequently mentioned in the literature include the following: (i) the limited development of shop steward systems, at the individual employment establishment level; (ii) the limited development of the personnel management function at the individual employment establishment level; (iii) sizeable individual bargaining units whose settlements are highly visible and well publicized, which has led incomes policies to pay particular attention to them; (iv) the proportion of working days lost through strike activity in the public sector tends to be greater than the number of strikes (i.e. strike frequency) which occur there; and (v) the size of the union relative wage effect is less than is the case with decentralized levels of collective bargaining. Some of these effects have already been mentioned in earlier chapters, the remainder will be discussed in later chapters. For the moment, however, I concentrate on the 'adverse effects' which the present government believes result from national-level bargaining arrangements in the public sector, and indeed in the system of industrial relations more generally. The essence of the government's claim is that national-level bargaining is 'remote and destroys jobs. It takes insufficient account of the different circumstances of individual enterprises, or of variations in the demand for workers and the cost of living in different parts of the country.'[19] In short, consistent with its belief in the need for relatively flexible labour market operations, the government case against national pay bargaining views such institutional arrangements as a wage transmission mechanism between regions which (i) limits the extent of inter-regional variation in earnings levels, (ii) makes such earnings levels relatively unresponsive to regional (and local labour) market pressures, and (iii) involves a loss of jobs in high unemployment regions where wage levels are set 'artificially high' due to their reflection of the pressures of low unemployment regions such as the South-East of England. And in an attempt to encourage bargaining structure changes in the direction desired by the government it has been stated that '. . . in the public sector . . . we will seek to gain acceptance of a wider geographical variation in pay rates'.[20]

In order to put this government criticism in context the following points should be noted:

1 the government's criticism of national-level bargaining arrangements is consistent with other measures they have taken (e.g. the

abolition of Schedule 11 of the Employment Protection Act 1975) to limit the coverage of industry-level collectively bargained wages;

2 the government is critical of the operation of both industry-level and company-level wage bargaining, and favours instead plant- or regional-level bargaining;

3 there is some evidence to indicate, at least for the coalmining industry,[21] that centralized bargaining arrangements are less sensitive to demand conditions (and hence facilitate the exercise of union power in terms of the size of wage settlements) particularly when labour markets are relatively loose; and

4 a number of existing studies of wage inflation have pointed to the role of national bargaining as a possible factor in the similarity of wage changes across regions.[22]

Furthermore, the present government is not unique in calling for more decentralized collective bargaining in the public sector, although earlier calls to this effect have based their case on rather different grounds. For example, the McCarthy review of the operation of the Whitley Council system in the NHS in 1976 contained a recommendation in favour of more regional-level bargaining.[23] The government case does, however, tend to suffer from the fact that it believes that there is one best (or least desirable) type of bargaining structure for the system of industrial relations as a whole, and, second, that the effectiveness of bargaining structures can be judged by reference to a single measure of performance (i.e. the impact on wages); both of these propositions would be strongly questioned by most industrial relations researchers.

The government's initial opposition to national-level bargaining in the public sector became obvious at the time of the reorganization of the water industry when the 1983 Water Act abolished the National Water Council. In that year a national strike in the water industry led employers to threaten to abandon national-level negotiations, a threat which resulted in the unions declaring their intention to generate a process of wage 'leap-frogging' by picking off the regional authorities one by one. Under the provisions of the 1983 legislation individual water authorities could withdraw from the national agreements after giving twelve months' notice of their intention to do so, and in 1985 the Thames Water Authority (with some 9,000 employees) withdrew from the senior officers' JNC, followed by four other authorities. Moreover, in anticipation of privatization of the industry, the water industry employers (as a group) came out in favour of ending national-level bargaining, a situation which has come to pass.

The continued maintenance of national-level bargaining arrangements have also been questioned in some other parts of the public sector. For example, following the passage of the Transport Act 1985, national bargaining has been abolished in the National Bus Company, the municipal undertakings and Passenger Transport Executives; a national forum still exists for municipal buses, but pay bargaining is now conducted at the individual company level. Furthermore, in late 1988 the British Railways Board proposed to end national-level bargaining, with the industry to be split into five occupational-based groups and negotiations to be conducted at the local level from the end of 1989;[24] the BR dispute in 1987 appears to have limited the pace of moves in this direction. In the NHS, the nurses' pay review award in 1987 included 9 per cent for working in Inner London, an element that has been viewed as the beginning of a move towards the introduction of regional pay,[25] while the ongoing proposals for reforming the NHS include a provision to allow large hospitals to opt out of central control, with such hospitals having the right to set their own rates of pay. In the civil service there has been the breakup of multi-union bargaining, with only four unions having negotiated together in 1987. The Treasury, in its negotiations with the individual civil service unions, has been seeking to introduce elements of performance-related pay, local pay additions and regional pay variations. Furthermore, the government's interest in reorganizing a substantial part of the civil service into executive agencies is viewed by the unions as posing a major threat to the maintenance of national-level negotiations.

It is, however, in local government that the most obvious pressures on the continued maintenance of national-level bargaining arrangements are apparent. In local government the operation of bonus schemes for manual employees in the 1970s and 1980s constituted the major element of the limited amount of individual authority-level bargaining which took place; the introduction of such schemes followed the recommendation of a report by the National Prices and Incomes Board in 1967, designed to deal with low pay in local government.[26] However, throughout the 1980s, government encouragement and local labour market pressures, particularly in the South-East of England, on levels of recruitment and retention have produced considerable questioning by local government management of the case for maintaining national-level bargaining. In Table 5.7 is a list of the major questions posed on this topic in a recent discussion document produced by LACSAB – the local authority employers' organization.

Since that document was produced, a national-level dispute (concerning the APT&C grades) occurred in the local government sector in the summer of 1987 over the employers' proposal to

Table 5.7 Questions concerning the future of national-level bargaining in local government

1 Is there still general support for the Whitley principles of collective bargaining?
2 Should local government continue to give emphasis to the 'merit principle'; to the desire to be a 'good employer'; and to provide equality of opportunity? Do these approaches need modification in the light of changing circumstances?
3 Should we maintain the principle that there is merit in close co-operation between authorities in pay and industrial relations matters (leaving aside for the moment how that co-operation is best achieved)? Or are authorities now ready to act independently?
4 Does the pay bargaining and industrial relations machinery need radical change?
5 Is there a case for local negotiations? If so, for which groups and on what topics?
6 Is there a desire for regional rates of pay? If so, for which groups? Should those rates be negotiated nationally or regionally?
7 Would authorities welcome more local discretion within a nationally agreed framework? If so, for which groups and on what topics?
8 Would more local discretion best be achieved by slimming down the national agreements; by distinguishing more clearly between matters which are mandatory and which are advisory; by accepting a change of status to the agreements; or by a combination of those approaches?
9 Should decentralization of decision-making be backed up by more employer advice and/or by LACSAB encouraging more experiment and innovation at local level?
10 Is the development of a more strategic or corporate approach to pay and conditions at national level desirable? If so, is it a practical proposition?
11 Should steps be taken to improve co-ordination between the separate employers' sides with a view to dealing more consistently with issues of common concern? How can this be achieved?
12 Do communications between those who work at the centre and local authorities need to be improved? If so, how?
13 At national level should we strive for a more systematic way of setting pay or is the present flexible approach the best, or only realistic, option?
14 If a more strategic approach is favoured, which topics need priority?

Source: *Industrial Relations Review and Report No. 408*, 19 January 1988

abolish all nationally agreed grades and age points, leaving only the existing 49-point pay spine subject to national negotiations. During the course of this dispute at least twelve district councils, largely Conservative-controlled ones in the South-East of England, reached separate settlements with their white collar staff; a number of these involved a local pay and grading structure outside the national agreement.[27] In the case of Brentwood District Council, for example, a new white collar pay and conditions package, which was not negotiated with NALGO, in late 1989 proposed a move to authority-level bargaining over pay and conditions;[28] this would involve a 'staff consultative forum' consisting of elected members of the council, relevant council officers and staff representatives (of NALGO, FUMPO (the Federalist Union of Managerial and Professional Officers) and non-union members). Furthermore, again in late 1989, the Conservative-controlled Kent County Council (with more than 11,000 white collar staff) became the first major local authority to break away from the national APT&C pay agreement.[29] The basic reason for this decision was the substantial difficulties experienced in attracting and retaining white collar staff in the tight labour market conditions of South-East England; the Council reported an annual turnover figure of some 20 per cent, with vacancy rates for professional staff in late 1989 ranging between 6 per cent for accountants and 24 per cent for planners.[30] More generally, a survey by the Association of District Councils of some 213 authorities in mid-1990 produced the findings set out in Table 5.8.

Table 5.8   Current status of national agreements by bargaining group (%), District Councils, 1990

	Local conditions	*Local conditions with some reference to national conditions*	*National conditions modified by local variations*	*National conditions unmodified*
Chief Executives	6.1	13.6	55.4	24.4
Chief Officers	5.6	13.6	54.9	25.8
APT&C	4.2	11.7	57.3	26.8
Manual	4.7	12.7	46.0	33.8
Craft and Chief Officers	3.3	11.3	43.7	38.0

Source: *NALGO Research*, July 1990, p. 20

The basic conclusion of the survey was that only a minority of these district councils rely solely on the nationally agreed terms and conditions of employment, with some form of locally determined conditions to cope with labour market difficulties being very much a feature of the APT&C grades in the South-East of England.

SUMMARY

In this chapter I have been very much concerned with the structures of collective bargaining, emphasizing the relatively high level of collective bargaining coverage and the traditional role and importance of national-level collective bargaining in the public sector in Britain. Chapter 6 turns to the processes of collective bargaining, with particular attention being paid to the issues of strike activity and third-party dispute resolution procedures.

Chapter 6

Bargaining processes, strikes and dispute resolution in the public sector

INTRODUCTION

In previous chapters my particular concern was with some of the leading structural aspects of industrial relations in the public sector. Nevertheless there were occasions to consider certain aspects of process and behaviour; the notion of changes in union character, the issue of who is the employer in the public sector and some limited reference to the level of strike activity in the public sector are all cases in point. In this chapter I take a much fuller look at some of the behavioural dynamics of public sector industrial relations by considering, in turn, the processes of collective bargaining, strikes and third-party dispute resolution facilities.

In order to appreciate certain distinctive features of the process of collective bargaining in the public sector it is useful to indicate some perspectives taken by researchers on the process of collective bargaining in general. There is in fact, as I will show, considerable literature on the process of collective bargaining, although this is overwhelmingly based on private sector experience and hence treats bargaining essentially as a bilateral process; in contrast there is relatively little uniquely public sector-based research that can be usefully summarized here, so that one is essentially in the position of having to identify certain individual issues and themes as being worthy of future research.

THE PROCESS OF COLLECTIVE BARGAINING AND THE PUBLIC SECTOR

The various, existing theories of the collective bargaining process tend, first, to reject any notion that the outcomes of bargaining are solely a function of environmental forces and, second, they seek to identify determinate solutions within the range of indeterminacy originally identified in early bilateral monopoly treatments of union–management wage bargaining.[1] The deductive theories along these lines, which include the Hicks economic model of employer concession and union resistance curves,[2] and game theory treatments of bargaining based on notions of rational, individual utility maximization in situations of interdependency of choice and pay-off,[3] make certain key assumptions about the nature of the bargaining process. And it is typically the 'unrealistic' nature of these assumptions which have led industrial relations researchers to question the insights and value of these deductive models for explaining and understanding the majority of 'real world' collective bargaining situations.[4]

In conceptual terms at least, industrial relations researchers have been much more favourably disposed towards the inductive theory based bargaining treatments of behavioural scientists. The most widely referenced and quoted behavioural study of collective bargaining is undoubtedly that of Walton and McKersie,[5] which was referred to briefly in chapter 5. This particular piece of work emphasized the essentially mixed-motive nature of bargaining relationships, with inter-party relationships rarely being either totally competitive or totally co-operative in nature. Indeed they identified the following four sub-processes involved in most bargaining relationships:

1 *Distributive* bargaining which involves conflict, with one party seeking to achieve gains at the expense of the other. In this particular sub-process a key determinant of the processes involved and outcomes achieved will be relative bargaining power as influenced by, among other things, the likelihood and costs of strike action.

2 *Integrative* bargaining which seeks to ensure mutual gains in areas where the parties have common interests. This particular joint problem-solving orientation will be influenced by factors such as the willingness of the parties to share information and the level of trust between them.

3 *Attitudinal structuring* which involves attempts to establish and maintain a desired, longer term working relationship between the two parties. The parties' preferences for a particular pattern or relationship here (i.e. some position along the distributive–integrative spectrum) are viewed as a function of overall strategic considerations, contextual factors, personalities and the social beliefs of the leading representatives of the two parties.

4 *Intra-organizational* bargaining, which involves the process of reconciling and accommodating the different interests within each of the individual parties involved in a bargaining relationship. The nature of these processes will be shaped by factors such as the authority and solidarity of the negotiating teams.

The second, major conceptual contribution of Walton and McKersie was in relation to the bargaining zone concept where they emphasized the role and importance of strategies and tactics by, for example, Party A in shaping Party B's perceptions of the needs, intentions and coercive capacity of A, although the objective determinants of, for instance, A's coercive capacity were unchanged. The result of their approach in this regard has been two-fold. First, most contemporary discussions of the concept of bargaining power view it as very much a perceptual or subjective-based concept,[6] which involves considerably more than, for example, the objective costs of any strike action. And second, many existing discussions of the collective bargaining process make substantial use of the contract zone notion in which the key concepts are the resistance points (i.e. bottom line positions) and target points (i.e. preferred settlement positions) of the parties, with the essence of the negotiating process being held to be that of (i) identifying the other party's resistance point (without revealing one's own) and (ii) influencing the other party to move from its initial resistance point to ensure an overlap of the two points in the positive contract zone; a move which significantly raises the probability of a settlement being achieved without resort to strike action.[7]

The major conceptual contribution that public sector industrial relations practice and, to a lesser extent, research has made to the literature on the process of collective bargaining has been the addition of the notion of multilateral bargaining. This concept is a recognition of the fact that public sector collective bargaining rarely involves a process in which only two separate, distinct and relatively homogeneous union and management parties are involved, largely as a result of divisions in the employer or management side of the process. The most comprehensive, detailed and formal studies of this particular concept have been conducted in the United States where research has shown that the existence and extent of multilateral bargaining is very much a function of the extent of internal conflict among management representatives.[8] As well as research on the determinants of multilateral bargaining the American literature stresses a number of effects which result from this particular process. For example, it has been observed that

> the result of this situation of dispersed management power and internal management conflict was that much of the bargaining between union representatives and those management officials who held the crucial decision-making power occurred away from the formal negotiating table. A whole new vernacular grew up for this practice – end runs, backdoor deals, two bites at the apple, double-dipping and so on.[9]

In addition to making for highly 'political' union tactics during the course of negotiations there have been questions raised about the outcomes of multilateral bargaining. A number of quantitative studies of the terms of collective agreements (i.e. not simply wage levels) have been conducted, although, as yet, there appears to be relatively little consensus as to whether the extent of multilateral bargaining in the public sector in the USA has generally produced relatively more (or less) favourable outcomes for the unions concerned.[10] Finally, some case study-based research in the USA indicates that the processes of multilateral bargaining can be a leading cause of complex and protracted strike actions in the public sector.[11]

The notion of multilateral bargaining is frequently referred to, either explicitly or implicitly, in studies of public sector industrial relations in other countries, although the particular sources or bases of intra-management divisions in bargaining authority or responsibility may differ from those in the USA. In the USA, multilateral bargaining is very largely discussed in terms of administrative staff vs elected officials, whereas in Britain it is more the paymasters vs actual employers (particularly in the NHS or local government sector) distinction which is emphasized. However, outside of the USA (and to a much lesser extent Canada) there has been remarkedly little systematic research concerning both the determinants and effects of multilateral bargaining in public sector industrial relations. Admittedly some studies of individual public sector strikes in Britain have pointed to the importance of this particular process. For example, an analysis of the national fire service dispute of 1977 (and its aftermath) revealed the extremely complicated negotiating processes which were involved on the management side as a result of: (i) changes in the political complexion of the employers' side of the National Joint Council; (ii) the different priorities of the local authorities and LACSAB; (iii) the different priorities of central and local government; and (iv) the different approaches and styles of the various central government departments involved.[12] As regards (ii) above, for instance, it was commented that

> the major source of conflict between the Associations and LACSAB lay in the link between grant and pay negotiations. For the Associations, limiting pay settlements to the specified cash limit, or obtaining Government commitment to cover any settlement in excess of the cash limit, was the main priority. For LACSAB, the priority was to negotiate a settlement which met this demand of the Associations *and* the demands of the Government and trade unions. Cash limits were a priority but not the only priority.[13]

Clearly further research on multilateral bargaining which goes beyond the details of individual instances of strike action in the public sector in Britain is essential.

In the public sector another important issue for future research concerns the nature of the relationship between the Walton and McKersie sub-processes of distributive and integrative bargaining. Traditionally in Britain, subjects where union–management aims are alleged to differ (e.g. wages) are deemed to be suitable for 'negotiation', whereas in subject areas where their aims are viewed as essentially similar in nature (e.g. workplace health and safety) the appropriate form of interaction is held to be that of 'consultation'. This distinction is often reflected in the provisions of particular pieces of industrial relations legislation in Britain, and has resulted in practice in the establishment of separate structures or committees for negotiation, joint consultation in general and consultation for specific subject areas, such as workplace health and safety. There has in fact been considerable discussion and debate in Britain in recent years as to the current status and future role of joint consultative committees,[14] with important questions being raised as to whether the extent of joint consultation committees has increased in the 1970s and 1980s, and whether their distribution, membership composition and subject coverage has become more heterogeneous through the course of time. This debate has been overwhelmingly confined to the private sector, particularly manufacturing industry, with work on joint consultative committees (as potential integrative bargaining arrangements) in the public sector being characterized by its essential absence. This state of affairs is, to say the least, somewhat surprising and disappointing, given that both joint consultative committees and joint health and safety committees are more widely established in the public than the private sector. For example, the 1984 workplace industrial relations survey revealed that some 48 per cent of public sector establishments had joint consultative committees (compared to 34 per cent of all sample establishments), while nearly 80 per cent of public sector establishments had a joint health and safety committee (although usually at a higher organizational level, rather than at the individual establishment level).[15]

The relatively well-developed consultative arrangements of the public sector, the issue of divisions within management representatives concerning responsibility and authority for bargaining, and the pressures for more decentralized bargaining in the public sector all need to be seen in the context of the general contention that national-level wage bargaining in the public sector in Britain has become increasingly 'adversarial' in nature throughout the 1970s and 1980s. In other words, the distributive bargaining element or sub-process has been held to have increasingly dominated the attitudes and behaviour associated with national-level wage negotiations relative to the integrative bargaining or joint problem-solving element. This has been evidenced by an increased incidence of national-level strike action in the public sector (see the next section) and by certain notable 'bargaining failures', such as the unsuccessful attempt to negotiate a new technology agreement throughout the civil service in the 1980s. An important exercise for researchers in the future will be to examine the extent to which the processes of national-level wage bargaining are either relatively self-contained in nature, or have 'spilled over' adversely to influence the union—management processes involved in lower level negotiating and consultative arrangements. A recent study of the local government sector in Britain has initiated the sort of research that could usefully be pursued along these lines.[16] Specifically, Laffin indicates that the environmental circumstances of the 1980s have increasingly drawn elected members into local level industrial relations arrangements, and that

cooptation and collaboration have declined as significant strategies with tightening financial pressures on local government. . . . there is a trend towards the substitution of corporatist arrangements within local authorities with collective bargaining type arrangements. Managements adopting a conciliatory strategy accept the basic legitimacy of the unions as partners in negotiation over service conditions and work practices. In consequence the institutional structures of joint committees and agreed procedures have grown in importance and become more formalised as authorities have turned to conciliation and away from cooptation or collaboration.[17]

However, the empirical basis for this broad statement is rather limited, and Laffin himself provides two case studies of vastly different local government management approaches towards unions and industrial relations matters more generally. Accordingly, we need considerably more research on the nature and determinants of the processes of union–management interaction at the local level in the public sector in Britain. Possibly some recent work in the USA concerning the determinants of integrative, as opposed to distributive, bargaining responses in relation to the introduction of new technology in parts of the public sector[18] can provide a useful starting point in this regard.

In summary, the processes of collective bargaining in the public sector is a subject area where practice is well ahead of research, particularly in countries outside the USA. Nevertheless if researchers begin systematically to pursue some of the topics outlined here, hopefully this gap will begin to close in the future, resulting in an important new input being made to the existing literature on the processes of collective bargaining which is still overly private sector dominated.

STRIKES IN THE PUBLIC SECTOR

In principle, researchers interested in the level of strike activity in the public sector in any country can adopt a number of possible reference points in their analysis and discussion. They can, firstly, consider how the level of strike activity (variously measured) in the public sector compares to that in the private sector. Second, they can consider whether the level of public sector activity has exhibited an upward trend over time. And third, in more recent years there has been an interest in the question of the level and changes in public sector strike activity across countries. In relation to the last issue, brief mention was made in chapter 1 of the view of some commentators that the level of strike activity has risen significantly in the public sector of a number of advanced industrialized economies during the course of the 1970s and 1980s. This is in fact a difficult proposition to test comprehensively and systematically for a variety of reasons. First, as mentioned in chapter 1, the definition and measurement of the public sector itself may vary between countries, with the role of public corporations being particularly important in this regard. Second, the definition and measurement of the public sector in an individual country may also change significantly over time if, for example, an extensive programme of privatization has been underway. Third, there are the well-known problems of comparing strike statistics across countries because of the considerable differences between countries in (i) the definitions of officially recorded strikes, (ii) the way in which the number of workers involved is calculated, and (iii) the methods by which strikes are identified for recording purposes. In general the particular dimension of strike activity which is held to be most suitable and appropriate for cross-country comparisons is that of workings days lost (adjusted for differences in workforce size). This is because a relatively small number of individually large-sized stoppages tends to account for a relatively high proportion of the total number of working days lost in individual countries over a given period of time, and such major disputes are the ones least likely to be missed in official figures, whatever the particular basis of the recording system. For instance, in Britain (where the official figures exclude 'political' strikes and include only those which lasted at least a day and involved at least ten workers) it has been calculated that nearly half (46 per cent) of all working days lost in the years 1960–79 were due to sixty-four large stoppages.[19]

The use of the working days lost measure to compare the public sector strike record of a number of countries will still, however, involve problems if, for example, the nature of bargaining structure in the public sector varies between countries; the point here is that with decentralized structures strikes may be relatively frequent, but involve few workers and be of short duration, whereas under more centralized bargaining arrangements there may be fewer strikes, but they are likely to involve more workers and last longer. (And the latter pattern is more likely to be fully picked up in the official recording procedures.)

Admittedly, some relatively long time series figures for strikes have been compiled in a number of countries by researchers interested in testing business cycle models of variation in strike activity. However, such work offers few insights to the researcher specifically concerned with public sector strike activity across countries because such models have overwhelmingly sought to explain variation in strike frequency, and have rarely included public sector status or the level of public sector employment as one of their potential explanatory variables. Further difficulties arise from the fact that the official strike figures for many countries do not explicitly identify and differentiate public sector strikes from those in the private sector. The extent of this particular problem was revealed in a recent ILO publication on public service industrial relations in seven countries in which the authors of contributions on the individual countries were asked to produce some figures for the trend in strike activity;[20] this request could rarely be complied with, at least to any comparable extent.

In Britain the perspective which has typically been adopted with regard to public sector strike activity has essentially been as follows:

It is difficult to provide a brief and accurate summary of the trends in public service industrial conflict in the United Kingdom. The official published data do not allow a clear separation of the public and private sectors, there is not complete record of non-strike sanctions, and there have been very sharp fluctuations in the pattern of conflict over the last 15 years. In this period, however, it is apparent that public service workers increasingly resorted to industrial action, usually as part of national pay campaigns when confronted with government policies that seemed to discriminate against the public sector. There has thus been a cyclical pattern of conflict that partly reflects different phases of government incomes policies. The image of public service trade union militancy that became established in the 1970s, and has been sustained since then, arises partly from the contrast with the 1950s and 1960s when public service labour relations were stable and predictable, and the employees seemed docile in comparison with those in manufacturing and some of the public corporations.[21]

Admittedly there is no single, continuous time series set of figures for public–private sector strike activity in Britain extending back over a number of decades. Nevertheless there have been certain individual research studies which do provide some useful pointers to the pattern of public sector strike activity in Britain. First, it is apparent that there has long been considerable variation in the extent of strike activity between the different parts of the public sector. For example, working days lost per 1,000 employees in the years 1949–73 averaged 47.5 in public administration, 64.1 in gas, electricity and water, 139.6 in railways and 579 in road passenger transport;[22] the relevant figure for all industries (excluding coal-mining) in these same years was 184.3. Second, in any given period of time the proportion of working days lost accounted for by the public sector is typically greater than its contribution to total strike frequency. In the years 1966–78, for instance, the public sector was responsible for an average of 26 per cent of all strikes, but for 36 per cent of all working days lost due to strikes;[23] this particular relationship is undoubtedly a reflection of the dominant role of national-level bargaining arrangements in the public sector. Third, the total number of working days lost in Britain can exhibit some substantial year to year variations, with much of this variation being due to the presence or absence of national-level disputes in the public sector. For example, the total number of working days lost in Britain in 1971 was 13,551,000 and 23,909,000 in 1972, with some 45 per cent of the latter figure being due to the national-level coal strike of that year.[24] Fourth, as the figures in Table 6.1 suggest, the proportion of total working days lost due to the public sector has tended to have increased over time.

The Department of Employment figures drawn from these two studies indicate that the public sector accounted for an average of 28.3 per cent of total working days lost in 1966–75 and for an average of 49.3 per cent in 1976–85; this upward movement needs to be seen in the context of a smaller sized public sector in Britain in the 1980s, largely as a result of the privatization of public corporations (see chapter 2). It should also be noted that a recent econometric analysis of strike activity in Britain for the years 1970–87 reported that (i) changes in industrial composition and a rise in unemployment reduced the number of strikes in the 1980s, (ii) the industrial relations legislation of the 1980s reduced the number of working days lost through strikes, although (iii) the number of working days lost fell by 30 per cent in the manufacturing sector, but increased by 30 per cent in the non-manufacturing sector;[25] the last increase was clearly very much a public sector phenomenon.

Public sector strikes were a major source of discussion and debate in the British system of industrial relations throughout the

Table 6.1   Public sector contribution to total working days lost, 1966–85

Year	Public sector proportion
1966	12
1967	17
1968	15
1969	30
1970	32
1971	50
1972	48
1973	21
1974	48
1975	10
1976	18
1977	26
1978	15
1979	21
1980	82
1981	44
1982	64
1983	49
1984	88
1985	87

Sources: C.T.B. Smith, R. Clifton, P. Makeham, S.W. Craigh and R.V. Burn, *Strikes in Britain*, DE Manpower Paper No.15, 1978, Table 13, p. 116, and 'Public sector trade unions', *IDS Public Sector Digest*, 187, London, Incomes Data Services, p. 8.

1970s and 1980s. This is because, first, a number of national disputes involved groups of workers that had never previously been on strike (e.g. civil servants in 1973 and firemen in 1977). Second, a considerable number of them were viewed as having constitutional overtones in that they were directed essentially against government policy of the day; certainly, virtually all episodes of incomes policy in Britain have been broken, at least formally, by public sector strikes, with groups of public sector employees spearheading the resulting 'pay explosions'. Third, these strikes have been alleged to be particularly high cost ones, being especially harmful to the public at large and in some cases raising the possibility of threats to public health and safety. And finally there is, of course, the increased incidence of strike activity in the public sector, as suggested by Table 6.1. This phenomenon, particularly among white collar groups of employees, is also apparent in the 1984 workplace industrial relations survey which, when comparing the positions in 1980 and 1984, reported that there was a substantial increase in white-collar strike action within the public services sector, from nine per cent to 38 per cent of establishments. As we might expect, much of the increase in strike action in the Education and Public Administration sectors reported above is accounted for by strike action among the white-collar workforce. In Public Administration, a half of workplaces with white-collar workers reported white-collar strike action in 1984, compared with only 13 per cent in 1980, and within the Education Sector the proportion reporting strikes increased from seven per cent in 1980 to 45 per cent in 1984.[26]

Since the Conservative government came to power in 1979, there have been instances of national strike action in the public sector in virtually every year. These national-level actions have mainly concerned wage questions, although the figures in Table 6.2 indicate that more localized, non-pay based stoppages have also been an important feature of the public sector industrial relations scene in recent years.

The miners' strike against pit closures in 1984—5 has been viewed as constituting the most direct challenge to overall government strategy in the public sector. This particular dispute involved over 26 million working days lost, the highest in any industry since 1926, and as a result the total number of working days lost through strike activity in Britain was the second highest (after 1979) since the war. The strike was estimated to have affected the GDP of the country by 1.25 per cent with the major impact being felt through stockbuilding and imports.[27] There have been numerous discussions and analyses of the merits of the miners' case, the tactical errors made during the course of the dispute and the wider implications for unions and management in the public sector.[28] There has also been considerable interest in the post-strike position in the industry as certain key individuals have moved on, further pit closures have occurred, disputes have continued to occur, management has imposed pay settlements on the workforce, national-level recognition has been accorded to the breakaway Union of Democratic Mineworkers, and the level of productivity in the industry has also risen dramatically since the strike.[29] The teachers' disputes, both north and south of the border, in the years 1985—6, have also been viewed as constituting important challenges to the government's 'efficiency—flexibility' approach in the public sector, with the outcomes having significant public expenditure implications. The most

Table 6.2   Selective list of more localized, non-pay stoppages in public administration, education and health services, 1985−9

Area	Began	Ended	Working days lost	Reported cause
Pentre, Mid-Glamorgan	11.12.84	30.1.85	26,000	over redundancy fears
Birkenhead	28.1.85	3.2.85	20,800	over redundancy fears
London	5.8.85	6.9.85	10,600	against the action of a supervisor
Sunderland	24.7.85	18.10.85	13,730	against proposed privatization plans
Greater London	3.4.86	3.4.86	8,000	over redundancy fears
Humberside	29.9.86	24.10.86	5,000	over dismissal of colleague
London	5.11.86	16.12.86	7,000	for additional staff
Various areas in England	25.5.87	27.11.87	12,000	for permanent opportunities for YTS trainees
Various areas in Gt Britain	27.5.87	4.11.87	20,000	for employment of additional permanent staff
London	16.6.87	16.6.87	13,000	against redeployment of teachers
Avon and London	4.1.88	30.3.88	29,000	over inadequate staffing
Various areas in Scotland	15.1.88	30.4.88	36,000	over privatization of hospital services
London	9.2.88	9.2.88	5,000	over redundancy fears due to budget cuts
Greater Manchester	16.5.88	3.6.88	9,000	over alleged driver shortage
Scotland	1.11.88	1.11.88	21,000	over redundancy fears
Merseyside	27.2.89	9.3.89	8,000	over dismissal of workers

Source: various issues of *Department of Employment Gazette*

obvious short-term outcome here was the passage of the Teachers' Pay Act 1987 which dismantled the Burnham Committee negotiating machinery and allowed the Secretary of State to impose his own pay settlement.

Major public sector disputes in Britain have frequently been followed by calls from various organizations for the introduction of 'no-strike clauses' in 'essential services' (a report to this effect by the Centre for Policy Studies in 1984 was referred to in chapter 1). The Conservative government was originally keen to proceed in this direction, although to date there has been little tangible outcome from discussions on this subject. This is presumably as a consequence of disagreements over the definition or scope of 'essential services' in the public sector and over the desirability of institutionalizing compulsory arbitration arrangements in return for removing the right to strike. The discussion of the right to strike in the public sector in Britain can be put into context by noting the following points. First, information from the ILO for 1985 suggests that less than twenty-five countries explicitly recognize the right to strike of public sector employees, although in some other countries, including Britain, it has been implicitly accepted.[30] Second, the case for restricting the right to strike in the public sector, regardless of the particular country concerned, invariably makes reference to the same three basic arguments, namely the notion of the government as a sovereign employer, the allegedly relatively strong bargaining position of public sector unions, and the contention that public sector strikes are particularly high cost ones to the public at large.[31] This last contention is the one which one hears most frequently these days, although it is one essentially made on a priori grounds (see chapter 3) as there has been very little systematic research conducted on the actual costs of public sector strikes in Britain or elsewhere. Table 6.3 indicates some of the gains and losses to the parties involved in the 1980 steel strike, a strike in which the government appeared to be the most obvious winner.

Finally, the decision to restrict the right to strike in the public sector in any country obviously raises questions as to whether the restrictions will be effective in practice, and whether there will be any significant costs attached to the operation of procedural arrangements, such as those of compulsory arbitration, which substitute for the right to strike. The American experience[32] here generally suggests that strike restrictions have been reasonably (if not totally) effective in practice, although concerns have been

Table 6.3 Checklist of gains and losses to the various parties in the 1980 steel strike in Britain

The unions (largely the Iron and Steel Trades Confederation)	*Management*	*The government*
(i) Short-term gains:	(i) Gains included:	(i) Gains included:
(a) national wage offer improved from 2% to 11%	(a) some resulting procedural changes in collective bargaining which meant that wage increases could, to some extent, be based on the criterion of local productivity	(a) the creation of an example of wage restraint in the public sector
(b) effective resistance to management's plan completely to change bargaining from national to local level	(b) this procedural change, as a means of reducing labour costs improved the corporation's image with the government	(b) the picketing involved and the original (later reversed on appeal) legal decision that the strike was a political one aided the passage of the Employment Acts 1980 and 1982 which substantially narrowed the definitions of a trade dispute
(c) improved inter-union relationships	(c) the moves towards joint union bargaining	
(ii) Longer term gains more doubtful as:	(d) a reduced workforce size and changed working practices	
(a) industrial restructuring proceeded with employment and union membership losses	(ii) However, management's handling of the negotiations reduced their credibility.	
(b) acceptance of management's wage offer in 1981 wage round (i.e. only a 3% average annual wage increase) and delay to the introduction of 39-hour week		

Source: Compiled from J. Hartley, J. Kelly and N. Nicholson, *Steel Strike,* London, Batsford, 1983, pp. 165–7

expressed that the operation of compulsory arbitration arrangements may limit the extent of genuine collective bargaining, place responsibility in the hands of individuals not directly responsible and accountable to the public at large, and result in relatively sizeable wage settlements. In Canada there have been some experiments in the public sector with the notion of a 'controlled' strike, in which strikes are permitted but a designated proportion of employees in the relevant bargaining unit must remain at work to provide essential services;[3] obviously the crucial and controversial issue here is just what proportion of employees fall into that designated group.

There is a considerable body of literature in Britain on the nature of media coverage of strike activity which has generally concluded that the media is overly preoccupied with strikes (compared to other industrial relations developments) and that the dominant value or normative premise in such coverage has invariably been support for non-disruption to the status quo.[34] The nature of media coverage of strikes in the public sector in Britain is particularly important because (i) the industry or national-level bargaining structure of the public sector makes for relatively sizeable, 'highly visible' strikes and (ii) the outcome of public sector strikes has been held to be strongly influenced by whether public opinion is generally well disposed (or not) towards the strikers' cause.[35] There have been a number of general discussions of the tactical dilemma faced by public sector unions in trying to ensure that their industrial action effectively exerts pressure on management (and ultimately on the government), but at the same time that it does not cause them to lose the support and backing of other union members and the public at large;[36] the result has often been the use of selective industrial action (as in the civil service dispute in 1981 and the NHS one in 1982) in an attempt to achieve some balance between or reconciliation of these two potentially conflicting objectives. However, the various instances of national-level industrial action in the public sector since the late 1970s have seen both unions and researchers making numerous critical comments concerning the role of media coverage in adversely conveying and projecting the essentials of the unions' side of the dispute(s) to the general public. This criticism was apparent during the so-called 'winter of discontent' in 1978–9,[37] but reached its high water mark during the miners' strike of 1984–5. During this dispute the National Coal Board spent a record amount of £4,566,000 on newspaper advertisements alone[38] which, with a media generally hostile to the miners' case,[39] undoubtedly helped to account for the fact that Gallup Opinion Polls reported that public sympathy for the miners in 1984 (26 per cent) was very much less than had been the case in the dispute of 1974 (52 per cent).[40]

In any consideration of the case for removing the right to strike in the public sector one must be aware of the fact that industrial conflict and action can be manifested in a variety of non-strike forms. And the costs of these alternative forms of action may not be inconsiderable in particular cases and circumstances; the electricity workers' overtime ban and work to rule of 1970, for example, resulted in the government taking special measures under the Emergency Powers Act 1920 (amended in 1964) to safeguard essential supplies and services. More generally, both the 1980 and 1984 workplace industrial relations surveys revealed that the most widely reported forms of non-strike action were the banning or restriction of overtime working and working to rule.[41] These forms of action were particularly associated with groups of white collar employees, with the 1980 survey concluding that

> in view of the growing proportion of non-manual workers in the national labour force, the results suggest that the incidence of strikes is no longer an adequate measure of the level of overt industrial conflict. Indeed, broadly speaking, less than one half of the establishments affected by any type of industrial action were affected by a strike which would have come within the definition used for the official records. Our findings show that the definition provides a particularly inadequate measure of industrial conflict in local and national government and, to a lesser extent, in . . . the health and education services.[42]

The importance of non-strike forms of industrial action among white collar employees in the public sector was also revealed by a survey of local authorities in the early 1980s.[43] This particular study, which enquired about industrial disputes over purely local issues in the period January 1980 to March 1982, reported that some 20 per cent of local authorities had experienced one or more instances of work to rule/withdrawal of co-operation by non-manual employees compared to only 8 per cent reporting strike action by such workers.

Finally, numerous comparative studies have indicated that the basic pattern of strike activity varies considerably between nations[44] which is a perspective that can also be applied to the public sector of many countries. The national-level disputes that increasingly characterized the public sector in Britain in the 1970s and 1980s clearly have had little counterpart elsewhere. As mentioned in chapter 1, in the United States, for example, the volume of public employee strikes grew rapidly during the late 1960s, fell in the mid-1970s, fell and rose again in the late 1970s, and fell again during the early 1980s.[45] Furthermore, public sector strikes in the USA overwhelmingly occur at the local government level, with teachers being among the major strike-prone groups of local government employees,[46] and tend to be of much shorter duration than those in the private sector, although they usually involve more workers per strike. There is even some research which suggests that they tend to follow a different cyclical pattern from private sector strikes, falling rather than rising in periods of business expansion.[47] In Canada the public sector accounted for some 18 per cent of total working days lost through strikes in the years 1973–85,[48] in Israel the public sector accounted for some 19 per cent of total working days lost in the years 1976–82,[49] while in Japan the number of strikes accounted for by the public sector has increased substantially from the 1960s, accounting for more than 60 per cent of all strikes in the early 1980s.[50]

THIRD-PARTY DISPUTE RESOLUTION IN THE PUBLIC SECTOR

Voluntary conciliation and arbitration facilities have a long history in Britain, with such arrangements having been placed on a formal, system-wide basis by the Conciliation Act 1896 and the Industrial Courts Act 1919. Traditionally conciliation, the most popular form of third-party dispute resolution, was operated by the Department of Employment, but its independence was held to have been compromised by the operation of incomes policies in the late 1960s and early 1970s; for example, the Conservative government in 1970–2 actually withheld conciliation services from disputes involving wage claims above the policy norm in those years. As a solution to this particular problem the Advisory, Conciliation and Arbitration Service (ACAS), with its tripartite council, was established in September 1974 and placed on a statutory basis by the Employment Protection Act 1975 which repealed the Conciliation Act 1896 and parts of the Industrial Courts Act 1919.

Collective (as opposed to individual) conciliation facilities are provided by ACAS under the provisions of Section 2 of the Employment Protection Act 1975, and in 1989 1,164 requests for collective conciliation were received (1,070 cases were completed), settlement or progress towards a settlement was achieved in 85 per cent of the completed cases, and the majority (i.e. 55 per cent) of completed cases concerned pay and terms and conditions of employment (13 per cent discipline and dismissal, and 13 per cent trade union recognition). However, the total number of requests for collective conciliation has fallen substantially over time, with a 58 per cent reduction in the years 1976–86. There have been no specialist studies of the extent and effectiveness of the usage of conciliation facilities in the public sector. The 1984 workplace industrial relations survey did, however, report, in the particular case of discipline and dismissal procedures, that 'private sector workplaces were more than three times as likely to specify ACAS within the procedure than those in the public sector'.[51] Nevertheless a breakdown of completed conciliation cases by industry group in 1986 and 1987 does indicate that ACAS conciliation is far from an unknown phenomenon in the public sector; national and local government, for example, accounted for approximately 9–10 per cent of the ACAS caseload in each of these years. Moreover recent annual reports of ACAS specifically cite a number of public sector disputes in which conciliation officers were involved; examples cited in the 1987 report include a dispute between a county council and the Fire Brigades Union, one between the Association of University Teachers and the Committee of Vice-Chancellors and Principals of Universities and one between the Inner London Magistrates Courts Committee of Magistrates and two civil service unions.

The last two disputes are particularly interesting ones in that the initial conciliation attempts were followed by the establishment of joint working parties. These joint working parties constitute a response to the possibility that the short-term settlement orientation of traditional conciliation may only deal with the particular manifestations, rather than the underlying causes, of problems in certain union–management relationships, particularly highly adversarial ones. The basic aim of joint working parties is 'to foster as far as possible a rational team approach to the solving of problems which yields results compatible with the objectives of both parties',[52] with the number in existence having grown from

74 in 1981 to 150 in 1986. These joint working parties, which seek to perform a preventive or strategic conciliation function, are operated by the advisory section of ACAS which in general deals with a wide range of subjects, although grievance procedures, disciplinary procedures, pay systems and individual employee rights matters have accounted for much of its workload in recent years. A substantial proportion of advisory work by ACAS arises out of prior conciliation contacts and as the 1987 annual report noted, the public sector has been a sizeable user of ACAS advisory services;[53] in 1986 and 1987 the public sector accounted for some 12 and 17 per cent of surveys, projects, joint working parties and training exercises conducted by ACAS in these two years. In view of the increasingly adversarial collective bargaining relationship at the national level in the public sector in Britain the potential of these joint working parties and advisory exercises as reform measures will be discussed in the final chapter.

The traditional back-up stage to conciliation in Britain has been the use of voluntary arbitration, with ACAS at the present time providing such facilities under the terms of Section 3 of the Employment Protection Act 1975. As the majority of arbitration cases arise out of unsuccessful, prior attempts at conciliation and the number of requests for conciliation has, as noted earlier, fallen in recent years, it is no surprise to find that the overall arbitration caseload is down in Britain; there has been a 43 per cent fall in the years 1976–86, with less than 200 cases going to arbitration per year from the mid-1980s. As to the extent of arbitration usage in the public sector, in 1986 and 1987 the electricity, gas and other energy industry group accounted for nearly one in three arbitration cases, a concentration of usage that certainly warrants some detailed investigation. The ACAS annual report of 1980 explicitly expressed the hope that arbitration would be used more extensively in the public sector,[54] a view that needs to be seen in the context of a government that is far from well-disposed towards arbitration in general, and to its use in the public sector in particular. The government has, for example, rejected the use of arbitration in a number of major public sector disputes in the 1980s, most notably in the civil service and NHS strikes of 1981 and 1982 respectively and in the ambulance dispute of 1989. In the 1982 NHS dispute, for instance, the then Health Minister Kenneth Clark was strongly opposed to the use of arbitration on the stated grounds that arbitrators are not ultimately accountable to the public at large and tend to try and fashion compromise solutions by splitting the difference between the positions of the two parties in dispute. Furthermore, a government report in the early 1980s which examined 17 arbitration agreements in the public sector recommended that in 11 of them the employers withdraw from and renegotiate the existing arrangements.[55] The essence of the recommended change was a move away from the right of unilateral reference to arbitration (traditionally much more a feature of the public than the private sector) on the grounds that the existing arrangements (i) encouraged irresponsibility among the parties (in that they had no responsibility for the final agreement and thus tended to hold their original bargaining positions), (ii) favoured the union side and (iii) were potentially inflationary in that they tended to undermine the effective operation of incomes policies and the system of cash limits. And in 1981, for example, this change was introduced in relation to the operation of the Burnham Committee for teachers in England and Wales.

ACAS provides the secretariat to several standing public sector arbitration tribunals, such as the Railway Staffs National Tribunal and the Police Arbitration Tribunal. Table 6.4 indicates some features of these standing arbitration arrangements, as well as those of other arbitration arrangements, in the public sector in Britain in the early 1980s.

The position of the NHS in Table 6.4 is a particularly interesting one,[56] in that when the General Whitley Council was established in 1948 there was considerable discussion about the need to insert an arbitration clause in the procedure agreement. This did not in fact occur, due to the failure of the parties to agree on the nature of the reference to arbitration – the staff side wanted the right of unilateral reference, while management favoured the case for joint reference. In practice, however, many pay settlements went to arbitration in the 1950s; fully 50 per cent of major pay settlements in the NHS in 1948–55 were resolved by arbitration.[57] In subsequent years the government response to disputes in the NHS has typically taken the form of establishing *ad hoc* committees of inquiry, such as the Halsbury Committee on Nurses' Pay in 1974 and the Clegg Comparability Commission on ancillary workers and ambulancemen in 1979. The absence of standing arbitration arrangements in the health service was highlighted in a report by the TUC Health Service Committee in the early 1980s,[58] which took as its model the Railway Staffs National Tribunal and proposed that (i) there be a

Table 6.4 Arbitration arrangements in the public sector in the UK at January 1983

Employer	Reference group	Nature of reference	Nature of award	Special tribunal	CAC/ACAS involvement through procedure agreement
British Airports Authority	7,500 airport workers	joint	binding	no	yes
BBC	ABS, NUJ, EETPU, SOGAT	joint	binding	no	yes
BBC	NATTKE*	unilateral	binding	no	yes
British Rail	(a) salaried conciliation – professional and technical staff	joint or unilateral/joint	non-binding	Railway Staffs National Tribunal	no
	(b) management staff	joint or unilateral/joint	binding	Chairman of Railway Staffs National Tribunal	no
British Waterways	wages grades and salaried staff	unilateral	non-binding	no	yes
British Steel	various manual unions	joint	binding	no	no
Civil Air Transport	British Airways and other private UK airlines	joint	binding	no	yes
Civil Service	non-industrial staff (550,000)	unilateral	binding 'subject to the overriding authority of Parliament'	Civil Service Arbitration Tribunal	no
Education (Soulbury)	industrial staff	joint	binding	no	yes
	3,000 LEA advisers	by independent chairman	binding	no	yes
Electricity supply	all grades, 178,000 people, 5 NJCs	joint	binding	no	yes
Gas supply	all grades, 103,000 people, 4 NJICs	unilateral	binding	no	yes

Local authorities					
(a)	manual workers, NJC	joint	as agreed in establishment of procedures	no	no
(b)	administrative, professional, technical, and clerical, NJC	unilateral	binding	no	yes
(c)	buildings and civil engineering, JNC	unilateral	open	no	yes
(d)	fire brigades	unilateral	open	no	yes
(e)	chief officers	unilateral	binding	no	yes
London Transport					
(a)	clerical, technical, railway classified supervisory, booking office, and conciliation staff, 23,500 people	unilateral or joint	binding only by prior agreement	Yes –London Transport Wages Board	no
(b)	railway workshop staff, 3,800 people	unilateral or joint	binding only by prior agreement	no	yes
Municipal Buses	all grades	joint	binding	no	yes
National Bus Co.	(a) non-manual staff	unilateral	binding	no	yes
	(b) manual	none	–	no	–
National Coal Board	All staff in 6 JNNCs	joint	binding	National Reference Tribunal	no
NHS	all staff in 1 national and 8 functional Whitley Councils	none	subject to ratification by Secretary of State	no	no
Police	all policemen	unilateral	recommendation, subject to approval of Home Secretary	Police Arbitatration Tribunal	yes
Post Office (until October 1981)	all post unions	unilateral	binding	Post Office Arbitration Tribunal	yes

continued overleaf

Table 6.4 – continued

Employer	Reference group	Nature of reference	Nature of award	Special tribunal	CAC/ACAS involvement through procedure agreement
Road Transport (BRS)	all staff below senior management (20,000) On 3 NJNCs	unilateral	binding	no	yes
National Carriers	all staff below senior management (8,000) On 3 NJNCs	joint, by appointing an independent chairman of the NJNC	binding	no	yes
Teachers (Burnham)	(a) teachers in schools	by chairman of committee	subject to review by Parliament	no	yes
	(b) Colleges of education, polytechnics in England	joint from 1981			
	(c) Similar arrangements in Scotland				
University Teachers Authority	all university teachers (37,000)	joint	binding	no	no
UK Atomic Energy Authority	non-industrial senior staff	joint	binding	no	no
	non-industrial below senior	unilateral	binding	no	no
	industrial	unilateral	binding	no	no
Water Industry (England and Wales)	all staff (74,000) in 4 NJCs	unilateral	binding	no	no

* List of acronyms used in table

CAC	Central Arbitration Committee	LEA	Local Education Authority
ABS	Association of Broadcasting Staffs	NJC	National Joint Councils
NUJ	National Union of Journalists	NJIC	National Joint Industrial Council
EETPU	Electrical, Electronic, Telecommunications and Plumbing Union	JNC	Joint Negotiating Committee
SOGAT	Society of Graphical and Allied Trades	JNNC	Joint National Negotiating Committee
NATTKE	National Association of Theatrical, Television and Kine Employees	NJNC	National Joint Negotiating Committee

Source: J.W. Leopold and P.B. Beaumont, 'Arbitration arrangements in the public sector in Britain', *The Arbitration Journal*, June 1983, pp. 54–5

three-person tribunal with an independent chairman, (ii) the tribunal be serviced by ACAS, (iii) reference to the tribunal should be as a 'last resort', (iv) joint reference, (v) binding awards on the government as well as on both parties and (vi) the operation of a status quo clause. Although no action followed the appearance of this report, the all-party Social Services Committee of the House of Commons produced a report in 1989 on the operation of Whitley Councils in the NHS, which recommended that

> the Government take the initiative in getting discussions started between the management and staff sides with the purpose of developing a mutually agreed arbitration procedure. We suggest that arbitration should be a last resort and that a strict timetable should be established and adhered to for issues referred to arbitration.[59]

In recent years there has been increased practitioner and researcher interest in the role that final-offer or pendulum arbitration arrangements can and should play in Britain. The essence of these procedures is that the arbitrator cannot make a compromise award, but rather must choose either the final offer of the employer or the final demand of the union; the belief underlying this practice is that it will mean greater potential costs for both parties in going to arbitration so that the 'chilling' (i.e. little movement from the original bargaining positions) and 'narcotic' (i.e. repeated reference to arbitration over the course of time) effects on collective bargaining of conventional arbitration should be eliminated or substantially reduced. The interest in this form of arbitration arrangements has largely been stimulated by their incorporation in the 'single recognition—no strike' package deals associated with the Electrical, Electronic, Telecommunication and Plumbing Union in the private sector, although the Institute of Directors has advocated their use in essential public services.[60]

In Britain there has been considerable initial a priori scepticism about, not to say criticism of, the alleged virtues of such arrangements. The points typically made in this regard include (i) a rejection of the view that conventional arbitration invariably involves compromise (i.e. split the difference) awards and (ii) an emphasis on the difficulties of precisely identifying final offers and operating such arrangements in complicated, multi-issue disputes.[61] On the former matter the 1968 annual report of ACAS referred to a particular study which confirmed that straight-choice or 'pendulum' arbitration, which has attracted particular attention in recent years, as a promising 'innovation' in industrial relations, has in fact a long history, going back at least to the turn of the century, when it was used in the Coal Industry Conciliation Boards. Since 1942 over 400 arbitrations dealing with pay and terms and conditions of employment, some 30 per cent of all such cases, have been handled in this way. It also showed that the common criticism made of arbitration, that it 'splits the difference', was ill-founded. Only one in four of all awards, and just over half of awards in cases involving pay or terms and conditions of employment, were a compromise, and even then the award was very rarely pitched half way between the union's claim and the employer's offer.[62]

Final-offer or pendulum arbitration arrangements are particularly associated with a number of public sector jurisdictions in the United States, where there has been considerable research as to its effectiveness. In general it appears that final-offer arbitration seems to encourage rather more collective bargaining activity than conventional arbitration, and that final offer (by package) arbitration tends to reduce the number of issues that are taken to arbitration.[63] In Canada there has been considerable discussion of final-offer arrangements, although such arrangements have not been adopted in the public sector there.

SUMMARY AND CONCLUSION

This chapter has provided an overview of the collective bargaining process, strikes and third-party dispute resolution facilities in the public sector in Britain. In general it was possible to provide numerous facts and figures under these various headings, but very little systematic research is available which could usefully be discussed. In short, there has been considerably more research on the structures of industrial relations in the public sector than there has been on the behavioural processes involved, an imbalance of treatment which clearly needs to change in the future.

Chapter 7

The criteria and outcomes of bargaining in the public sector

INTRODUCTION

In the discussion of industrial relations in the public sector so far I have considered, in turn, the external environmental context, union organizational characteristics, management organizational characteristics, bargaining structure and the process of bargaining, together with the issues of industrial disputes and third-party dispute resolution facilities. This chapter completes the sequential examination of structure, process and performance by examining the outcomes of bargaining. The outcomes of bargaining are important in a number of ways. First, they provide some indication as to whether the various parties concerned have achieved their particular aims in a given period of time. Second, such indications of the degree of goal attainment have important implications for the patterns of behaviour one can expect to see exhibited in subsequent periods of time. And third, outcomes themselves will feed back into the environment which will, in turn, influence the process of bargaining in subsequent periods, strongly shape perceptions of the performance of public sector industrial relations and hence influence the content of any proposed policy changes to the system.

In Britain the performance of public sector industrial relations tends to be overwhelmingly seen in terms of wage outcomes (together with the associated issue of strike activity) with the vast majority of 'necessary changes' in the system concentrating on the nature of wage determination arrangements. This perspective leads me to discuss here the issues of wage criteria in the public sector, public sector wage levels (and changes) in comparison with those in the private sector, and the relationship between wage bargaining outcomes and the operation of incomes policies and the system of cash limits; there will also be some lesser reference to the issue of union relative wage effects and the non-wage outcomes of bargaining. It is important to note too that the issue of wage determination, and strike activity and dispute resolution, tend to be very much the basic terms in which the public sector industrial relations is seen and discussed in other countries.[1]

WAGE CRITERIA IN THE PUBLIC SECTOR

It is generally conceded that both traditional wage theory and private sector practice offer relatively little guidance to either the understanding or operation of wage determination arrangements in the public sector. The comparative remoteness of product market forces, the difficulty of measuring productivity in many parts of the public sector, the lack of a straightforward analogy between the ability to pay in the public and private sectors and the existence of certain public sector-specific groups of employees are among the leading reasons why the direct role of economic forces in public sector wage determination is fairly limited. In order both to effectively recruit and retain labour in the public sector, and to ensure some degree of inter-sectoral equity for employees, some notion of wage comparability with the private sector would seem, at least in principle, an appropriate and useful criterion; although time lags would be involved, this criterion could be the means through which market forces can indirectly influence public sector wage determination. In reality, however, the wide variation in wages paid for essentially similar jobs in the private sector (due to differences in, for example, the ability to pay) is just one of several factors likely to make for considerable difficulties in translating this criterion into an operational formula whose outcomes are acceptable to all the parties concerned.

In Britain the role of comparability (with the private sector) in wage determination has been most explicitly institutionalized in the case of the civil service, and has also been important in the operation of a number of both standing and *ad hoc* commissions and pay review bodies in the public sector. There has also frequently been an important intra-public sector dimension to comparability with, for example, such a relationship existing between the wages of manual employees in the NHS and local government prior to 1980. However, its role and strength in the public sector in both Britain and elsewhere[2] has always been highly controversial in nature. In the civil service in Britain, for example, Fry has argued that the suggested principles of civil service wage determination over time have fallen into four basic groups: (i) follow the market, paying sufficient effectively to recruit and retain labour (position A); (ii) the extreme version of the model employer notion, with the civil service acting as a wage leader for the private sector (position B); (iii) fair comparison (a more modest version of the model employer notion), with civil service pay being comparable to that of good, outside employers (position C); and (iv) compromise with the market (position D).[3]

The third position above was that taken by the Report of the Priestley Committee of Inquiry into the Civil Service in 1955.[4] However, the subsequent operation of their recommended arrangements led to frequent criticisms that civil servants were being 'over-paid' set against many groups of comparable private sector employees. This alleged over-payment of civil servants was held to be the result of biases associated with the measure of compensation used and biases associated with the scope of the survey.[5] With regard to the first set of biases it was argued that, although the comparability surveys conducted by the Civil Service Pay Research Unit did collect information on the non-pecuniary aspects of employment, the relatively favourable position of civil servants in such matters was consistently undervalued when making the appropriate wage adjustments. This particular argument overwhelmingly centred around pension arrangements as (i) a relatively high proportion of civil servants were covered by such schemes, (ii) the civil service schemes mainly involved non-contributory arrangements, and (iii) civil service pensions provided for automatic increases in line with changes in the cost of living.[6] The comparability procedures provided for a wage deduction to take account of these facts (i.e. a 1.75 per cent deduction prior to 1979), but to some outside commentators a more appropriate-sized deduction would have been of the order of about 10 per cent.[7] The second source of the alleged bias in the operation of the comparability procedures was the extent of intra-public sector comparisons and the over-representation of very large-sized organizations; in 1978, for example, only some 20 per cent of the outside organizations surveyed had less than 2,000 employees, with fully 45 per cent having more than 10,000 employees. The flavour of this particular line of criticism can be gauged from the following:

It is bad enough that civil servants themselves decide which jobs in industry and commerce are analogous to those in the Civil Service. It is worse that they draw their comparisons solely from those firms which are closest in structure to the Civil Service in companies like ICI, Shell, BP, Unilever, and the big banks and insurance companies. These are inevitably also the best paid. British civil servants thus enjoy a ratchet system which in normal times ensures that their salaries are linked to those in the most efficient sectors of British industry and commerce – even though they work, generally speaking, in more congenial and less hazardous circumstances, and are much less accountable for the results of their decisions than businessmen.[8]

In the USA the comparability procedures for federal employees expressly preclude intra-public sector comparisons and stipulate a minimum size of survey establishment which appears to be considerably below the size range which was typically used by the Civil Service Pay Research Unit in Britain.[9] However, despite such differences between the two systems, essentially similar points and criticisms to those made above have also been made of the operation of the federal sector comparability procedures in the USA.

In Britain the strongest criticism of the role of comparability in public sector wage determination has typically been associated with the operation of incomes policies. The National Board for Prices and Incomes, for example, which operated in the years 1965–70, was a notable critic of this particular wage setting principle. For instance, in its examination of the pay position in the railways it was highly critical of (i) the inadequate identification of the jobs used for comparisons, (ii) the assumption that relationships that existed in 1960 should continue thereafter, (iii) the fact that comparisons of pay rates could lead to quite different patterns of earnings, and (iv) the potential of the criterion for generating a process of wage leap-frogging.[10] In other public sector pay references (e.g. busmen and the industrial civil service) the board sought to encourage the development of productivity-based payment schemes relative to the use of comparability. The operation of incomes policies in the 1960s and 1970s in Britain had a number of significant implications for the operation of the comparability criterion in the civil service. For example, during the incomes policy standstill of 1966 the Labour government stipulated that in future no more than six months' retrospection should be permitted in any civil service pay increase. Following this announcement the survey cycle of the pay research unit was reduced to three years in 1967, and to two years in 1971. However, civil servants due for a pay review in January 1973 were caught out by the imposition of the Conservative government's Incomes Policy standstill. In considering the case for granting the non-industrial civil service a special wage increase under the anomalies provision of this policy, the Pay Board devoted considerable attention to the wider question of the compatibility of the pay research system with the needs and pressures of a continuing incomes policy. The view of the Pay Board was that

> although the pay research system is intended to ensure that the pay of civil servants is determined by the pay for comparable outside employments, the nature of the system is such that the pay of civil servants inevitably lags behind. Civil servants normally have to wait two years before they can catch up to the full extent permitted by the system although they receive interim increases in intermediate years. They cannot attempt to change the timing to their advantage.[11]

The report went on to suggest certain possible reforms to the pay research system, notably the use of an annual survey cycle and the involvement of outside interests in the survey procedure. These views were influential in the new pay formula for civil servants which was initiated in 1975 in an attempt to avoid large periodic catch-up wage increases. This new formula involved two important changes: the introduction of an annual pay research cycle and provision for the wage information gathered by the Pay Research Unit to be updated between the date of reporting and the date of settlement. The settlement for non-industrial civil servants in 1975 involved an increase of 32.5 per cent which was held to be justified on catch-up grounds, although its size was undoubtedly an embarrassment to a government committed at the time to a policy of wage restraint. The whole system of pay research was in fact suspended in 1976 as part of the incomes policy in operation at the time, and its reintroduction in 1978 (as preparation for an April 1979 settlement) incorporated yet another set of structural changes, most notably the establishment of the Pay Research Unit Board whose basic function was to make the survey aspect of the wage determination process more independent and open to public scrutiny.

Beyond the civil service, the comparability criterion in public sector wage determination appeared to make certain advances during the 1970s. These largely took the form of the establishment of certain *ad hoc* courts and committees of inquiry into pay for particular groups of public sector employees under both Conservative and Labour administrations; the Wilberforce Courts of Inquiry in electricity (1971) and coal (1972) and the Houghton Committee of Inquiry for non-university teachers (1974) and the Halsbury Committee of Inquiry for nurses and midwives (1974). Furthermore in March 1979 the Clegg Comparability Commission was established, in order to ward off damaging public sector strikes, and it produced a number of reports which recommended relatively large-sized public sector awards for 'catch-up' purposes: local authority manuals (10.2 per cent), health service staff (8.4 per cent), ambulancemen (21.6 per cent), nurses and midwives (19.6 per cent) and teachers (18.2 per cent).

The present Conservative government, however, has been strongly opposed to the role of comparability in public sector wage determination and has taken a number of special actions to try and reduce the extent of its influence. First, it abolished the Clegg Comparability Commission in August 1980. Second, it established the Scott Committee in 1980–1 to investigate whether the pay determination arrangements by civil servants took too little account of their relatively favourable pension position, although

> to the Government's chagrin and to the delight of the unions, the committee evaded the issue by suggesting that the way out of the situation in which in pension terms there were 'two nations' – one indexed and one not – was for everybody to have inflation-proofed pensions.[12]

Third, in 1981 the government terminated its agreement with the national staff side in the civil service and was prepared to accept a 21-week strike so as to keep the size of the pay settlement down. The final settlement package included the establishment of the Megaw Committee of Inquiry into Civil Service Pay. The Megaw Committee reported in July 1982 and recommended that pay comparisons should have less influence than previously, with the major influence in wage determination to be that of paying sufficient to recruit, retain and motivate staff. Fourth, the government reluctantly established a pay review body for nurses and midwives in 1983, but has strongly opposed any proposals to establish similar standing or *ad hoc* review bodies for other groups in the public sector. And finally, employees in the police and fire services have had their pay linked, albeit in different ways, to average earnings movements in recent years, but the government is known to be unhappy with these arrangements, particularly in the case of the fire service.

The Conservative government is in favour of more decentralized pay bargaining arrangements in which pay levels and changes should be increasingly related to skills, merit, performance and local market conditions. And the years under the Thatcher premiership witnessed a number of changes and developments along these favoured lines. For example, a number of intra-public sector wage relationships have ended, such as that between manual workers in local government and the NHS in 1980; in the years 1980–6 the pay of local authority manuals increased by 64 per cent, compared to only 47 per cent for the NHS ancillary grades.[13] Second, prior to 1985, major and even minor salary structure adjustments were relatively few and far between in the public sector. However, in response to the increased bunching of white-collar staff at the top of salary stuctures in a number of areas of the public sector, and the government's desire to see pay related more closely to performance and market forces, the 1985 pay round witnessed (i) merit- or performance-related pay proposals, (ii) salary restructuring moves to alleviate pressure at the top and (iii) special pay additions in hard-to-fill vacancy areas.[14] Subsequent pay rounds have seen similar changes along these lines.

In the civil service, for instance, the development of performance pay schemes and pay targeting initiatives from the mid-1980s has been noted.[15] Indeed by the 1989 pay round approximately 400,000 civil servants (out of a total civil service of 585,000) had some part of their pay determined by performance appraisal.[16] Table 7.1 contains a summary outline of the civil service performance pay schemes.

In the civil service, all employees except the most senior ones are covered by longer term pay agreements. In addition, there exist local pay additions (up to £1,000 from mid-1989) which can be paid to staff at the discretion of individual civil service departments, a new special bonus scheme (to reward individuals for specific short-term achievements) covering all civil servants was introduced in early 1989, while in a number of the newly established agencies in the civil service (ten have been established, covering 7,700

Table 7.1 Performance pay schemes in the civil service

Bargaining groups	Type of staff and numbers covered	Type of scheme	Number of discretionary increments
Grade 2–3	top civil servants 600	performance-based incremental scales with additional discretionary points	3
Grades 5–7	senior civil servants 23,000	performance-based incremental scales with additional points	4
IPMS	professional and technical staff 55,000	performance-based incremental scales with additional discretionary points	4
IRSF	Inland Revenue staff 60,000	performance-based incremental scales with additional discretionary points	3
NUCPS	executive staff 109,000	performance-based incremental scales with additional discretionary points	3
CPSA	clerical staff 195,000	incremental scales with two additional discretionary half increments	2 × 0.5 increments

Source: IDS Public Sector Unit, *Public Sector Pay: Review of 1989 and Prospects for 1990*, London, Incomes Data Services, 1990, p. 20

employees, although more are planned), special incentive bonus arrangements have been established (e.g. Companies House and the Vehicle Inspectorate). Moving outside of the civil service, the following pay-related developments were also noted by the time of the 1989 pay round:

1 In the NHS, discretionary pay supplements were introduced for administrative and clerical staff; these pay supplements, worth up to 30 per cent in the South-East of England (20 per cent in the rest of the country), can be attached to hard-to-fill posts. A £5

million pilot scheme to target pay supplements at hard-to-fill posts has also been introduced following the recommendation of the 1989 Nurses' and Midwives' Pay Review Body.

2 In the local government sector, a variety of developments have occurred particularly in the South-East of England. As noted in chapter 5, some councils have broken away from the national-level bargaining arrangements, while others have made adaptations and modifications to the national agreement. The latter include the addition of special location or market supplements, the spread of new benefit packages and the introduction of performance-related pay schemes. A survey by Incomes Data Services indicated that around one in four local authorities in England and Wales had, or were planning to have, performance-related pay, while LACSAB reported that 60 per cent of authorities in the South-East made some use of such arrangements.[17] Table 7.2 sets out the details of the white collar pay and conditions package in Brentwood District council, a council which broke away from the national negotiating arrangements in 1989.

3 In British Rail, regional pay incentives have been introduced. For example, in 1989 a package for staff working within 40 miles of Charing Cross in London included residential travel (i.e. free travel from home to work and back, for up to 40 miles), a shift supplement (i.e. a flat payment of £5–£10 per week for irregular and unsocial hours shift working) and skills retention payments. The latter involves a payment of £300 per quarter for certain grades with interchangeable fitter and electrician skills, with satisfactory performance and attendance records.

4 In Post Office, special recruitment and retention supplements have been introduced for staff in areas with a local unemployment rate of less than 5 per cent and where turnover rates have exceeded 15 per cent.[18]

In general, most of these pay flexibility initiatives and developments have been confined to managerial and white collar staff in the public sector; this is especially the case in the local government sector, although the Post Office is an important exception here. Moreover a number of the initiatives have been of an essentially *ad hoc* nature, particularly in local government. Indeed there has been some concern expressed that some of the special payments or allowances to meet specific problems will become 'blanket payments',[19]

Table 7.2   White collar pay and conditions package, Brentwood District
Council, 1989

● *A move to authority-level bargaining over pay and conditions*. In future discussions on annual pay increases will take place at a 'staff consultative forum'. This will consist of elected members of the council, relevant council officers and staff representatives. Representatives of NALGO, of the non-TUC affiliated union FUMPO, and of employees who are not union members will be included in this forum.

● *A no-strike clause*. The new arrangements at Brentwood mean that when there is a failure to agree at local level, the next and final stage of the procedure is binding pendulum arbitration by the conciliation service, ACAS.

● *The implementation of a local disputes procedure*. The new procedure replaces the national and regional appeals machinery by 'in-house' only arrangements, the highest level of appeal resting with a sub-committee of elected members.

● *The introduction of new local allowances*. As part of the initial deal the council gave a commitment to its staff that it would implement in full the national 1989 pay settlement (PABB 239) when it was finally agreed. This has been done and in addition employees receive two local pay supplements in exchange for acceptance of the new deal. The first, called 'Brentwood local conditions allowance', is a 3% addition to national pay rates. Under the terms of the second – the 'Brentwood local area allowance' – the nationally agreed outer fringe allowance of £282 is frozen and paid together with an extra supplement of 2% of salary.

● *The introduction of 'linked grading' for lower paid staff*. In a response to the issue of 'low pay' the council has introduced a linked grading system covering Administrative, Professional, Technical & Clerical (APT&C) grades one to six. Staff in these grades are no longer limited to the grade which is attached to their job. They may move into a higher grade subject to the attainment of experience, training, qualifications, or exemplary performance. This reinforces the council's earlier decision to end automatic progression through the pay scales, and to promote a system of 'performance-only' salary progression.

● *Other merit payments introduced*. Other forms of performance-related payments, such as 'payments for special work' and so on are extended across the board. Recommendations for salary progression and other performance payments are made by the respective chief officers and authorized by the council's chief executive.

● *The potential for a move to more flexible working arrangements*. Under the terms of the new package the authority is now able to introduce more flexible working patterns which, for example, address, the variable workloads of particular departments and the prevailing operational requirements.

Table 7.2 – continued

● *Private medical insurance for all white collar staff*. This already applies to senior officers, but is now extended to all staff.

● *Car leasing scheme extended*. Brentwood already operated a car leasing scheme for staff designated as 'essential car users'. This scheme has been extended, and is now available to all employees on scale six and above (£12,960 pa and over, under the national agreement).

● *Car loan scheme extended*. Car loan facilities, previously a benefit offered to senior employees and essential car users, are now available across the board.

● *Interest-free season ticket loan facility introduced*.

● *Free life assurance introduced*. This benefit, equal to annual salary, is available to all staff.

Source: *Industrial Relations Review and Report*, No. 458, February 1990

while a recent newspaper article on teacher recruitment difficulties commented that:

> Essex's experience is typical of the brinkmanship involved in teacher recruitment this summer. Most authorities think they will fill their vacancies – almost. But it has cost millions of pounds and thousands of hours of staff time to achieve, and there are serious doubts about repeating the feat year after year.[20]

The sort of pay-related developments in the public sector discussed above need to be seen in the context of (i) growing labour market pressures on recruitment and retention levels, (ii) increasingly decentralized organizational changes, (iii) criticisms and concerns about the adequacy, value and future of national pay bargaining and (iv) government attempts to limit the size of the public sector wage bill. As regards the last, the government sought to have to pay settlements of around 8 per cent in 1990/1, 5.5 per cent in 1991/2 and 5 per cent in 1992/3, at least according to the public expenditure White Paper in early 1990.[21]

COMPARISONS WITH PRIVATE SECTOR WAGES

In view of the fact that the relationship between public and private sector wages has been seen in many countries as the central determinant of the overall 'state of public sector industrial relations' it is interesting to note the following:

Public employees today tend to receive higher salaries and wage-related benefits than do employees in the private sector. In part, higher wages reflect higher qualifications, and jobs requiring skill and responsibility: in part, they reflect more generous wage settlements by government as an employer. In pay bargains in the public sector, unions have two advantages lacking in the private sector: the threat of political embarrassment to politicians if a favourable settlement is not made, and the employers' lack of a need to make a profit, for wage increases can be paid by raising taxes.[22]

The basic empirical evidence cited in support of this very strong statement is set out in Table 7.3. In fact, public and private sector wage comparisons are a much less straightforward exercise than is implied by the quote cited above. This is acknowledged in an IMF report which, having posed the issue of whether public sector wages are too high, went on to comment that

The obvious question is high in relation to what? Generally, public sector wages are measured against private sector wages and are perceived as 'too high' or 'too low' relative to remuneration for equivalent services performed in the private sector. . . . The basis of comparison is obviously central to this issue. . . . Central government wages may be high relative to those prevailing at the state and local governmental level or in the nonfinancial public enterprise sector. Moreover, any analysis of the sectoral distribution of pay which solely examines the public and private sectors in total will mask considerable heterogeneity within each sector. Again, the overall evidence on pay for any one country shows that there are considerable fluctuations in the relative pay of workers in the public and private sectors. Comparisons of pay in single years or even two or three year averages can therefore be particularly misleading and results can be very sensitive to the benchmarks chosen.[23]

This comment, plus many others, suggests that in any attempt to compare public and private sector wages in an individual country, researchers must pay considerable attention to the following issues and questions: (i) is a comparison of average wages in the two sectors really appropriate, if the wages of public sector employees have traditionally been compared with those of particular, private sector groups; (ii) is it appropriate to treat the public sector as if it

Table 7.3 Rates of earnings per public employee to earnings of private
sector for wage and salary earner, various countries

	1960	1965	1970	1974	1975	1976
Australia	—	—	1.80	1.63	—	—
Belgium	1.34	1.23	1.25	1.27	1.35	—
Canada	—	1.03	1.14	1.16	1.17	1.18
Denmark	1.11	1.26	1.24/1.09	1.17	1.20	—
Finland	—	1.56	1.21	1.31	1.32	1.31
France	1.22	1.29	1.24	—	—	—
Germany	1.44	1.31	1.33	1.31	1.29	1.25
Italy	1.76	1.76	1.35/1.48	1.28	1.20	—
Netherlands	1.33	1.59	1.56/1.53	1.51	1.52	1.50
Norway	—	—	1.07	1.00	1.00	1.02
Sweden	—	—	0.95	0.95	0.94	—
Switzerland	—	—	1.35	—	—	—
United Kingdom	1.09	1.04	0.92	0.93	0.96	0.91
United States	0.88	0.91	0.96	0.99	0.99	0.98

Source: *Employment in the Public Sector*, Paris, OECD, 1982, p. 34

were a single, homogeneous group for wage determination
purposes; (iii) what is the appropriate time scale over which
comparisons should be made; (iv) can differences in the composition of the workforces in the public and private sectors be
adequately taken into account or controlled for; (v) can the
differing impacts (if any) of unions in the two sectors be identified;
and (vi) can any differences in non-pecuniary terms and conditions
of employment be identified which may be a source of compen-
sating wage differentials.

Prior to the 1970s the available wage information in Britain provided little direct evidence concerning the relative movements of
public and private sector wages. Nevertheless, some wage series for
male manual employees were constructed by researchers which
suggested that earnings in the two sectors moved reasonably closely
together throughout the 1950s and 1960s, that the public sector
tended to lag behind the private sector in peaks in the earnings
series, and that private sector earnings generally rose more than
public sector earnings in the upswing of the cycle, but rose by less in
the downswing of the cycle.[24] The appearance of the annual *New
Earnings Survey* in the 1970s has been a major source of information on public and private sector wage movements, with one
examination of this particular source for the years 1970–9
concluding that

1 only public sector male manuals were 'better off' compared to their private sector counterparts at the end of the 1970s than they had been at the beginning. For women manual workers there was essentially the same relative wage relationship between the public and private sectors in 1979 that had existed in 1970, while for non-manual workers (both men and women) in the public sector there was a relative wage loss over the course of the decade.

2 all public sector employee groups substantially improved their relative wage position in 1974–5, a movement maintained in 1976 for non-manual but not for manual workers.

3 subsequent to the relative wage gains of the public sector in 1974–5, there was a movement back in favour of the private sector for all four groups in each year since 1975 (manual men and women) or 1976 (non-manual men and women) which, except for male manuals, more than offset the mid-1970s gains for the public sector.[25]

Table 7.4 shows this pattern of change for male workers (both manual and non-manual), together with an indication of the nature of change in the early to mid-1980s. There are no obvious, long run trends in the figures, although substantial short-term changes in the relative position of the two sectors are clearly much in evidence:

Table 7.4 Public sector pay as percentage of private sector pay (full-time males over 21, comparison of median weekly earnings), 1971–84

Year	Manual	Non-manual
1971	94.4	106.3
1972	96.2	110.5
1973	97.3	106.5
1974	96.4	108.5
1975	105.2	113.4
1976	104.2	118.2
1977	102.7	114.6
1978	100.0	107.3
1979	99.1	104.2
1980	104.6	108.0
1981	107.4	113.4
1982	106.2	110.8
1983	106.7	109.6
1984	103.8	105.6

Source: R. Layard, 'Public sector pay: the British perspective', London, Centre for Labour Economics, LSE, Discussion Paper No. 229, January 1986, p. 10

witness the public sector manual gains in 1975, the public sector non-manual gains in 1975 and 1976, the public sector relative losses in the late 1970s, the relative gains for the public sector in 1980 and 1981, and then the subsequent losses, particularly for non-manuals in the public sector. In a similar exercise Trinder examined public services pay relative to average earnings (for the whole economy) for the years 1972−3 to 1987−8 and concluded that (i) significant public service gains had occurred in the years 1975−6, 1980−1 and 1987−8, which were years of major 'comparability awards', and (ii) the public sector suffered a relative wage loss for five successive years from 1980−1, which amounted to a cumulative gap of some 10 per cent.[26] The *New Earnings Survey* data is also important in permitting a more disaggregated view of the public sector. Accordingly, Table 7.5 sets out some relative wage information for individual parts of the public sector for male employees in the 1980s.

In 1980 male non-manuals in central government and both male manuals and non-manuals in public corporations enjoyed relative wage gains over their respective private sector counterparts. However, the relative wage movement against the public sector in the 1980s has been such that only the male manuals in public corporations continued to enjoy such a position by 1989. Table 7.6 produces a similar set of wage information for women workers.

In the case of women workers all public sector groups, except the local authority manuals, enjoyed a relative wage advantage over the private sector in 1980, with some particularly sizeable advantages being apparent. These wage gains in general were reduced in size by 1989, although positive differentials still existed for central government and local government non-manuals and for both groups in public corporations, while the relative position of the local authority manuals in 1989 had improved over that in 1980. In summary, the contents of Tables 7.5 and 7.6, which are only 'crude' comparisons of gross weekly earnings (i.e. there are no controls for differences in workforce characteristics, for example), indicate first, a relative wage movement against virtually all public sector groups throughout the 1980s (women manual workers in local government are something of an exception), although, second, women workers in the public sector were more likely than men in the public sector to enjoy a relative wage advantage over their private sector counterparts at both the beginning and end of the decade.

Table 7.5 Pay for individual parts of the public sector as percentage of private sector pay (full-time males, comparison of gross weekly earnings), 1980–9

Year	Central government		Local government		Public corporations	
	manuals	non-manuals	manuals	non-manuals	manuals	non-manuals
1980	94.8	108.1	91.3	98.1	110.7	103.2
1981	94.5	104.4	91.4	106.1	114.9	108.3
1982	98.8	100.7	87.3	102.2	116.0	107.6
1983	93.5	98.6	86.9	101.0	115.5	106.7
1984	90.7	95.5	85.6	98.1	114.2	106.2
1985	88.6	93.4	83.7	95.7	112.5	103.6
1986	90.0	92.7	83.4	93.9	113.6	103.8
1987	88.0	90.9	83.3	92.2	112.2	100.2
1988	88.0	88.4	84.4	92.0	111.1	95.4
1989	83.2	88.9	84.1	88.8	106.6	95.9

Source: Table I, Part A of *New Earnings Survey*, relevant years

Table 7.6 Pay for individual parts of the public sector as percentage of private sector pay (full-time females, comparison of gross weekly earnings), 1980–9

Year	Central government		Local government		Public corporations	
	manuals	non-manuals	manuals	non-manuals	manuals	non-manuals
1980	108.3	122.4	97.6	135.9	135.0	117.2
1981	105.6	116.5	100.8	150.4	133.3	120.8
1982	103.2	113.2	100.5	141.5	132.3	121.5
1983	104.6	114.9	100.1	139.9	131.9	123.0
1984	101.4	107.3	99.1	132.5	134.1	120.0
1985	97.8	105.6	97.8	128.2	137.1	115.1
1986	97.0	105.3	99.2	128.9	135.1	115.6
1987	96.0	103.7	99.3	125.5	131.7	113.0
1988	93.9	101.3	99.8	125.6	130.4	106.9
1989	94.0	108.4	101.7	121.2	138.1	109.8

Source: Table I, Part A of *New Earnings Survey*, relevant years

Table 7.7 Public sector pay settlements 1983–9

April–March each year	1983/4	1984/5	1985/6	1986/7	1987/8	1988/9	1989/90
Inflation (at start of period)	4.0	5.2	6.9	3.0	4.2	3.9	8.0
Average earnings (underlying at start of period)	7.5	7.7	7.5	7.5	7.75	8.5	9.25
Central government							
Armed Forces (review body)	3.9–9.9	6.5–9	4–8.5	5.5–9.5	4.7	6.4	6.8
Civil service (staff)	4.9*	4.55*	4.9*	6	4.25 (basic)	4.5 (admin staff)	4 + new pay structure (admin staff)
NHS							
Nurses (review body)	–	6–8	4–14.7	7.9–9.5	9.5	15.3*	6.8*
Doctors (review body)	9	3 + 6.9	6.2 (avg.)	6.9–7.2	8.25	7.9	8
Ancillaries	4.8–3.5	4.8–3.5	4.7*	6*	5*	6	7.7*
Admin and clerical	4.5	4.5	4.7	6	5	5	6.25 × 3.25 for restructuring
Local government							
Manuals	4.1–5.1	5.7–4.7	12.0–6.7	7.2–6.3	10.6*	5.6*	8.8*
APT&C staffs	4.6–5.5	4.6–5.6	5.25	6.0	7.1–8.8 (staged)	5.4	8.8 (avg.)
Police (indexed)	8.4	5.4	7.5	7.5	7.75	8.5	9.25
Fire (indexed)	7.8	7.2	7.2	7.3	7.3	8.6	8.6
Teachers (E&W)	4.8	5.1	6.9 + 1.6	5.5	16.4 (staged) (15 mths)	4.2	6**

Public corporations							
British Coal (miners)	5.2	5.2	5.1–3.8	2.6–3.6	4.3 (2 yr deal)	5–6.1	7.64
Electricity (manuals)	4.5–6.1	5.2	4.8–6.7	6.5	5.6	7	9.2
Water (manuals)	7.3	4.6	5–5.5	5	5	5	cons + 7.5
British Rail (manuals)	4.5	4.9	4.8	5	4.5	5	8.8
Post Office (postmen)	5 + 1	5.2	5 + 0.5	5.3*	5*	5*	8.1*

The earnings increase is the DE estimated 'underlying increase' (whole economy).

* Paybill increase
** Heads and deputies received 7.5%

The increase in settlements shown should be seen as a guide to the settlements in each period, rather than as an exact description.

Source: IDS Public Sector Unit, *Public Sector Pay: Review of 1989 and Prospects for 1990*, London, Incomes Data Services, 1990, p. 5

Since the mid-1980s there has been a variety of institutional arrangements for determining pay in the different parts of the public sector: review bodies for the armed forces and for nurses, indexing formulas (albeit different in nature) for both the police and fire services, and national-level negotiations for other groups such as the local authority manuals and NHS ancillaries. This diversity of arrangements has predictably produced some not inconsiderable variation in the size of wage increases enjoyed by different groups within the public sector, thus raising some issues of intra-sectoral equity. Table 7.7 sets out some relevant information for the pay settlements of individual public sector groups in the years 1983−9.

As the table indicates, the police, with their special indexation arrangements, have been individually the most successful public sector group in wage settlement terms throughout the 1980s, while more generally the contents of the table tend to suggest that the groups covered by indexing arrangements and review bodies have fared better than the (other) public sector 'negotiating' or bargaining groups: this being said, the government in early 1990 decided to stage the awards recommended by pay review bodies.[27] As a result questions have increasingly been raised about the problems of intra-public sector equity which have arisen from different-sized settlements being associated with the operation of review bodies and negotiating arrangements. For example in its report on the NHS the all-party Social Services Committee of the House of Commons observed that

the disruption of pay relativities in the NHS caused by the different outcomes of Pay Review Body and Whitley Council settlements is significant. The point is well illustrated by considering the pay of Physiological Measurement Technicians (PMTs), though many other examples could be given. In 1982 newly qualified State Registered Nurses (SRNs) and the various Professions Allied to Medicine (including radiographers, chiropodists and physiotherapists) earned (on average) only slightly more than a newly qualified PMT. By 1988 the differential had increased to over 20 per cent. Similarly, a State Enrolled Nurse (SEN) in 1982/3 earned 10 per cent less than a newly qualified PMT. Now SENs earn over 15 per cent more than PMTs.[28]

In the light of this, and other evidence the committee went on to argue that there was a problem of pay comparability within the health service (as well as externally) and that, rather than extend the coverage of pay review bodies, 'there is a strong case for some selective investment in improving pay and conditions for Whitley Council staff.'[29]

The general tendency in Britain to use the *New Earnings Survey* to make comparisons of the level of (and changes in) the average earnings of public and private sector employees needs to be seen in the light of (i) the April position revealed by the survey is less comprehensive for the public than for the private sector (due to more settlements occurring later in the calendar year) and (ii) average earnings differences between the two sectors reflect more than simply pay settlement differences. The latter point has been especially emphasized by Elliott and Murphy, whose analysis of the period 1970–84, when adjustments were made for certain 'compositional' differences between the two sectors of employment, revealed some important differences from the picture suggested by average weekly earnings comparisons;[30] in particular they found that the relative pay loss of non-manual workers (especially women) in the public sector was considerably greater than was suggested by a simple average earnings comparison. Admittedly there has been some limited analysis conducted on wage data sources other than the *New Earnings Survey* which have shed some light on public– private sector wage relationships. For example, a recent cross-sectional, multi-variate analysis of the (grouped) wage data contained in the 1984 workplace industrial relations survey suggested that 'nationalised industries pay wages up to 10% higher, *ceteris paribus*, while the rest of the public sector pay up to 15% less, *ceteris paribus*. These findings suggest that further exploration of the UK public/private distinction would be fruitful.'[31]

There is a limited amount of information on public–private sector wage movements in other countries which indicates that changes in relative wages (between the two sectors) are apparent over time, although both the nature and timing of such changes do vary between countries. First, for example, in Sweden average wages increased more in the private than the public sector in 1970–6, whereas in 1976–9 the exact opposite occurred, while in 1979–82 there was little difference apparent between the two sectors.[32] Second, in the case of Italy it has been reported that public sector employees earned on average more than their private sector counterparts to the end of the 1960s, a difference that was reduced in the 1970s which, in turn, resulted in above-average increases in the public sector in the early 1980s.[33] And finally in the USA for the 1982—6 period, it was noted that

> annual changes in compensation were greater for public than for private sector workers throughout this period, although the rates of increase for both groups declined from the beginning to the end of the period. Both white-collar and blue-collar employees of state and local government experienced more rapidly rising compensation rates than their respective counterparts in industry. This contrasts markedly with the experience of the mid-1970s to the early 1980s, when rates of public employee pay increases in the United States were well and consistently below the rates of pay increase for private workers.[34]

In the United States there has been a considerable body of research which has gone well beyond simple comparisons of the levels of, and changes in, average wages in the public and private sectors. The concern of this reserch has been essentially to see first, whether there is a positive wage return to public sector employment status, *ceteris paribus*, and second, whether the size of the union relative wage effect in the public sector differs significantly from that in the private sector. There is a very sizeable body of literature on these two issues in the USA, with some important methodological differences between some of the earlier and later studies. On the former question, one of the most recent studies suggests that 'overall, public sector workers seem slightly underpaid given their characteristics and selection'.[35] And, for the second question, of the size of the union relative wage effect, the weight of evidence tends to suggest that this effect is somewhat smaller in the public than in the private sector in the USA.[36] This sort of finding seems to cast doubt on the view that unions in the public sector, at least in the USA, enjoy rather greater bargaining power than unions in the private sector. However, it also needs to be noted that public sector unions in the USA have tended to raise fringe benefit levels more than they have raised wages[37] and that there is some limited evidence which suggests that public sector unions have positively influenced employment levels at the individual department level in local government;[38] the latter is the sort of public sector specific research which, as was noted in chapter 1, needs to be increasingly undertaken. The other country in which there has been considerable interest in whether a public sector wage premium exists in Canada, with one recent paper suggesting a rise in this premium between 1970 and 1980.[39]

The question of whether unionized workers enjoy a wage premium over comparable non-union workers, *ceteris paribus* (i.e. the union relative wage effect), has led to a number of studies appearing in Britain during the 1970s and 1980s. In general it seemed that the size of this effect had shown some tendency to increase through time (i.e. 8 per cent in the 1970s and 11 per cent in the early 1980s), although this effect was much smaller than that observed in America. The initial British studies were largely confined to male workers in the manufacturing sector, with little attention being given to the public sector, although the individual findings[40] which indicated (i) relatively little relationship between the size of this effect and the level of union density at the individual industry level and (ii) a relatively greater wage return to unions under decentralized collective bargaining arrangements seemed to imply that the union relative wage effect in the public sector might be somewhat limited. However, one study using data contained in the 1980 workplace industrial relations survey produced the estimates set out in Table 7.8.

Table 7.8 Wage gaps in Britain, 1980 (%)

	Manual		Non-manual	
	semi-skilled	skilled	clerical workers	middle managers
Britain	10.2	−0.4	0.7	4.0
Manufacturing	2.0	−0.7	3.0	2.6
Non-manufacturing	14.0	−0.9	−0.5	3.5
Private sector	7.8	−1.0	1.3	2.3
Public sector	25.5	6.7	12.4	3.5

Source: D. Blanchflower, 'What effect do unions have on relative wages in Great Britain?', *British Journal of Industrial Relations*, 24, 2, July 1986, p. 200

Blanchflower, the author of the study, expressed some surprise at the relatively sizeable effect apparent in the public sector, and went on to suggest that this might have resulted from some unmeasured differences in both establishment and workforce characteristics between 'union' and 'non-union' establishments within the public sector. Indeed, given the comparatively highly unionized nature of the public sector in Britain, there would seem considerable merit in his observation that 'establishments which do not recognise unions in the public sector are marginal to the industry in which they are located'.[41] A second analysis of this same data set produced much less dramatic differences between the public and private sectors in that (i) the public sector variable was insignificant in both the union and non-union equations for semi-skilled manual workers, while (ii) 'public sector pay in the union sector is significantly below that in comparable private sector establishments for skilled workers'.[42] In short, given the sensitivity of such estimates to particular data sets, the presence or absence of particular control variables and the particular estimating techniques employed, there is clearly a need for considerably more research before any reasonable consensus can be reached concerning the size of the union relative wage effect in the public sector in Britain.

PUBLIC SECTOR WAGES, INCOMES POLICIES AND CASH LIMITS

In general discussion of the operation of incomes policies in Britain it has been widely contended that governments of both political persuasions have sought to enforce the policies most vigorously on public sector employees. There have in fact been episodes of incomes policies solely or overwhelmingly directed at the public sector (e.g. the 1961–2 pay pause, the 'N–1' years of 1970–2), while in other policy periods there have been an above-average number of public sector wage claims referred to the body responsible for administering the policy (e.g. the 1965–70 Price and Incomes Board period). The relatively high labour cost ratio of public sector employment, the national-level bargaining structures and the pressure to provide an example of wage restraint to the private sector are among the leading factors which have both motivated and facilitated attempts along these lines.

The intent of governments to act in this way is little disputed in Britain. However, different commentators have differing views as to whether governments have successfully achieved their aims in this regard. There appear to be three different schools of thought here. The first generally argues that public sector employees have experienced a relative wage loss under incomes policies due to factors such as policy norms in flat rate terms squeezing income differentials, and the limited ability of public sector bargaining groups to achieve exceptional increases through productivity and efficiency gains. The second group is likely to emphasize the fact that most incomes policies in Britain have 'failed', largely as a result of a substantial wage catch-up phenomenon at the end of the life of an individual policy. And here reference is made to the fact that most episodes of incomes policy in Britain have been broken, at least formally, by public sector strikes (e.g. the coal strikes of 1972 and 1974) with groups of public sector employees having been particularly prominent in the sizeable wage increases which have occurred immediately after an incomes policy episode. The third and final group of commentators takes rather more of a contingency approach by arguing that incomes policies in Britain have been a very heterogeneous set of instruments, with public sector employees making relative gains under some policies and relative losses under others.

These differing views need to be seen in the light of the fact that any attempt to identify whether *all* groups of public sector employees have experienced a relative wage loss under *all* periods of incomes policy is a far from straightforward exercise. The first point to note here is that any government attempt particularly to hold down the level of wage settlements in the public sector can, at least to some extent, be limited or partially offset by certain actions and occurrences at the operational level. For example, Fry suggests that promotion, 'grade drift' and a shortening of incremental scales were all significant occurrences in the civil service under the incomes policies of the 1960s and 1970s, which means that a simple concentration on the level of (and changes in) basic wage rates may tell only part of the story.[43] More generally, as noted above, we need to recognize the fact that incomes policies in Britain have been anything but a homogeneous instrument in terms of their manner of introduction, content, and administration. Indeed Burton, writing as early as 1972, aptly noted that Britain 'has gone through a veritable Kama Sutra of incomes policy experiments and variations in the last couple of decades'.[44] As an illustration of such variation, Table 7.9 sets out some basic information on the incomes policies of the 1970s in Britain.

In view of such variation in incomes policies it should occasion little surprise that their overall effectiveness has been reported to be highly variable in nature.[45] What is more, there has been considerable discussion and debate about the appropriate methodology of studies designed to assess the overall effectiveness of such policies, *ceteris paribus*. And some commentators have contended

Table 7.9 Wage inflation and incomes policies in the 1970s in Britain

Incomes policy		Change in average weekly earnings (%)	
		(i) prescribed by the policy	*(ii)* actual
November 1972–April 1973	freeze	0	1.8
April 1973–November 1973	£1 + 4% (£5 max.)	6.7	10.3
November 1973–August 1974	£2.25 or 7% (£7 max.) + 'threshold'	13.0	14.9
August 1974–August 1975	no limit	no limit	25.9
August 1975–August 1976	£6	10.4	14.3
August 1976–August 1977	5% (£2.50) min., £4 max.)	4.5	7.3
August 1977–August 1978	10%	10.0	13.9

Source: R. Layard, *How To Beat Unemployment*, Oxford, Oxford University Press, 1986, p. 128

that 'precise quantification of incomes policy . . . cannot, in the present state of knowledge, be obtained. Assessments of the efficacy of incomes policy are therefore judgements rather than accurate measurements'.[46]

There are not insubstantial data difficulties facing any study designed to look at the impact of incomes policies in the public sector,[47] and certainly some studies have done little more than look at changes in the relationship between average wages in the public and private sectors during such policy periods, with little attempt being made to control for the influence of any other relevant wage determination factors. In more recent years there seems to have been some increased consensus among researchers to the effect that the impact of such policies on the public sector cannot be discussed in general or aggregate terms, as considerable variation has been apparent between different policies and between different public sector groups under individual policies. Indeed one of the most comprehensive examinations of the subject has gone a little further in concluding that the key to an understanding of the impact of successive incomes policies on pay differentials and relativities in the public sector lies in the analysis of the mechanisms which govern and control pay determination in that sector. . . . Only when these mechanisms are explicitly and forcefully replaced or suspended (as in the case of the suspension of the PRU in the mid-1970s) do we see any real evidence of a pattern of settlements which differs from that which could be predicted *a priori*. Even in the cases where the Government has taken steps (either explicitly or de facto) to hold the public sector to the terms of an incomes policy, and there is considerable circumstantial evidence to support the assertion that this has taken place in practice . . . , the evidence . . . indicates that in the period following an incomes policy the reinstatement of the traditional mechanisms has led to the restoration of the original set of relativities and differentials via 'catch up' settlements. The only significant instance of a shift in established differentials would seem to be the long-run decline in the relative position of non-manual workers, and even this phenomenon cannot be said to be peculiar to the public sector. [And] . . . although this process was exacerbated by the incomes policies of the late 1960s and during the first half of the 1970s, it was not in essence the product of incomes policies.[48]

The Conservative government is the first one to have operated without a formal system-wide incomes policy for nearly twenty years in Britain. However, this statement needs to be seen in the light of, first, frequent ministerial statements calling for the exercise of 'responsible' wage behaviour and, second, the use of the system of cash limits in the public sector, which was inherited from the previous Labour government. The cash-limits approach arose because governments of both political persuasions in the 1970s faced continual problems in trying to control public expenditure because the actual growth in GDP was less than that forecast and because the existence of the relative price effect whereby the price of public services increased more rapidly than prices in general.[49] These comparatively longstanding problems, together with the strong relative wage movement in favour of the public sector in 1974–5, seriously damaged the credibility of volume planning. The result was the introduction of cash limits in 1976 (to supersede volume control of public spending) in order to try and ensure a closer correspondence between what was planned to be spent and out-turn expenditure, and more closely to control government borrowing as part of the increasing emphasis on limiting the growth of the money supply.

Under the Conservative government the cash-limits approach has involved a number of individual measures. These include the government's *prior* announcement of a pay provision figure for central government services (i.e. 4 per cent in 1981–2, 3.3 per cent in 1982–3, 3 per cent in 1983–4, 3 per cent in 1984–5 – this practice was discontinued from 1985–6), strict limits in the Rate Support Grant and rate-capping for any 'overspending' authorities in local government and the use of external financing limits to constrain the spending of public corporations. The prior pay provision figures have been widely held to constitute an implicit or backdoor form of incomes policy for the public sector. As to their 'success', the contents of Table 7.10 offer some guidance.

Table 7.10   Pay factors, out-turns, inflation and average earnings, 1980s (annual percentage increases)

Year	Pay factor	Public services pay out-turn	Inflation (RPI)	Average earnings (whole economy)
1981–2	6.0	9.5	11.0	12.0
1982–3	4.0	6.5	7.5	9.0
1983–4	3.5	5.5	4.5	7.5
1984–5	3.0	5.5	5.0	6.5
1985–6	3.0	6.5	6.0	8.5
1986–7	–	7.5	3.25	7.5
1987–8	–	8.75	4.0	6.5

Source: C. Trinder, 'Public sector pay in the 1980s: an economic overview', in R. Saran and J. Sheldrake (eds), *Public Sector Bargaining in the 1980s*, Aldershot, Avebury, 1988, p. 71

This table clearly indicates that public service pay increased considerably more than was assumed in the public expenditure plans, although the government has claimed that the pay factors may have helped to lower the level of public sector wage settlements in these years: from a range of, for example, 13 to 20 per cent in 1981–2 to 4.5 to 6.5 per cent in 1984–5. Moreover, in individual parts of the public sector the adverse effects of cash limits (broadly defined) on the process of negotiations have been highlighted. For example, in 1986 the Committee of Inquiry into the pay and conditions of service of school-teachers in Scotland commented as follows:

The most common complaint put to us was that the SJNC had failed to yield satisfactory pay settlements because of the unduly tight financial constraints set by Central Government through controls over local authority expenditure in advance of the negotiations. As part of its policy for controlling public expenditure the Government has sought to restrain local authority expenditure by a variety of means. COSLA informed us that the limits set each year since 1981 by the guidelines for individual local authorities' expenditure have included assumptions for teachers' pay that have run consistently at half the rate of increase in average earnings. Although the authorities have been able to settle at figures higher every year than those assumed by Government, teachers' pay has failed to keep pace with movements in average earnings, and realistic negotiations about conditions of service have not been possible. This point was echoed by all the teachers' asociations and a number of other interested bodies.[50]

In keeping with this point, a number of academic commentators have pointed to the adverse implications of the government setting unrealistically low 'pay factors' in the public sector.[51] Although primarily introduced as a means of public expenditure planning, the cash-limits approach has significant implications for public sector wage settlements, given that some 60 per cent of public expenditure is accounted for by public sector pay; one can in fact view the approach as seeking to reduce union power in wage negotiations by increasing the elasticity of demand for labour in the public sector (see chapter 3). However, the cash-limits approach of the Conservative government under Mrs Thatcher's leadership changed in certain respects over the course of the 1980s. For example, the use of a single, prior announced central government pay factor was, as mentioned earlier, abandoned after some five years of usage, and subsequently the government has sought to influence the future growth of public sector pay through the mechanisms of departmental running costs (which includes the pay of civil servants) and 'public service pay' (which includes the pay and pension costs of directly employed staff in the non-trading public sector).

A BRIEF NOTE ON NON-WAGE TERMS AND CONDITIONS

The material presented in this chapter has very much reflected the fact that public sector industrial relations in Britain, and indeed elsewhere, tends to be very much viewed and discussed in terms of wage settlement machinery, criteria and outcomes. However, to round off the chapter, it seems useful to make one or two comments about non-wage terms and conditions of employment or bargaining outcomes. The first point to make under this heading is that the British public sector is fairly unusual in the sense of having relatively few legal restrictions on the scope or subject matter of collective bargaining. In general, the scope of collective bargaining in the public sector in Britain is very much up to the parties concerned to determine, with only the scope of negotiable matters in the case of the police being specified by statute, and certain items in the fire service (e.g. procedures and qualifications for appointment and promotion) being deemed by statute, as consultative, rather than negotiating, issues. This position is quite different to that in, for example, the USA and Canada where, as shown in chapter 2, the scope of negotiation is frequently highly regulated by the provisions of public sector specific legislation.

The second point to note is that the issue of fringe benefits (broadly defined) in the public sector cannot be treated independently of wage levels. As stated earlier in this chapter, particularly in relation to the civil service, critics of public sector wage determination arrangements have frequently argued that such arrangements have continually taken insufficient account of the relatively favourable position of public sector employees as regards job security, pension scheme coverage and content, etc. In fact, information on fringe benefit provision in Britain is far from satisfactory in nature, with researchers having to make use of sources of information that are frequently partial, fragmented and rather dated in nature. However, it is worth noting first, that the regular Department of Labour Costs Survey reveals that the percentage of labour costs due to holiday, sickness and maternity pay and to voluntary social welfare payments was consistently higher in the gas, electricity and water industries in the 1970s and 1980s than was the case in the manufacturing sector, and second, that an analysis of information in the General Household Survey for 1976 indicated that both sick pay entitlement and pension entitlement were significantly and positively associated with public sector employment status.[52] Furthermore, the 1984 workplace industrial relations survey contained some information on the extent of joint regulation of non-wage items.[53] And the information provided by management respondents suggested that (i) there had been a general reduction in the scope of bargaining over non-pay matters, particularly at the workplace level, for both manual and non-manual groups in the years 1980–4, although (ii) this was least marked in the case of the nationalized industries, and (iii) public administration was the only sector where the extent of such bargaining was greater for non-manual employees than for manual ones.

CONCLUSIONS

In this chapter I have reviewed a number of the leading, individual issues concerned with the wage outcomes of public sector employees. These issues included the criteria of wage determination, public–private sector wage relationships and the impact of incomes policies and cash limits. Although it would be highly desirable to see more research on the non-wage outcomes of public sector collective bargaining, the reality is, as I have continually stressed, that public sector industrial relations are seen very much in terms of wage determination arrangements. In view of this fact it is important to observe that Britain in the 1980s has witnessed a strong government attack on traditional wage criteria, such as comparability, and a significant relative wage loss by many groups of public sector employees. This is an important part of the background to the final chapter, which discusses the future of public sector industrial relations.

Chapter 8

Changes in public sector industrial relations?

INTRODUCTION

In its various roles as macro-economic manager, paymaster and employer, the present Conservative government has accorded a relatively high priority to bringing about change in public sector industrial relations. Indeed during the course of the 1981 civil service strike it has been reported that the then Prime Minister Margaret Thatcher used the threat of personal resignation to ensure that a divided Cabinet remained opposed to the unions' pay claim.[1] The importance the government attaches to this particular task would seem to suggest that public sector industrial relations have experienced a not inconsiderable amount of change during the course of the 1980s. Furthermore, individual instances of proposed change in existing institutional arrangements in the public sector employment area continue to appear at a very rapid rate under the present regime: the much reduced role of the Civil Service Commission in the selection and recruitment of new employees,[2] and the proposal to transfer a further thirty civil service departments (with some 211,480 staff) to executive agency status by the end of 1991[3] are all important actual and proposed changes in recent times.

However, the public sector needs to be seen in the wider context of the debate about the extent and nature of change in both the economy and industrial relations system as a whole during the Thatcher years. One recent economic assessment of those years, for example, has argued that the reduction in inflation, the stabilization of public finances and the growth in productivity were the most conspicuous economic successes, with the most obvious failure being the level of unemployment.[4] Although others may disagree with this assessment, and certainly we do not know how the economy would have fared under a different government in the 1980s, the reference to stabilization of public finances would seem highly suggestive as regards the state of public sector industrial relations. Turning to the industrial relations arena, a number of commentators have raised major questions about the extent of actual industrial relations change, whether the changes observed are all in the direction desired by the government, whether they are solely, or even largely, due to the effects of government policy, whether they are sustainable in the longer term, and whether the costs of any change have outweighed the benefits. This wider, on-going debate has considerably influenced the contents of this final chapter, which examines some studies of industrial relations change in the public sector, highlights some major constraints on the possibility of the government fully achieving its aims, points to some costs of their approach and outlines a number of recent proposals for 'reform' in public sector industrial relations. In addition it raises some questions about whether there has been a 'values shift' against the public sector, whether private sector human resource management developments have a future in the public sector, and whether public sector unions will increasingly influence the overall union movement in Britain.

In the immediate future under the present Conservative government the basic environment in which public sector collective bargaining operates is likely to be one characterized by restrictions on public expenditure growth, further employment reductions, increased privatization and competitive tendering initiatives, public sector wage constraints and pressures to decentralize wage bargaining arrangements. The nature of this environment raises some major questions about the future shape of public sector industrial relations in Britain. Specifically, what (if any) is the extent and nature of change from the existing pattern of collective bargaining structure, process and outcome that one can expect to observe? There are in fact two major problems involved in trying to provide an answer to this question. The first is that there is not a sizeable, systematic body of research on recent changes in public sector industrial relations which can usefully be drawn on for the purpose of providing some 'signposts' for the future. And second, there is a very real need for researchers to be quite explicit and precise about the number and nature of indicators or measures of change which they regard as meaningful and significant in studies of this type.

The importance of the latter point will, hopefully, become apparent as a result of the ensuing discussion.

SOME STUDIES OF CHANGE IN THE PUBLIC SECTOR

Under this heading reference can be made to the findings of some general survey studies, the movements in some aggregate statistics and the results of one or two more detailed studies of individual parts of the public sector. For example, some survey findings by Batstone and Gourlay suggests that management in the civil service (and in British Telecom) have sought to bring about more intensive work effort levels than in the private sector.[5] Furthermore, a number of nationalized industries (e.g. British Rail, British Coal) have reported much improved levels of productivity in recent years. Indeed Table 8.1 sets out some productivity figures for the nationalized industries as a group, alongside those for the manufacturing sector.

Table 8.1 Annual percentage change in output per person employed, 1975–87

Year	Nationalized industries	Manufacturing sector
1975–6	−5.1	−2.8
1976–7	2.1	6.1
1977–8	1.2	−0.3
1978–9	3.2	1.7
1979–80	0.1	0.9
1980–1	−0.5	−5.3
1981–2	6.5	6.9
1982–3	2.4	6.4
1983–4	7.2	8.3
1984–5	6.0	4.8
1985–6	9.6	2.4
1986–7	6.2	4.8

Source: D. Metcalf, *Water Notes Dry Up*, London, Centre for Labour Economics, LSE, Discussion Paper No. 314, July 1988, p. 38.

The contents of the Table 8.1 indicate that in the last three years cited the extent of productivity increase in the nationalized industries was considerably greater than that achieved in the manufacturing sector. These figures do, however, need to be viewed in the light of the companion volume (on technical and organizational change) to the 1984 workplace industrial relations survey which reported that the rate of technical and organizational change in the public sector was below that of the private sector.[6] Furthermore an examination of the civil service has argued that functional flexibility developments in working arrangements and practices lag substantially behind those in outside industry.[7] In short, these studies have all tended to concentrate on a single measure of change (i.e. productivity, technical change, flexible working) and, when taken together, suggest that the public sector (or at least some part of it) is leading or lagging the private sector, depending on which single measure of change is being considered.

A number of detailed in-depth studies of particular parts of the public sector have been carried out which, although lacking a comparative focus with the private sector, are important in highlighting some of the important constraints on the government's attempt to bring about changes in public sector employment and industrial relations practices. First, for instance, Fry's examination of the impact of the financial management initiative in the civil service concluded that 'while developments such as performance pay represent a potentially important incursion into traditional arrangements, at the end of the second Thatcher Administration it is still the case that the "old civil service" recognisably survives'.[8] The limited scale of the initiative, the lack of sufficient, supportive changes (e.g. devolved power to line managers), the maintenance of a career bureaucracy and the inherent, practical difficulties of closely monitoring activities in operations on the scale of the civil service were all cited as factors responsible for the limited degree of change achieved. Second, a study of industrial relations in British Rail reached a number of conclusions which are of particular interest here.[9] In general it was critical of the view that changes in industrial relations in British Rail in the 1980s were largely the result of the Thatcher government having increasingly exposed the industry to market forces. Such a view was rejected because a number of more market-oriented influences on British Rail predated the Thatcher administration; reductions in the real value of the block grant, the introduction of cash limits and profit targets being individual examples cited in this regard. In addition, because the state of industrial relations in the nationalized industries was a real priority with the Thatcher administration the government was, despite the rhetoric to the contrary, highly interventionist in the industrial relations of British Rail. For example, the government has frequently stated that any increased investment in the industry is contingent upon significant increases in productivity being achieved, while more specifically the issue of flexible rostering and the decision to separate the pay and productivity issues in the closing stages of the 1984 pay round constituted well-known cases of government intervention. A number of other actions by British Rail management may also be the result of more discreet forms of government intervention or attempts (by management) to anticipate and limit such potential intervention, management's lodging a claim under the 1984 Act for damages following the unions' institution of industrial action without a membership ballot, the decision to institute a depot closure review procedure at national level, and the recently stated intention to do away with national-level collective bargaining were all cited as supporting cases. More generally, the union–management relationship at the national level which sought to limit government intervention in the 1970s has changed and become much less effective in this regard during the course of the 1980s. In addition, Richardson and Wood's examination of the recent sizeable increases in productivity in the coalmining industry, following the 1984–5 dispute, suggests that the reassertion of managerial authority, tighter performance standards, substantial employment reductions, a change in the wage payment system and attempts to cut into restrictive work practices have all been important in this respect.[10] However, fundamental changes in worker attitudes and new institutional arrangements were much less in evidence. Finally, Edwards and Heery, having outlined the two schools of thought on industrial relations change in Britain, conducted a case study of a subsidiary of British Rail which led them to conclude:

> Freightliner's experience of recession falls between the two general interpretations of recent developments in British industrial relations. . . . The effect of recession on the company was to alter industrial relations outcomes but this was not accompanied by radical change in other elements of the industrial relations system. There was innovation in the structure of institutional regulation but this amounted more to a reform than a break with collective bargaining, and, though the unions were prepared to negotiate change, neither they nor their members had embraced the more innovative elements of the new realism.[11]

What does all this add up to? There are in fact a variety of questions that need to be posed here. These include: is there any change, is it large-scale change, is it all in the direction desired by the government, is the change taking place in institutional forms, attitudes or in outcomes? The limited volume of systematic research conducted to date precludes definitive answers being given to each and all of these questions at this stage. However, one or two tentative observations and suggestions can certainly be put forward here in what will undoubtedly remain an important, on-going debate. First, studies based on single measures of change are more likely to be supportive of the general case that change has actually occurred. Increases in productivity, effort levels, and the spread of performance-related pay are all single indices of change which can be pointed to in the public sector. Second, the evidence for change tends to rely heavily on output-orientated measures; productivity being a major case in point. Third, not all of the government's initiatives have produced change in the direction that it desires. The high proportion of competitive tendering initiatives in the NHS and local authorities which have resulted in successful 'in-house' bids (at least currently) is an obvious example. Fourth, the various measures of output change do not appear to be widely underpinned by significant attitudinal and institutional change. In this sense many instances of change appear to be relatively self-contained in nature, which raise doubts about whether they can be sustained through time. Indeed the public sector continues to remain the most highly unionized part of the economy so there is certainly no question of the dominant role of collective bargaining arrangements being significantly reduced in scope or coverage, or being increasingly bypassed or challenged by an alternative set of non-complementary, institutional arrangements for determining and regulating the terms and conditions of employment. Furthermore, the nature of the attitudes and behavioural patterns associated with collective bargaining in the public sector do not suggest that the integrative sub-process of bargaining is gaining relative to the distributive sub-process. That is, collective bargaining, particularly at the national level, is certainly not becoming more co-operative, more joint problem-solving and less adversarial in nature or orientation; if anything, a change in exactly the opposite direction is suggested by the increased proportion of working days lost through strike activity which is accounted for by the public sector. In short, the government has not transformed public sector industrial relations in Britain to anything like the extent that it has sought; the extent of institutional and values changes has been relatively limited in comparison to changes in the outcomes of industrial relations processes, with the latter largely deriving from a shift in bargaining power in favour of management. The next section offers a number of reasons for the limited degree of change and 'success' in this regard.

SOME CONSTRAINTS ON AND COSTS OF THE CONSERVATIVE GOVERNMENT'S APPROACH

In some ways the difficulties which the present Conservative government has encountered in trying fundamentally to change the nature of public sector industrial relations should not be entirely a matter of surprise. For example, as discussed in chapter 7, it was apparent that governments of both political persuasions had frequently sought to impose the restrictions of incomes policies most tightly and rigorously on public sector employees, but in practice it was clear that not all groups of public sector employees had suffered an actual relative wage loss under all periods of incomes policy. The phenomenon of 'grade drift' was simply one instance of union–management collaborative action at the operational level which had sought to get round or limit the adverse consequences of such policy restrictions. The reason for this type of action is simply that public sector management – itself a highly unionized body, operating in a highly unionized environment – will frequently have a different agenda and priorities to that of the government as employer and paymaster.

The importance of this difference in the aims and objectives of the government and management is that the latter can seriously impede the process of translating government objectives into practice. In short, as Ferner has argued in the case of British Rail,[12] there is essentially a bargaining relationship between the government and the management of nationalized industries in which the latter is not entirely without power. As a consequence, government control mechanisms in the public sector are not so all-pervasive and powerful in nature that one can automatically assume that government objectives will be fully and effectively put into practice and realized. The importance of relatively blunt control mechanisms in limiting the full achievement of government objectives has also been emphasized in a number of discussions of attempts to restrain public expenditure levels in local government. For example, Newton and Karran have argued that one 'should be careful to distinguish between the rhetoric and the reality of grant reductions, for in spite of all the tough talking and apparent energy with which the Conservative government has tried to cut since 1979, its success has been muted'.[13] Specifically, Newton and Karran contend that the central government's mechanisms of financial control are not sufficiently sensitive to distinguish effectively between individual local authorities which they favour (or do not) in political terms, and that local authorities have been able to take some actions to offset the effects of such cuts by turning to alternative sources of income.[14]

In short, *any* government seeking to effect a fundamental transformation of public sector industrial relations will face certain *inherent* problems in trying to carry out such a task. These problems basically stem from the fact that their control mechanisms permit considerable scope for various forms of offsetting action at lower, operational levels of decision-making in the public sector. These control mechanism limitations provide the *ability* to take such action, while the *incentive* to take it stems from the fact that lower level management will frequently have different aims and objectives to that of the government. These differences in agendas are not simply the result of political differences (in the party sense of the word), but stem from the fact that the operating environment of local level public sector management imposes certain constraints on them, not least that they are situated in a highly unionized area of employment.

These are problems and constraints that would confront any government seeking to bring about large-scale changes in public sector industrial relations in Britain. However, a number of commentators have suggested that the Conservative government's basic approach to change in the public sector has generated a number of specific problems for achieving its stated objectives. The first is the general contention that too many individual change and reform proposals have been initiated, which has hindered the achievement of any change in depth. The second is that the Conservative government has not in fact produced a consistent, coherent strategy for change in public sector industrial relations. Instead it has only produced a hybrid model of change which in some cases 'goes too far', in the sense of running ahead of local managers' desire for change, whereas in other cases it has not gone far enough, in the sense of linking change in one area with other necessary complementary forms of change (the latter point was certainly one made in Fry's explanation of the limited impact of the financial management initiative in the civil service);[15] while more generally several commentators in favour of the Thatcher approach have argued that political considerations have over-ridden economic logic and pre-vented a number of changes going far enough.[16] A *Times* editorial in early 1990, for example, argued that the government has 'yet to identify successful strategies for public sector pay',[17] the limited move away from national-level bargaining and the role of cost of living considerations in wage settlements being particularly singled out for criticism. The third contention is that there have been various costs or 'negative externalities' associated with the nature of changes in public sector industrial relations which have posed problems for local level management and, at the same time, have limited the desire of private sector management to emulate and follow the government's leadership by example model in the public sector. The most obvious cost or 'negative externality' of the government's programme of change in the public sector has been the increased role of the public sector in strike action in recent years, a phenomenon noted in a number of studies and discussed at some length in chapter 6.

In addition to this form of collective cost, the public sector in the 1980s has frequently experienced costs at the level of the individual employee, with problems of (i) recruitment and retention and (ii) low morale being increasingly reported. For example, the annual reports of the Civil Service Commission have increasingly referred to recruitment difficulties in recent years. In 1984 it was reported that executive officer grade vacancies had increased by 29 per cent from the previous year, but that applications had only risen by 7 per cent,[18] while in the 1988 annual report reference was made to the fact that some 2,100 job offers had been made to applicants but only 927 of these were accepted.[19] Such recruitment difficulties are particularly acute for more senior staff in tight labour market areas of the country; at the end of 1988 the Department of Customs and Excise had a vacancy rate of 23 per cent for higher executive officers in the London and Reading areas, a figure up from 17 per cent nine months previously.[20] In addition, a number of studies indicate quite substantial turnover and retention problems in particular parts of the public sector. For example, a survey of turnover among ancillary staff in the NHS (excluding London) reported a weighted average figure of nearly 45 per cent, with the figure in Milton Keynes in 1987/8 being more than 100 per cent.[21] Finally, a variety of sources have made reference to increased problems of employee morale in various parts of the public sector. For example, the 1988 report of the Top Salaries Review body stated that morale was 'unsatisfactory' among grades 5 to 7 of the senior structure of the civil service,[22] while an ACAS report on the ambulance service in London revealed that staff had relatively negative views of the organization and management, were relatively dissatisfied with their levels of pay and that increased manifestations of work-related stress were becoming apparent.[23] Table 8.2 lists some recent facts and figures concerning labour market pressures in the public sector.

Table 8.2 Indications of labour market pressures in the public sector

1 32,504 civil servants resigned in 1988/9, compared to 31,403 in 1987/8. Resignation rates in the Inland Revenue Service were 23.8 per cent in London, 21.6 per cent in the South-East of England and 10.1 per cent in the rest of the country.

2 A survey of 8 NHS regions and 47 districts in 1987/8 revealed average turnover rates of 25.3 per cent for all non-medical staff and 20.2 per cent for nurses and midwives. The NHS currently needs to recruit 1 in every 4 suitably qualified school leavers for its nursing needs.

3 The shortage of NHS administrative and clerical staff, particularly in the South-East, has led to the increased use of agency staff, with the cost of such staff having risen from £10.3 million to £31.2 million in the period 1983/4–1986/7.

4 The extent of the failure to meet target staffing levels in the NHS is indicated by a rise in the shortfall figure, from 3,300 in 1985 to 17,600 in 1988.

5 The school teacher turnover rate averaged 7.4 per cent for the country as a whole in 1987.

Source: IDS Public Sector Unit, *Public Sector Pay: Review of 1989 and Prospects for 1990*, London, Incomes Data Services, 1990, pp. 9–10.

The government is certainly not unaware of these sorts of costs and problems in the public sector at the present time. Indeed it has its own agenda of reform designed to deal with them, such as the attempt to encourage the break-up of national-level bargaining arrangements in order to introduce more local pay flexibility as a means of dealing with labour recruitment and retention difficulties. However, the next section of this chapter briefly outlines one or two reform proposals of a rather different nature to those currently being contemplated in government circles.

SOME REFORM PROPOSALS

As was noted in chapter 7, public sector industrial relations in Britain are overwhelmingly viewed and discussed in terms of wage settlements and wage determination machinery. As a result it is not surprising that individual reform proposals and suggestions in this particular subject area continue to emerge with considerable frequency. The starting point for such pay-orientated reforms is frequently the concern that public—private sector wage relativities have exhibited a very erratic pattern of short-term movements throughout the 1970s and 1980s. As Trinder, for example, has commented

> The considerable fluctuations in the relative pay of public servants observed in recent years is not new. The fluctuations can be long and wide. They involve much more than just one group falling behind slightly one year and catching up the next. But trend stability always seems to be restored in the end, usually by pay comparability awards such as those of the Clegg inquiries of 1980. There is a danger, however, that the piecemeal nature of these inquiries and the way in which they come about and are implemented stores up as many problems for the future as it solves. It may be a good idea if the falling behind could be averted, if it is to be merely temporary, but if catching up is to take place it must involve a comprehensive focus with a clear strategy involving all the main groups and implemented over the medium term, hopefully with all-party support, and not to left to somewhat random and certainly haphazard swings in the popularity and favour of the different groups of public servants.[24]

Trinder's own proposals to deal with this particular problem are that (i) the recommendations of existing pay review bodies should be automatically implemented on the due dates, (ii) pay review body coverage should be extended to all non-covered groups (certainly all white collar groups, and possibly the manual worker groups), (iii) information and evidence on public sector pay movements should be more comprehensively gathered and publicized by a Standing Public Service Pay Commission (with independent members), and (iv) a common policy approach is necessary to deal with the low pay problem in the public sector as a whole. A rather different approach to the same basic problem has been put forward by Layard and Nickell.[25] They advocate the introduction of a tax-based incomes policy which will essentially apply to the private sector and the nationalized industries. In addition they argue the need for establishing a publicly responsible pay information board for the whole of the public sector, with the government accepting the presumption that public sector employees will receive a wage increase equal to the reference level for the growth of average hourly earnings in the private sector and nationalized industries (beyond which a firm suffers a tax penalty) plus a catch-up amount equal to the difference between the previous year's private sector pay growth and the previous year's reference level.

Industrial relations problems in the public sector stem not only from relative wage losses and erratic wage movements in relation to the private sector. There are also problems of intra-public sector equity in wage terms, a theme that has been particularly emphasized in a number of recent documents concerning the NHS.[26] Indeed the House of Commons Social Services Committee produced a recent report, which was mentioned in the previous chapter, that particularly emphasized the wage inequities arising between NHS employees covered by collective bargaining arrangements and those covered by the awards of the pay review body for nurses.[27] The report contained a number of recommendations concerned with wage-determination arrangements, but also put forward some suggestions designed to improve some of the non-wage aspects of industrial relations in the NHS. These included the need to develop a mutually agreed arbitration procedure, the development of good practice guidelines in relation to competitive tendering, a review of the composition of staff sides of Whitley Councils, more co-ordination between the workings of the Whitley Councils and the establishment of an independent management secretariat for such councils.

The joint working parties established by ACAS (mentioned in chapter 6) constitute an interesting, on-going attempt to build more co-operative union–management relationships in the public sector. These arrangements seek to develop mutually acceptable solutions to problems particularly through the medium of attitude change. However, industrial relations researchers have frequently questioned whether such behavioural science-orientated interventions can produce lasting changes in collective bargaining relationships. And this questioning, not to say scepticism, is likely to be even more acute given the multilateral, as opposed to bilateral, nature of collective bargaining in the public sector. Nevertheless, such working parties are likely to be increasingly prevalent in the public sector in the future, and their role and impact should be of considerable interest to both practitioners and researchers.

It is widely recognized that many aspects of the traditional pattern of public sector industrial relations in Britain began to be increasingly questioned and changed in the 1970s, a process that accelerated and intensified in the 1980s.[28] As a result, the public sector industrial relations scene is currently an awkward mixture of relatively long-established procedural arrangements, a more assertive management strategy and a great deal of political and public questioning about the appropriate balance between efficiency and social considerations in public sector decision-making – and indeed about the appropriate boundary between the public and private sectors.[29] The one safe prediction that can be made about this situation is that public sector industrial relations will continue to remain central to so many discussions and debates about the future of the British industrial relations system, economy and society at large. This is a proposition I illustrate by discussing, in turn, the issues of human resource management, a values shift against the public sector, and public sector unions and the larger union movement.

SOME FUTURE SCENARIOS FOR PUBLIC SECTOR INDUSTRIAL RELATIONS

One of the major reasons why the Conservative government under Margaret Thatcher had a reputation of being 'anti-public sector' was its desire increasingly to import private sector employment practices into the public sector. This was most obviously observed in relation to the introduction of performance appraisal systems and performance-related pay elements, as well as the attempt to bring about more decentralized pay bargaining arrangements in the public sector. However, beyond these sorts of individual arrangements, practices and criteria is the much larger issue of the potential place and role of human resource management in the public sector.

There is in fact a considerable on-going debate in the British industrial relations literature as to the meaning of this term, what its major elements are, whether it is anything more than personnel management with a new name, whether it is anti-union and just how widespread and systematic has been its adoption in the private sector. A recent paper, which essentially saw the term as involving a corporate strategy, an emphasis on obtaining individual employee commitment, a more individual orientation towards the conduct of industrial relations and an increased role for line management, raised the question of its potential for adoption in the *public* sector.[30] The general verdict reached was as follows:

> The constraints upon a widespread adoption of human resource management in the public sector should not necessarily be seen as insurmountable barriers. Rather, they should be seen for what they are: indicators that principles and approaches, refined originally within large, and exceptional private sector organisations, such as IBM, should not be expected to translate easily into organisations in very different settings. This being so, it is perhaps not surprising that the overall verdict on the state of play for human resource management in the public sector at the present time has to be one which declares: extensive discussion and diverse experimentation but as yet, with a somewhat limited impact upon staff attitudes and behaviour.[31]

The leading constraints which were identified as having the potential to limit a sizeable and effective emulation of private sector human resource management practices in the public sector were: (i) the relatively high level of union density in the public sector; (ii) the heterogeneous nature of human resources in parts of the public sector, such as the NHS (where some groups have a strong professional, college orientation); (iii) the relatively limited education/training levels of managers; (iv) the 'political' nature of strategic objectives in the public sector; and (v) the distinctive nature of public sector management. On the last point, Steward and Ranson, for example, have argued that 'one reason why models drawn from other sectors distort the nature of management is that they assume the dilemmas (which characterize management in the public domain) do not exist or do not have the depth implied, because they do not do so in other sectors'.[32] Interestingly, a number of leading individual practitioners and groups in the public sector have recently begun to express concerns about the relatively uncritical importation and acceptance of private sector management models, concepts and practices in the public sector; for example, in early 1990 the Society of Chief Personnel Officers in Local Government debated the question of the need for different personnel management 'styles' in the two sectors of employment.

The likelihood of a general election in Britain in 1992 raises the all-important questions of whether the Labour Party will be returned to office and, if so, whether it seeks to change many of the developments which have been observed in public sector industrial relations in the 1980s. These questions need to be seen in the wider context of whether over a decade of Conservative government under Margaret Thatcher (it is too soon to assess what effect, if any, John Major's leadership will cause) has produced a funda-mental values shift in British society at large which will limit both the incentive and ability of any incoming Labour government to reverse many of the public sector developments initiated by the Thatcher government. For obvious reasons this is a difficult subject area to examine in a systematic manner. However, Phelps Brown has recently argued that there has been a move away from the public and electorate supporting notions of collectivism towards more of an acquisitive individualistic orientation.[33] As a specific instance of this change he argues that the inefficiencies, deficits and poor industrial relations record of the nationalized industries have produced an adverse reaction on the part of the public to maintain-ing, much less enhancing, this particular part of the public sector. In contrast, Ivor Crewe talks of a values crusade that has failed, arguing that

> much of Thatcherism will die with Thatcher. Its permanent legacy at the level of the mass public will be very limited. It will not have killed off popular socialism, at least not in its welfarist forms. A post-Thatcher Labour Government will inherit an electorate as friendly to its major objectives as the 1979 electorate was to those of the Conservatives.[34]

In support of this conclusion, Crewe cites a wide variety of public opinion poll data concerning attitudes towards taxes vs social services, unions and nationalization. Although Crewe does not envisage a large-scale re-nationalization programme by any Labour government, he nevertheless notes that

> Mrs Thatcher came to power when the public was firmly in favour of privatisation: between 1979 and 1983 the majority preferring privatisation to nationalisation hovered around 20 per cent, a peak for the post-war period. By 1987 the majority was a mere 4 per cent and the proportion believing that nationalised industries are less efficient than private companies has steadily

declined during the Thatcher decade. A more recent survey in August 1988, asking a similarly phrased question, reports a net majority in favour of more public ownership rather than more privatisation (with a substantial proportion supporting the status quo). A majority is as heavily opposed to the privatisation of the remaining public industries – electricity, water, coal, and railways – as it was to the previous privatisations. Once again, Thatcherism appears to have paid the price of its own achievements, as loss-making nationalised industries become a thing of the past, public ownership has become more attractive again.[35]

Crewe also cites public opinion data indicating that the proportion of the electorate in favour of tax cuts has fallen from 37 per cent in May 1979 to 11 per cent in October 1987, compared to figures of 37 per cent (May 1979) and 66 per cent (October 1987) in favour of extending social services, and, second, that proportion which thinks trade unions are a good thing has risen from 55 per cent (in the years 1974–8) to 70 per cent in 1987–8. In view of the latter set of figures it is interesting to consider the future role of the public sector unions within the wider union and labour movement.

As evidence in earlier chapters shows, the proportion of total union membership accounted for by the public sector has risen quite significantly in a number of advanced industrialized economies in the 1970s and 1980s. The result is that the trade union movement of such countries is becoming much less blue collar, male, manufacturing sector and large plant dominated. The public sector, white collar unions are becoming much more well represented in the senior decision-making circles of the relevant trade union confederations of a number of countries. Indeed it is highly likely that public sector trade unions will begin increasingly to replace the engineering and metal workers unions as the 'intellectual' leader or spokesman of such union movements. Such movements and tendencies are, however, likely to be a source of some tension and difficulties within the union and wider labour movement. For example, it is not so obvious that a future trade union movement heavily influenced by the concerns of the public sector unions will be as interested in establishing corporatist or tripartite labour market arrangements as was the case in the past, when unions in the export-orientated sector tended to be much more influential. These potential difficulties between trade union confederations and labour or social democratic governments may be particularly acute in Britain when it is recalled how white collar, public sector union affiliation to the TUC was rarely a simple and easy matter because of membership concern about the TUC–Labour Party connection.

In sum, as was argued earlier in this chapter, it is a reasonably safe bet that public sector industrial relations relations will be as interesting an area of development, albeit perhaps different in nature, in the 1990s, as it was in the 1980s and 1970s.

Notes

Preface

1 A.W.J. Thomson and P.B. Beaumont, *Public Sector Bargaining: A Study of Relative Gain*, Farnborough, Saxon House, 1978.
2 This point is well illustrated by the sort of material contained in, for example, A. Ponak and M. Thompson, 'Public sector collective bargaining' in J.C. Anderson, M. Gunderson and A. Ponak (eds), *Union–Management Relations in Canada*, Don Mills, Ontario, Addison-Wesley, second edition, 1989, 373–406.

1 Introduction

1 D. Boyd, 'Foreword' to B. Towers (ed.), *A Handbook of Industrial Relations Practice*, London, Kogan Page, first edn, 1987, xiv.
2 N. Millward and M. Stevens, *British Workplace Industrial Relations 1980–1984*, Aldershot, Gower, 1986, 314.
3 'Public Sector Trade Unions', *IDS Public Sector Digest*, London, Incomes Data Services, May 1987, 8.
4 CPS, *Essential Services – Whose Rights?*, London Centre for Policy Studies, May 1984.
5 E. Hobsbawm in M. Jacques and F. Mulhern (eds), *The Forward March of Labour Halted?*, London, Verso, 1981, 14.
6 E. Cordova, 'Strikes in the public service: some determinants and trends', *International Labour Review*, 124, 2, March–April 1985, 164–5.
7 D. Lewin, 'Public employee unionism and labor relations in the 1980s: an analysis of transformation', in S.M. Lipset (ed.), *Unions in Transition*, San Francisco, ICS Press, 1986, 246.
8 Cordova, op. cit.
9 ibid., 171.
10 ibid., 172.
11 T.A. Kochan and H.C. Katz, *Collective Bargaining and Industrial Relations*, Homewood, Ill., Irwin, second edn, 1988, 152.

12 M. Gunderson and N.M. Meltz, 'Recent developments in the Canadian industrial relations system', *Bulletin of Comparative Labour Relations*, 16, 1987, 82.
13 R. Freeman, 'On the divergence in unionism among developed countries', Cambridge, Mass., mimeograph, Harvard University, 1988, 6.
14 ibid., 7.
15 Kochan and Katz, op. cit., 448.
16 T. Treu, 'Labour relations in the public service: a comparative overview', in T. Treu *et al.*, *Public Service Labour Relations*, Geneva, ILO, 1987, 42.
17 ibid., 42–3.
18 R.B. Freeman and C. Ichniowski, 'Introduction: the public sector look of American unionism', in R.B. Freeman and C. Ichniowski (eds), *When Public Sector Workers Unionize*, Chicago, National Bureau of Economic Research, University of Chicago, 1988, 13.
19 This discussion is very much based on L. Pathirane and D.W. Blades, 'Defining and measuring the public sector: some international comparisons', *The Review of Income and Wealth*, 28, 3, September 1982, 261–89.
20 ibid., 275.
21 P.S. Heller and A.A. Tait, *Government Employment and Pay: Some International Comparisons*, Occasional Paper No. 24, Washington, International Monetary Fund, 1984, 2–4.
22 K. Newton and T.J. Karran, *The Politics of Local Expenditure*, London, Macmillan, 1985, 12–13.
23 OECD, *Employment in the Public Sector*, Paris, OECD, 1982, 10.
24 A. Fleming, 'Employment in the public and private sectors 1982–1988', *Economic Trends*, 422, December 1988, 122.
25 See, for example, M. Ross, 'Employment in the public domain in recent decades', London, The Economic and Social Research Institute Paper No. 127, April 1986, 3.
26 *Civil Service Statistics 1987*, London, HM Treasury, 1987, 33.
27 J.L. Perry and H.G. Rainey, 'The public–private distinction in organization theory: a critique and research strategy', *Academy of Management Review*, 2, April 1988, 182–201.
28 D.S. Pugh and D.J. Hickson, *Organizational Structure in its Context: The Aston Programme*, Aldershot, Gower, 1976.
29 R.B. Freeman, 'Unionism comes to the public sector', *Journal of Economic Literature*, 24, March 1986, 44.
30 See, for example, Freeman, ibid., 50.
31 A. Ferner, 'Political constraints and management strategies: the case of working practices in British Rail', *British Journal of Industrial Relations*, 23, 1, March 1985, 47–50.
32 A. Ponak and M. Thompson, 'Public sector collective bargaining', in J.C. Anderson, M. Gunderson and A. Ponak (eds), *Union–Management Relations in Canada*, Don Mills, Ontario, Addison-Wesley, second edn, 1989, 380.
33 T.A. Kochan, *Collective Bargaining and Industrial Relations*, Homewood, Ill., Irwin, 1980, chapter 2.

34 D. Lewin, P. Feuille, T.A. Kochan and J.T. Delaney (eds), *Public Sector Labor Relations*, Lexington, Mass., Heath, third edn, 1988, 4.

2 The environment of public sector industrial relations

1 J.T. Dunlop, *Industrial Relations Systems*, New York, Holt, 1958.
2 T.A. Kochan, H.C. Katz and R.B. McKersie, *The Transformation of American Industrial Relations*, New York, Basic Books, 1986.
3 For an exception see A. Ferner, *Governments, Managers and Industrial Relations*, Oxford, Blackwell, 1988, chapter 2.
4 R. Scase, 'Introduction', in R. Scase (ed.), *The State in Western Europe*, New York, St Martin's Press, 1980, 11.
5 J. O'Connor, *The Fiscal Crisis of the State*, New York, St Martin's Press, 1973.
6 For a useful summary see P. Edwards, *Conflict at Work*, Oxford, Blackwell, 1986, chapter 5.
7 R. Bacon and W. Eltis, *Britain's Economic Problem: Too Few Producers*, London, Macmillan, second edn, 1978.
8 K. Newton and T.J. Karran, *The Politics of Local Expenditure*, London, Macmillan, 1985, 21.
9 For example, Newton and Karran, ibid., chapter 2.
10 Cited in P. Jackson, 'Perspectives on practical monetarism', in P. Jackson (ed.), *Implementing Government Policy Initiatives: The Thatcher Administration 1979–83*, London, Royal Institute of Public Administration, 1985, 37.
11 Jackson, op. cit., 36.
12 See, for example, D. Kavanagh, *Thatcherism and British Politics*, Oxford, Oxford University Press, 1987.
13 Jackson, ibid., 36–7. See also D. Heald, *Public Expenditure*, Oxford, Martin Robertson, 1983.
14 'The British economy since 1979', *National Institute Economic Review*, 122, November 1987, 42.
15 P. Jenkins, *Mrs Thatcher's Revolution*, London, Pan, 1989, 280–3.
16 K. Matthews and P. Minford, 'Mrs Thatcher's economic policies 1979–1987', *Economic Policy*, 5, October 1987, 68–70.
17 Kavanagh, op. cit., 293.
18 I. Crewe, 'Values: the crusade that failed', in D. Kavanagh and A. Seldon (eds), *The Thatcher Effect: A Decade of Change*, Oxford, Clarendon Press, 1989, 248–9.
19 D. Steel and D. Heald, 'The privatisation of public enterprises 1979–83', in Jackson (ed.), op. cit., 70–3.
20 *OECD Economic Outlook*, 43, June 1988, 105.
21 *OECD Economic Outlook*, 40, December 1986, 14–17.
22 *OECD Economic Outlook*, 43, June 1988, 72.
23 P. Jackson, 'Policy implementation and monetarism: two primers', in Jackson (ed.), op. cit., 29.
24 P.S. Heller, 'Analysing and adjusting government expenditure in LDCs', *Finance and Development*, 22, 2, June 1985, 5.
25 J. Sheahan, *Patterns of Development in Latin America*, Princeton, Princeton University Press, 1987, 112.

26 F. Gould, 'The development of public expenditures in western indus-
    trialised countries: a comparative analysis', *Public Finance*, 38, 1, 1983,
    38–69.
27 C.V. Brown and P.M. Jackson, *Public Sector Economics*, Oxford,
    Blackwell, third edn, 1986, 99–104.
28 See, for example, R. Rose, *Understanding Big Government*, London,
    Sage, 1984.
29 See, for example, R. Rose, *Do Parties Make a Difference?*, London,
    Macmillan, second edn, 1984, 119–20.
30 OECD, *Employment in the Public Sector*, Paris, OECD, 1982, 26.
31 See, for example, *Economic Survey of Europe in 1986–87*, Geneva,
    Economic Commission for Europe, 1987, 102.
32 *Social Trends*, 18, London, HMSO, 1988, 112.
33 *Social Trends*, 19, London, HMSO, 1989, 111.
34 *Social Trends*, 20, London, HMSO, 1990, 105.
35 *The Times*, 31 January 1990.
36 *The Times*, 2 November 1988.
37 *Social Trends*, 18, op. cit., p. 110.
38 *The Times*, 21 October 1988.
39 *National Institute Economic Review*, 119, February 1987, 16.
40 Newton and Karren, op. cit., 120.
41 P. Dunleavy and R.A.W. Rhodes, 'Government beyond Whitehall',
    in H. Drucker, P. Dunleavy, A. Gamble and G. Peele (eds),
    Developments in British Politics, London, Macmillan, second edn,
    1986, 119.
42 P.S. Heller and A.A. Tait, 'Government employment and pay: some
    international comparisons', Occasional Paper No. 24, Washington,
    International Monetary Fund, 1984, 7.
43 National Economic Development Office, *A Study of UK Nationalised
    Industries*, London, HMSO, 1976.
44 S.N. Woodward, 'Performance indicators and management per-
    formance in nationalised industries', *Public Administration*, 64,
    Autumn 1986, 303–17.
45 N. Foster, S. Henry and C. Trinder, 'Public and private sector pay: a
    partly disaggregated study', *National Institute Economic Review*, 107,
    February 1984.
46 A. Zabalze, 'Comments on public and private sector pay: a partly
    disaggregated study', London, Centre for Labour Economics, LSE,
    Working Paper No. 611, 1984.
47 A. Pendleton, 'Markets or politics? The determinants of labour
    relations in a nationalised industry', *Public Administration*, 66, 3,
    Autumn 1988, 279–96.
48 A. Ferner, *Governments, Managers and Industrial Relations*, Oxford,
    Blackwell, 1988.
49 A. Ferner, 'Ten years of Thatcherism: changing industrial relations in
    British public enterprises', *Warwick Papers in Industrial Relations No.
    27*, Warwick, Industrial Relations Research Unit, University of
    Warwick, 1990.
50 M. Thompson and A. Ponak, 'Industrial relations in Canadian public

enterprises', *International Labour Review*, 123, 5, September–October 1984, 647–63.
51 ibid., 659.
52 Heller and Tait, op. cit., 35.
53 OECD (1982), op. cit., 12.
54 P. Saunders and F. Klau, 'The role of the public sector', *OECD Economic Studies*, 4, Spring 1985, 63.
55 R. Rose, 'The significance of public employment', in R. Rose (ed.), *Public Employment in Western Nations*, Cambridge, Cambridge University Press, 1985, 1–53.
56 Ponak and Thompson in Anderson, Gunderson and Ponak (eds), op. cit., 374.
57 Heller and Tait, op. cit., 14–16.
58 M. Masters and J. Robertson, 'The impact of organized labor on public employment: a comparative analysis', *Journal of Labor Research*, 9, 4, Fall 1988, 347–62.
59 Rose in Rose (ed.), op. cit.
60 OECD (1982), op. cit., 29.
61 T. Karren, 'The local government workforce: public sector paragon or private parasite?', *Local Government Studies*, 10, July/August 1984, 39–58.
62 OECD (1982), op. cit., 39–41 and Rose in Rose (ed.), op. cit., 37.
63 R.F. Elliott and P.D. Murphy, 'The relative pay of public and private sector employees, 1970–1984', *Cambridge Journal of Economics*, 11, 1987, 117.
64 See B.A. Hepple and P. O'Higgins, *Public Employee Trade Unionism in the United Kingdom: The Legal Framework*, Ann Arbor, University of Michigan Press, 1971.
65 S. Fredman and G.S. Morris, *The State as Employer: Labour Law in the Public Services*, London, Mansell, 1982, 2.
66 Lord Wedderburn, *The Worker and the Law*, Harmondsworth, Penguin, third edn, 1986, 135–6.
67 K.W. Wedderburn, *The Worker and the Law*, Harmondsworth, Penguin, second edn, 1971, 70.
68 G. Morris, 'Industrial action in public enterprises – the legal issues', *Public Administration*, 63, Summer 1983, 227–36.
69 Ponak and Thompson in Anderson, Gunderson and Ponak (eds), op. cit., 386–91.
70 Thompson and Ponak, op. cit., 651–2.
71 R.B. Freeman, 'Unionism comes to the public sector', *Journal of Economic Literature*, 24, March 1986, 45–9.
72 J.F. Burton and T. Thomason, 'The extent of collective bargaining in the public sector', in B. Aaron, J. Najita and J. Stern (eds), *Public Sector Bargaining*, Madison, Wisconsin, Industrial Relations Research Association, second edn, 1988, 17–27.

3 Unions in the public sector

1 S. and B. Webb, *The History of Trade Unionism 1666–1920*, London, Longman, 1920, 507.
2 A. Marsh and V. Ryan, *Historical Directory of Trade Unions: Vol. I, Non-Manual Unions*, Aldershot, Gower, 1980, xii–xiii.
3 E. Wigham, *From Humble Petition to Militant Action*, London, Civil and Public Services Association, 1980, 218.
4 Marsh and Ryan, op. cit., xvii.
5 H.A. Clegg, *A History of British Trade Unions Since 1889: Vol. II, 1911–1933*, Oxford, Clarendon Press, 1985, 545.
6 G.S. Bain and R. Price, 'Union growth revisited: 1948–74 in perspective', *British Journal of Industrial Relations*, 14, 3, November 1976, 339–55.
7 H. Clegg, *Trade Unionism under Collective Bargaining*, Oxford, Blackwell, 1976, 23–7.
8 D. Lockwood, *The Blackcoated Worker*, London, Allen & Unwin, 1958, 142–4.
9 P. Seglow, *Trade Unionism in Television*, Farnborough, Saxon House, 1978, 265.
10 M.B. Gregory and A.W.J. Thomson, 'The coverage mark up, bargaining structure and earnings in Britain, 1973 and 1978', *British Journal of Industrial Relations*, 19, 1, March 1981, 28.
11 M. Poole, R. Mansfield, P. Frost and P. Blyton, 'Why managers join unions: evidence from Britain', *Industrial Relations*, 22, 3, Fall 1983, 426–44.
12 G.S. Bain, *The Growth of White Collar Unionism*, Oxford, Oxford University Press, 1970, 124.
13 H. Parris, *Staff Relations in the Civil Service*, London, Allen & Unwin, 1973, chapter 1.
14 See, for example, *Staff Relations in the Civil Service*, London, HMSO, 1949, 3.
15 See, for example, the reference for local government cited in G. Routh, 'White collar unions in the United Kingdom', in A. Sturmthal (ed.), *White Collar Trade Unions*, Urbana, University of Illinois Press, 1967, 187.
16 W.W. Daniel and N. Millward, *Workplace Industrial Relations in Britain*, London, Heinemann, 1983, 21–2.
17 K. Prandy, 'Professional organizations in Great Britain', *Industrial Relations*, 5, 3, Fall 1965, 73.
18 'Public Sector Trade Unions', *IDS Public Sector Digest*, London, Incomes Data Services, May 1987.
19 Office of Population Census and Statistics, *General Household Survey 1983*, London, HMSO, 101.
20 G.S. Bain, D. Coates and V. Ellis, *Social Stratification and Trade Unionism*, London, Heinemann, 1973, 4.
21 R.M. Blackburn, *Union Character and Social Class*, London, Batsford, 1967.
22 R. Undy, V. Ellis, W.E.J. McCarthy and A.M. Halmos, *Change in Trade Unions*, London, Hutchinson, 1981, 259.

23 P. Joyce, D. Corrigan and M. Hayes, *Striking Out: Trade Unionism in Social Work*, London, Macmillan, 1988, 75.
24 K. Walsh, 'Emerging bureaucracy; industrial relations systems in local authorities', *Public Administration Bulletin*, 40, December 1982, 58.
25 Joyce, Corrigan and Hayes, op. cit., 2.
26 N. Millward and M. Stevens, *British Workplace Industrial Relations, 1980–1984*, Aldershot, Gower, 1986, 85–6.
27 P.B. Beaumont and M. Partridge, *Job Satisfaction in Public Administration*, London, Royal Institute of Public Administration, 1983.
28 G.K. Fry, *The Changing Civil Service*, London, Allen & Unwin, 1985, 131.
29 J.F. Burton and T. Thomason, 'The extent of collective bargaining in the public sector', in B. Aaron, J. Najita and J.L. Stern (eds), *Public Sector Bargaining*, Madison, Wisconsin, Industrial Relations Research Association, second edn, 1988, 2–3.
30 J.L. Stern, 'Unionism in the public sector', in Aaron, Najita and Stern (eds), ibid., 72–8.
31 A. Ponak and M. Thompson, 'Public sector collective bargaining', in J.C. Anderson, M. Gunderson and A. Ponak (eds), *Union–Management Relations in Canada*, Don Mills, Ontario, Addison-Wesley, second edn, 1989, 375–80.
32 T. Treu, 'Italian industrial relations in the past ten years', in *Bulletin of Comparative Labour Relations*, 16, 1987, 172.
33 R. Taylor, *The Fifth Estate*, London, Pan, 1980, 353.
34 See P.B. Beaumont and J. Elliott, 'Individual employees choice between unions: some public sector evidence from Britain', *Industrial Relations Journal*, 20, 4, Winter 1989, 119–27.
35 J. Leopold, 'Moving the status quo: the growth in trade unions political funds', *Industrial Relations Journal*, 19, 4, Winter 1988, 286–95.
36 K. Mayhew, *Trade Unions and the Labour Market*, Oxford, Martin Robertson, 1983, 74–7.
37 J.T. Dunlop, *Wage Determination Under Trade Unions*, New York, Macmillan, 1944, and A.M. Ross, *Trade Union Wage Policy*, Berkeley, University of California Press, 1948.
38 C. Mulvey, *The Economic Analysis of Trade Unions*, Oxford, Martin Robertson, 1978, 145–7.
39 T.A. Kochan and H.C. Katz, *Collective Bargaining and Industrial Relations*, Homewood, Ill., Irwin, second edn, 1988, 425–6.
40 N.W. Chamberlain, *Collective Bargaining*, New York, McGraw-Hill, 1951.
41 N.W. Chamberlain and J.M. Schilling, *The Impact of Strikes: their Social and Economic Costs*, New York, Harper, 1954.
42 G.H. Hildebrand, 'An economic definition of the national emergency dispute', in Irving Bernstein, H.A. Enarson and R.W. Fleming, (eds), *Emergency Disputes and National Policy*, New York, Harper, 1955.
43 H.H. Wellington and R.K. Winter, *The Unions and the Cities*, Washington, Brookings, 1971.
44 J.F. Burton, 'Can public employees be given the right to strike?',

Proceedings of the Industrial Relations Research Association, Spring 1970, 474.
45 C.J. Wheelan, 'Military intervention in industrial disputes', *Industrial Law Journal*, 8, 1979.
46 Institute of Personnel Management and IDS Public Sector Unit, *Competitive Tendering in the Public Sector*, London, Institute of Personnel Management/Incomes Data Services, 1986, 7.
47 IDS Public Sector Unit, *Public Sector Pay, Review of 1986 and Prospects for 1987*, London, Incomes Data Services, 1987, 13.
48 IDS Public Sector Unit, *Public Sector Pay, Review of 1987 and Prospects for 1988*, London, Incomes Data Services, 1988, 16.
49 K. Ascher, *The Politics of Privatisation*, London, Macmillan, 1987, 268.
50 Institute of Personnel Management and IDS Public Sector Unit, op. cit., 66.
51 Ascher, op cit., 102–3.
52 ibid., 124–5.
53 ibid., 125.
54 ibid., 125–32.
55 IDS Public Sector Unit, *Public Sector Pay, Review of 1989 and Prospects for 1990*, London, Incomes Data Services, 1990, 41.
56 ibid., 12.

4 Management organization for industrial relations purposes in the public sector

1 A. Ponak and M. Thompson, 'Public sector collective bargaining', in J.C. Anderson, M. Gunderson and A. Ponak (eds), *Union–Management Relations in Canada*, Don Mills, Ontario, Addison-Wesley, second edn, 1989, 381.
2 Quoted in G.K. Fry, *The Changing Civil Service*, London, Allen & Unwin, 1985, 72.
3 ibid., 1985, 72.
4 C. McCleod, *All Change: Railway Industrial Relations in the Sixties*, London, Gower, 1970, 119.
5 A. Ferner, *Governments, Managers and Industrial Relations*, Oxford, Blackwell, 1988, 153.
6 ibid., 155.
7 Lord McCarthy, *Making Whitley Work: A Review of the Operation of the Whitley Council System in the National Health Service*, London, HMSO, 1976, 11.
8 ibid., chapter 2.
9 A. Spoor, *White Collar Union*, London, Heinemann, 1967, chapter 23.
10 R. Saran, 'Schoolteachers' pay and conditions of employment in England and Wales', in R. Saran and J. Sheldrake (eds), *Public Sector Bargaining in the 1980s*, Aldershot, Avebury, 1988, 13.
11 K. Newton and T.J. Karran, *The Politics of Local Expenditure*, London, Macmillan, 1985, 109.

12 ibid., 110.
13 ibid.
14 ibid., 111–12.
15 P. Dunleavy and R.A.W. Rhodes, 'Government Beyond Whitehall', in H. Drucker, P. Dunleavy, A. Gamble and G. Peele (eds), *Developments in British Politics*, London, Macmillan, second edn, 1986, 126–9.
16 ibid., 143.
17 D. Lewin, P. Feuille, T.A. Kochan and J.T. Delaney (eds), *Public Sector Labor Relations: Analysis and Readings*, Lexington, Mass., Heath, third edn, 1988, 582.
18 T.D. Jick and V.V. Murray, 'The management of hard times; budget cutbacks in public sector organizations', *Organization Studies*, 3, 2, 1982, 141.
19 See, for example, H. Glennerster, 'Social service spending in a hostile environment', in C. Hood and M. Wright (eds), *Big Government in Hard Times*, Oxford, Martin Robertson, 1981, 174–96. Also A. Midwinter, 'Local budgetary strategies in a decade of retrenchment', *Public Money and Management*, 8, 3, Autumn 1988, 21–8.
20 Quoted in Fry, op. cit., 72.
21 A. Ferner, 'Industrial relations and the meso-politics of the public enterprise', *British Journal of Industrial Relations*, 25, 1, March 1987, 49–75.
22 For something of an exception see M.R. Godine, *The Labour Problem in the Public Service*, New York, Russell & Russell, 1951, chapter 2.
23 T. Treu, 'Labour relations in the public service: a comparative overview', in T. Treu *et al.*, *Public Service Labour Relations: Recent Trends and Future Prospects*, Geneva, ILO, 1987, 18–19.
24 P.B. Beaumont, 'The government as a model employer: A change of direction in Britain?', *Journal of Collective Negotiations in the Public Sector*, 16, 3, 1987, 187–9.
25 *Royal Commission on the Civil Service 1929–31*, London, HMSO, Cmnd 3909, para 311, chapter 11.
26 Godine, op. cit., 32–40.
27 See, for example, M. Gunderson, 'The public/private sector compensation controversy', in M. Thompson and G. Swimmer (eds), *Conflict or Compromise: The Future of Public Sector Industrial Relations*, Toronto, The Institute for Research on Public Policy, 1984, 8.
28 *Royal Commission on the Civil Service 1953–55*, London, HMSO, Cmnd 9613, para 146, 39.
29 For further details see P.B. Beaumont, *Government as Employer – Setting an Example?*, London, Royal Institute of Public Administration, 1981.
30 M. Thompson and A. Ponak, 'Industrial relations in Canadian public enterprises', *International Labour Review*, 123, 5, September–October 1984, 656.
31 M.A. Gordon, 'The emergence of co-determination in Australian government employment', *International Labour Review*, 124, 4, July–August 1985, 470.

32 B. Hepple, 'Labour law and public employees in Britain', in W. Wedderburn and W.T. Murphy (eds), *Labour Law and the Community*, London, Institute of Advanced Legal Studies, University of London, 1982, 78.
33 *The Sunday Correspondent*, 11 March 1990.
34 P.B. Beaumont and J. Leopold, 'Public sector industrial relations: recent developments', *Employee Relations*, 7, 4, 1985, 33–4.
35 See, for example, D. Kavanagh, *Thatcherism and British Politics*, Oxford, Oxford University Press, 1987, chapter 8.
36 G.K. Fry, 'The Thatcher government, the financial management initiative and the new civil service', *Public Administration*, 66, 1, Spring 1988, 4.
37 IDS Public Sector Unit, *Public Sector Pay: Review of 1986 and Prospects for 1987*, London, Incomes Data Services, March 1987, 12.
38 D. Thomas, 'Privatisation and the unions', *New Society*, 21 June 1984, 479.
39 *Industrial Relations Review and Report*, No. 458, February 1990.
40 M. Derber, 'Management organization for collective bargaining in the public sector', in B. Aaron, J. Najita and J. Stern (eds), *Public Sector Bargaining*, Madison, Wisconsin, Industrial Relations Research Association, second edn, 1988, 103.
41 T.A. Kochan, 'Determinants of the power of boundary units in inter-organizational bargaining relations', *Administrative Science Quarterly*, 20, September 1975, 434–52.
42 I.M. Brown, *Personnel Management in Five Public Services: Its Development and Future*, Birmingham, Institute of Local Government Studies, University of Birmingham, 1982, 47.
43 A. Fowler, *Personnel Management in Local Government*, London, Institute of Personnel Management, 1975, 141.
44 See, for example, R.A.W. Rhodes, 'Corporatism, pay negotiations and local government', *Public Administration*, 63, Autumn 1985, 287–307.
45 Brown, op. cit., chapter 2.
46 H.A. Clegg, *The Changing System of Industrial Relations in Great Britain*, Oxford, Blackwell, 1979, 128.
47 *The New Local Authorities: Management and Structure*, Report of the Study Group, 1972, 21.
48 P.B. Beaumont and M. Ingham, 'Bargaining structure and the personnel industrial relations management function in British local government', *Journal of Collective Negotiations in the Public Sector*, 14, 2, 1985, 101–10.
49 D. Guest and R. Horwood, 'Characteristics of the successful personnel manager', *Personnel Management*, May 1981, 30.
50 J.W. Leopold and P.B. Beaumont, 'Personnel officers in the National Health Service in Scotland: development and change in the 1970s', *Public Administration*, 63, 2, Summer 1985, 219–26.
51 W. Brown (ed.), *The Changing Contours of British Industrial Relations*, Oxford, Blackwell, 1981, 32–4.
52 L. Mackay, 'Personnel management in the public and private sectors', *Industrial Relations Journal*, 17, 4, Winter 1986, 312.

53 N. Millward and M. Stevens, *British Workplace Industrial Relations*, Aldershot, Gower, 1986, chapter 2.
54 I.M. Brown, ibid., 4–8.
55 J.S. Cassells, *Review of Personnel Work in the Civil Service*, London, HMSO, 1983, 38–9.
56 IDS Public Sector Unit, *Public Sector Pay: Review of 1989 and Prospects for 1990*, London, Incomes Data Services, 1990, 27.
57 *Industrial Relations Review and Report*, No. 458, February 1990.
58 J. Storey, 'Human resource management in the public sector', *Public Money and Management*, 9, 3, Autumn 1989, 19–24.

5 Collective bargaining coverage and structure in the public sector

1 A. Flanders, 'Collective bargaining: a theoretical analysis', *British Journal of Industrial Relations*, 6, 1, March 1968, 1–26.
2 N.W. Chamberlain, *Collective Bargaining*, New York, McGraw-Hill, 1951, 121.
3 R.E. Walton and R.B. McKersie, *A Behavioural Theory of Labor Negotiations*, New York, McGraw-Hill, 1965.
4 R. Hyman, *Industrial Relations: A Marxist Introduction*, London, Macmillan, 1974.
5 A. Flanders, *Collective Bargaining: Prescription for Change*, London, Faber, 1967, 19–26.
6 See the various papers in Lord Wedderburn of Charlton and W.T. Murphy (eds), *Labour Law and the Community*, London, Institute of Advanced Legal Studies, University of London, 1982.
7 H.A. Clegg, *A History of British Trade Unions since 1889: Vol. II, 1911–1933*, Oxford, Clarendon Press, 1985, 549.
8 Flanders, op. cit., 13.
9 P.B. Beaumont and M.B. Gregory, 'The role of employers in collective bargaining in Britain', *Industrial Relations Journal*, 11, 5, 1980, 47.
10 R. Freeman, 'On the divergence in unionism among developed countries', Cambridge, Mass., Harvard University, October 1988.
11 Clegg, op. cit., 549.
12 M. McIntosh, 'The negotiation of wages and conditions for local authority employees in England and Wales: part 3 – structure and scope', *Public Administration*, 33, Summer 1955, 151.
13 ibid.
14 W. Brown (ed.), *The Changing Contours of British Industrial Relations*, Oxford, Blackwell, 1981, chapter 2.
15 N. Millward and M. Stevens, *British Workplace Industrial Relations 1980–1984*, Aldershot, Gower, 1986, 229–44.
16 I. Boraston, H. Clegg and M. Rimmer, *Workplace and Union*, London, Heinemann, 1975, chapter 8.
17 D. Lewin, P. Feuille, T.A. Kochan and J.T. Delaney (eds), *Public Sector Labor Relations*, Lexington, Heath, third edn, 1988, 159.
18 P. Feuille, H. Juvis, R. Jones and M.J. Jedel, 'Multiemployer bargaining among local governments', *Proceedings of the Industrial*

Relations Research Association, Madison, Wisconsin, Winter 1977, 123–31.
19 *IDS Report No. 495*, April 1987.
20 Kenneth Clark, quoted in *The Times*, 12 February 1987.
21 P. Cappelli, 'Bargaining structure, market forces and wage outcomes in the British coal industry', *Industrial Relations*, forthcoming.
22 A. Thirlwall, 'Regional Phillips curves', *Bulletin of Oxford Institute of Economics and Statistics*, 31, 1, February 1970, 19–32.
23 Lord McCarthy, *Making Whitley Work: A Review of the Operation of the Whitley Council System in the National Health Service*, London, HMSO, 1976.
24 *The Times*, 2 November 1988.
25 *The Times*, 2 November 1988.
26 P.B. Beaumont and M. Ingham, 'Low pay, productivity, and collective bargaining in local government in Britain', *Journal of Collective Negotiations in the Public Sector*, 12, 3, 1983, 243–57.
27 IDS Public Sector Unit, *Public Sector Pay: Review of 1989 and Prospects for 1990*, London, Income Data Services, 1990, 40.
28 *Industrial Relations Review and Report*, No. 458, February 1990.
29 *IDS Report*, No. 561, January 1990.
30 *IDS Report*, No. 558, Supplement, December 1989.

6 Bargaining processes, strikes and dispute resolution in the public sector

1 For a useful summary of this literature see S.B. Bacharach and E.O. Lawler, *Bargaining Power, Tactics and Outcomes*, San Francisco, Jossey-Bass, 1981, chapter 1.
2 J.R. Hicks, *The Theory of Wages*, London, Macmillan, second edn, 1963, chapter 7.
3 See, for example, H. Raiffa, 'A strike game', in C. Kerr and P.D. Standohar (eds), *Industrial Relations in a New Age*, San Francisco, Jossey-Bass, 1986, 239–43.
4 T.A. Kochan, *Collective Bargaining and Industrial Relations*, Homewood, Ill., Irwin, 1980, 240.
5 R.E. Walton and R.B. McKersie, *A Behavioural Theory of Labor Negotiations*, New York, McGraw-Hill, 1965.
6 Bacharach and Lawler, op. cit.
7 Kochan, op. cit., 243–4.
8 T.A. Kochan, G.P. Huber and L.L. Cummings, 'Determinants of intraorganizational conflict in collective bargaining in the public sector', *Administration Science Quarterly*, 20, 1, March 1975, 10–23.
9 D. Lewin, P. Feuille, T.A. Kochan and J.T. Delaney (eds), *Public Sector Labor Relations: Analysis and Readings*, Lexington, Mass., Heath, third edn, 1988, 10.
10 R.B. Freeman, 'Unionism comes to the public sector', *Journal of Economic Literature*, 24, March 1986, 53.
11 T.A. Kochan, 'Dynamics of dispute resolution in the public sector', in

B. Aaron, J.R. Grodin and J.L. Stern (eds), *Public Sector Bargaining*, Madison, Wisconsin, Industrial Relations Research Association, 1979, 163–7.

12 R.A.W. Rhodes, 'Corporatism, pay negotiations and local government', *Public Administration*, 63, Autumn 1985, 287–307.

13 ibid., 303.

14 For a summary of this debate see P.B. Beaumont, *Changing Industrial Relations*, London, Routledge, 1989, chapter 9.

15 N. Millward and M. Stevens, *British Workplace Industrial Relations 1980–1984*, Aldershot, Gower, 1986, pp. 139 and 149 respectively.

16 M. Laffin, *Managing under Pressure: Industrial Relations in Local Government*, London, Macmillan, 1989.

17 ibid., 38–9.

18 Lewin *et. al.*, op. cit., 286–7.

19 'Large industrial stoppages 1960–1979', *Department of Employment Gazette*, 88, 1980, 994–9.

20 T. Treu *et al.*, *Public Service Labour Relations: Recent Trends and Future Prospects*, Geneva, ILO, 1987.

21 D. Winchester, 'Labour relations in the public service in the United Kingdom', in Treu *et al.*, ibid., 210–11.

22 J.W. Durcan, W.E.J. McCarthy and G.P. Redman, *Strikes in Post War Britain*, London, Allen & Unwin, 1983, 176.

23 C.T.B. Smith, R. Clifton, P. Makeham, S.W. Creigh and R.V. Burn, *Strikes in Britain*, London, DE Manpower Paper No. 15, 1978, 116.

24 Calculated from R. Undy, V. Ellis, W.E.J. McCarthy and A.M. Haknos, *Change in Trade Unions*, London, Hutchinson, 1981, 35, Table 4.

25 S. McConnell and L. Takla, 'Mrs Thatcher's trade union legislation': has it reduced strikes?' London, Centre for Labour Economics, LSE, Discussion Paper No. 374, January 1990.

26 N. Millward and M. Stevens, *British Workplace Industrial Relations 1980–1984*, Aldershot, Gower, 1986, 67.

27 *National Institute Economic Review*, No. 111, February 1985, 22.

28 See, for example, P. Hain, *Political Strikes*, Harmondsworth, Penguin, 1986, chapter 9.

29 See R. Richardson and S. Wood, 'Productivity change in the coal industry and the new industrial relations', *British Journal of Industrial Relations*, 27, 1, March 1989, 33–56.

30 E. Cordova, 'Strikes in the public service: some determinants and trends', *International Labour Review*, 124, 2, March–April 1985, 164–5.

31 See P.B. Beaumont, 'The right to strike in the public sector: the issues and evidence', *Public Administration Bulletin*, 35, April 1981, 21–38. Also L.J. McFarlane, *The Right to Strike*, Harmondsworth, Penguin, 1981, chapter 6.

32 See, for example, C.A. Olson, 'Dispute resolution in the public sector', in B. Aaron, J. Najita and J.L. Stern (eds), *Public Sector Bargaining*, Madison, Wisconsin, Industrial Relations Research Association, second edn, 1988, 160–88.

33 A. Ponak and M. Thompson, 'Public sector collective bargaining', in J.C. Anderson, M. Gunderson and A. Ponak (eds), *Union–Management Relations in Canada*, Don Mills, Ontario, Addison-Wesley, second edn, 1989, 397–8.

34 P.K. Edwards, 'The awful truth about strife in our factories: a case study in the production of news', *Industrial Relations Journal*, 10, 1, 1979, and T. Lane and K. Roberts, *Strike at Pilkington's*, London, Collins, 1971, 76.

35 V.L. Allen, *Trade Unions and the Government*, London, Longman, 1960, 213 and 216.

36 See, for example, E. Hobsbawm, *The Forward March of Labour Halted?*, London, Verso, 1981, 14.

37 P. Edwards, 'Britain's changing strike problem?', *Industrial Relations Journal*, 13, 2, Summer 1982, 16.

38 N. Jones, *Strikes and the Media*, Oxford, Blackwell, 1986, 207.

39 See, for example, B. Towers, 'Posing larger questions: the British miners' strike of 1984–85', *Industrial Relations Journal*, 16, 2, Summer 1985, 21–2.

40 *New Statesman*, 18 January 1985.

41 Millward and Stevens, op. cit., 315.

42 W.W. Daniel and N. Millward, *Workplace Industrial Relations in Britain*, London, Heinemann, 1983, 292.

43 M. Ingham, 'Industrial relations in British local government', *Industrial Relations Journal*, 16, 1, Spring 1985, 6–15.

44 See, for example, M. Poole, *Industrial Relations: Origins and Patterns of National Diversity*, London, Routledge & Kegan Paul, 1986, chapter 6.

45 D. Lewin, 'Public employee unionism and labor relations in the 1980s: an analysis of transformation', in S.M. Lipset (ed.), *Unions in Transition*, San Francisco, ICS Press, 1986, 246.

46 P. Feuille, 'Unions and employers in government: more conflict than co-operation', Paper presented to the International Industrial Relations Association, Hamburg, 1986, 136.

47 Freeman, op. cit., 66–7.

48 Ponak and Thompson in Anderson, Gunderson and Ponak (eds), op. cit., 393.

49 R.B. Israel, 'Co-operation and conflict in public sector labour relations in Israel', in A. Gladstone, R. Lansbury, J. Stieber, T. Treu and M. Weiss (eds), *Current Issues in Labour Relations*, Berlin, De Gruyter, 1989, 357.

50 T. Hanami, 'Co-operation and conflict in public sector labour relations in Japan', in Gladstone *et al.*, ibid., 363.

51 Millward and Stevens, op. cit., 180.

52 *ACAS Annual Report 1981*, London. HMSO, 1982, 56.

53 *ACAS Annual Report 1987*, London, HMSO, 1988, 44.

54 *ACAS Annual Report 1980*, London, HMSO, 1981, 25–6.

55 See J.W. Leopold and P.B. Beaumont, 'Arbitration arrangements in the public sector in Britain', *The Arbitration Journal* 38, 2, June 1983, 57.

56 This draws on Leopold and Beaumont, ibid., op. cit., 58–9.
57 H. Clegg and T.A. Chester, *Wage Policy and the Health Service*, Oxford, Blackwell, 1961, 91–5.
58 TUC Health Service Committee, *Improving Industrial Relations in the NHS*, London, TUC, 1981, chapter 6.
59 Social Services Committee of the House of Commons, Third Report, *Resourcing the National Health Service: Whitley Councils*, Vol. I, London, 1989, para. 155.
60 Institute of Directors, *Settling Disputes Peacefully*, London, Institute of Directors, 1984.
61 See, for example, Sir John Wood, 'Last offer arbitration', *British Journal of Industrial Relations*, 23, 3, November 1985, 415–24.
62 *ACAS Annual Report 1986*, London, HMSO, 1987, 45.
63 Lewin *et al.*, 343.

7 The criteria and outcomes of bargaining in the public sector

1 See, for example, A. Ponak and M. Thompson 'Public sector collective bargaining', in J.C. Anderson, M. Gunderson and A. Ponak (eds), *Union–Management Relations in Canada*, Don Mills, Ontario, Addison-Wesley, second edn, 1989, 374.
2 See. for example, S.B. Goldenberg, 'Public sector labor relations in Canada', in B. Aaron, J.R. Grodin and J.L. Stern (eds), *Public Sector Bargaining*, Madison, Wisconsin, Industrial Relations Research Association, 1979, 267–8.
3 G. K. Fry, *The Changing Civil Service*, Allen & Unwin, London, 1985, 96–8.
4 See, for example, P.B. Beaumont, *Government as Employer – Setting an Example?*, London, Royal Institute of Public Administration, 1981, 31–2.
5 These terms are borrowed from S.P. Smith, *Equal Pay in the Public Sector: Fact or Fantasy*, Princeton, Industrial Relations Section, Princeton University, 1977, 26.
6 Beaumont, op. cit., 33–4.
7 *The Economist*, 5 February 1944, 89.
8 *The Times*, 6 September 1977.
9 G.L. Stenlutto, 'Federal pay comparability: facts to temper the debate', *Monthly Labor Review*, June 1979.
10 Cited in A.W.J. Thomson and P.B. Beaumont, *Public Sector Bargaining: A Study of Relative Gain*, Farnborough, Saxon House, 1978, 55.
11 Pay Board Advisory Report No. 1, *Anomalies*, Cmnd 5429, 1973, 1.
12 Fry, op. cit., 113.
13 C. Trinder, 'Public sector pay in the 1980s: An economic overview', in R. Saran and J. Sheldrake (eds), *Public Sector Bargaining in the 1980s*, Aldershot, Avebury, 1988, 75.
14 P.B. Beaumont 'Industrial relations in the public sector', in B. Towers (ed.), *A Handbook of Industrial Relations Practice*, London, Kogan Page, 1989, 43.

15 K. Chivers, 'Flexible pay in the civil service', *Public Money and Management*, 8, 4, Winter 1988, 51–4.
16 IDS Public Sector Unit, *Public Sector Pay: Review of 1989 and Prospects for 1990*, London, Incomes Data Services, 1990, 11.
17 IDS Public Sector Unit, ibid., p. 39.
18 IDS Public Sector Unit, ibid.
19 *IDS Report No. 9, Labour Market Supplement*, December 1989.
20 *The Times*, 3 September 1990.
21 *The Times*, 31 January 1990.
22 R. Rose, *Understanding Big Government*, London, Sage, 1984, 146.
23 P.S. Heller and A.A. Tait, 'Government Employment and Pay: Some International Comparisons', Occasional Paper No. 24, Washington, International Monetary Fund, March 1984, 17.
24 A.J.H. Dean, 'Earnings in the public and private sectors 1950–1975', *National Institute Economic Review*, No. 74, November 1975, 60–70.
25 A. Dean, 'Public and private sector pay and the economy', in J.L. Fallick and R.F. Elliott (eds), *Incomes Policies, Inflation and Relative Pay*, London, Allen & Unwin, 1981, 55.
26 Trinder, op. cit., 68–9.
27 *The Times*, 2 February 1990.
28 Social Services Committee of the House of Commons, Third Report, *Resourcing the National Health Service: Whitley Councils*, London, 1989, xiii.
29 ibid.
30 R.F. Elliot and P.D. Murphy, 'The relative pay of public and private sector employees, 1970–1984', *Cambridge Journal of Economics*, 11, 1987, 108.
31 D. Blanchflower, A. Oswald and M. Garrett, 'Insider power in wage determination', London, Centre for Labour Economics, LSE, Discussion Paper No. 319, August 1988, 17–18.
32 T. Seth, 'Labour relations in the public sector in Sweden', in T. Treu *et al.*, *Public Service Labour Relations: Recent Trends and Future Prospects*, Geneva, ILO, 1987, 179.
33 T. Treu, 'Labour relations in the public service in Italy', in Treu *et al.*, ibid., 115–16.
34 D. Lewin, P. Feuille, T.A. Kochan and J.T. Delaney (eds), *Public Sector Labor Relations: Analysis and Readings*, Lexington, Mass., Heath, 1988, 436.
35 D. Belman and J.S. Heywood, 'Government wage differentials: A sample selection approach', *Applied Economics*, 21, 1989, 436.
36 D.J.B. Mitchell, 'Collective bargaining and compensation in the public sector', in B. Aaron, J.M. Najita and J.L. Stern (eds), *Public Sector Bargaining*, Madison, Wisconsin, Industrial Relations Research Association, second edn, 1988, 137. Also R.B. Freeman, 'Unionism comes to the public sector', *Journal of Economic Literature*, 24, March 1986, 53–9.
37 Freeman, ibid.
38 J.S. Zax, 'Employment and local public sector unions', *Industrial Relations*, 28, 1, Winter 1989, 21–31.

39 D.M. Shapiro and M. Stelener, 'Canadian public–private sector earnings differentials, 1970–1980', *Industrial Relations*, 28, 1, Winter 1989, 72–81.
40 See, for example, M. Stewart, 'Relative earnings and individual union membership in the UK', *Economica*, 50, 2, May 1983.
41 D. Blanchflower, 'What effect do unions have on relative wages in Great Britain?', *British Journal of Industrial Relations*, 24, 2, July 1986, 200.
42 M.B. Stewart, 'Collective bargaining arrangements, closed shops and relative pay', *Economic Journal*, 97, March 1987, 149.
43 Fry, op. cit., 111–12.
44 J. Burton, *Wage Inflation*, London, Macmillan, 1972, 78.
45 S.B. Wadhwani, 'Wage inflation in the United Kingdom', *Economica*, 52, 1985, 201.
46 D. Robinson and K. Mayhew, 'Introduction', in D. Robinson and K. Mayhew (eds), *Pay Policies for the Future*, Oxford, Oxford University Press, 1983, 6.
47 Dean in Fallick and Elliott (eds), op. cit., 61.
48 J.L. Fallick and R.F. Elliott, 'Incomes policy and the public sector', in Fallick and Elliott (eds), op. cit., 122.
49 See D. Heald, *Public Expenditure*, Oxford, Martin Robertson, 1983, chapter 8.
50 *Committee of Inquiry Report into the Pay and Conditions of Service of School Teachers in Scotland*, Edinburgh, HMSO, Cmnd 9893, 1986, 140–1.
51 Trinder in Saran and Sheldrake (eds), op. cit., 70.
52 F. Green, G. Hadjimatheon and R. Smail, 'Fringe benefit distribution in Britain', *British Journal of Industrial Relations*, 23, 2, July 1985, 261–80.
53 N. Millward and M. Stevens, *British Workplace Industrial Relations 1980–1984*, Aldershot, Gower, 1986, 248–53.

8 Changes in public sector industrial relations?

1 J. Prior, *A Balance of Power*, London, Hamish Hamilton, 1986, 142–3.
2 *The Times*, 14 April 1989.
3 *The Times*, 20 August 1990.
4 C. Bean and J. Symons, 'Ten years of Mrs T', London, Centre for Labour Economics, LSE, Discussion Paper, No. 370, January 1990.
5 E. Batstone and S. Gourlay, *Unions, Unemployment and Innovation*, Oxford, Blackwell, 1986, 149.
6 W.W. Daniel, *Workplace Industrial Relations and Technical Change*, London, Frances Pinter, 1987.
7 *Industrial Relations Review and Report*, No. 408, 19 January 1988, 10–12.
8 G.K. Fry, 'The Thatcher government, the financial management initiative and the new civil service', *Public Administration*, 66, 1, Spring 1988, 18.

9 A. Pendleton, 'Markets or politics? The determinants of labour relations in a nationalised industry', *Public Administration*, 66, Autumn 1988, 279–96.

10 R. Richardson and S. Wood, 'Productivity change in the coal industry and the new industrial relations', *British Journal of Industrial Relations*, 27, 1, March 1989, 33–56.

11 C. Edwards and E. Heery, 'Recession in the public sector: industrial relations in Freightliner 1981–85', *British Journal of Industrial Relations*, 27, 1, March 1989, 69.

12 A. Ferner, *Governments, Managers and Industrial Relations*, Oxford, Blackwell, 1988.

13 K. Newton and T.J. Karran, *The Politics of Local Expenditure*, London, Macmillan, 1985, 110.

14 Newton and Karran, ibid. See also A. Midwinter, 'Local budgetary strategies in a decade of retrenchment', *Public Money and Management*, 8, 3, Autumn 1988, 21–8.

15 Fry, op. cit., 17.

16 See, for example, K. Matthews and P. Minford, 'Mrs Thatcher's economic policies 1979–1987', *Economic Policy*, 5, October 1987, 92.

17 *The Times*, 1 May 1990.

18 *Industrial Relations Review and Report*, No. 344, May 1985.

19 *The Times*, 1 May 1989.

20 *IDS Report No. 540*, Supplement, London, Incomes Data Sources, March 1989, 4.

21 ibid., 3.

22 IDS Public Sector Unit, *Public Sector Pay: Review of 1988 and Prospects for 1989*, London, Incomes Data Sources, 1989, 18.

23 ibid.

24 C. Trinder, 'Public Service Pay', in M.S. Levitt (ed.), *New Priorities in Public Spending*, Aldershot, Gower, 1987, 81–2.

25 R. Layard and S. Nickell, 'An incomes policy to help the unemployed', *The Economic Review*, 5, 2, November 1987, 16.

26 See, for example, J. Leopold and P.B. Beaumont, 'Pay bargaining and management strategy in the NHS', *Industrial Relations Journal*, 17, 1, Spring 1986, 32–45.

27 Social Services Committee of the House of Commons, Third Report, *Resourcing the National Health Service: Whitley Councils*, London, 1989.

28 B. Hepple, 'Labour law and public employees in Britain', in Lord Wedderburn of Charlton and W.T. Murphy (eds), *Labour Law and the Community*, London, Institute of Advanced Legal Studies, University of London, 1982, 67–84.

29 M. Fogarty with D. Brooks, *Trade Unions and British Industrial Development*, London, Policy Studies Institute, 1986, 177–82.

30 J. Storey, 'Human resource management in the public sector', *Public Money and Management*, 9, 3, Autumn 1989, 19–24.

31 ibid., 24.

32 J. Stewart and S. Ranson, 'Management in the public domain', *Public Money and Management*, 8, 2, Spring/Summer 1988, 17.

33 H. Phelps Brown, 'The counter-revolution of our time', *Industrial Relations*, 29, 1, Winter 1990, 1–14.
34 I. Crewe, 'Values: the crusade that failed', in D. Kavanagh and A. Seldon (eds), *The Thatcher Effect: A Decade of Change*, Oxford, Oxford University Press, 1989, 250.
35 ibid., 248–9.

Index

Note: All references are to Great Britain unless otherwise indicated